Saving Marriage
by Applying
Biblical
Wisdom

Saving
Marriage
by Applying
Biblical
Wisdom

Drs. Trevor and Edith
FRASER

Benson Prigg, PhD. Editor

WinePressPublishing
Great Books, Defined.

Unless otherwise noted, all Scriptures are taken from the *Holy Bible, New International Version®, NIV®*. Copyright © 1973, 1978, 1984 by Biblica, Inc.™ Used by permission of Zondervan. All rights reserved worldwide. www.zondervan.com

Scripture references marked NLT are taken from the *Holy Bible, New Living Translation*, copyright © 1996, 2004 by Tyndale Charitable Trust. Used by permission of Tyndale House Publishers, Wheaton, Illinois 60189. All rights reserved.

Scripture references marked KJV are taken from the *King James Version* of the Bible.

Scripture references marked NASB are taken from the *New American Standard Bible*, © 1960, 1963, 1968, 1971, 1972, 1973, 1975, 1977, 1995 by The Lockman Foundation. Used by permission.

Scripture references marked THE MESSAGE are taken from *The Message Bible* © 1993 by Eugene N. Peterson, NavPress, PO Box 35001, Colorado Springs, CO 80935, 4th printing in USA 1994. Published in association with the literary agency—Alive Comm. PO Box 49068, Colorado Springs, CO 80949. Used by permission.

Scripture references marked NAB are taken from the *New American Bible with Revised New Testament and Revised Psalms* © 1991, 1986, 1970 Confraternity of Christian Doctrine, Washington, D.C. and are used by permission of the copyright owner. All Rights Reserved.

ISBN 13: 978-1-4141-1875-8
ISBN 10: 1-4141-1875-9
Library of Congress Catalog Card Number: 2010909846

Contents

Foreword

TREVOR AND EDITH Fraser, in a most engaging way, address an extremely critical need in society—saving marriages. Today's shocking statistics underscore the disturbing truth that marriage is on the critical list, if not life-support, and in need of extraordinary care.

In this book the Frasers apply biblical wisdom to address that need. With the lure of provocative titles, they use personal narrative and an array of relevant experiences to unpack and plainly illustrate biblical truths. While their 40 years of married life, as well as the experiences of others, are a helpful resource, they clearly indicate that the principles contained in the Bible, and their relationship to them, are the essential key.

Skillfully using the needle of biblical models and metaphor, they have woven a tapestry of biblical truth on marriage that deserves a central, featured place in every relationship. This book can serve as a wise preparation for marriage, as well as a useful tool to strengthen a marriage, or—as the title indicates—to save a marriage.

—**Benjamin F. Reaves, D.Min.**
Vice President of Mission and Ministries
Adventist Health System

Introduction

TREVOR AND I were at church when the inspiration for this book occurred. I was talking with a young woman who, in the course of our conversation, looked at me and said, "You and your husband are the perfect match."

"What does that mean?" I said.

She talked of her own failed marriage and the many marriages she had seen fall apart. Then she explained that our marriage worked because Trevor and I were the perfect match. As she continued, it became obvious that in her mind, being the perfect match was a matter of finding the "right person for you," that marriages are about being connected with the perfect person. It did not seem to matter about being the perfect person. Somehow the implication was that we did not have problems. Things worked for us magically.

The perfect match? I thought. *Is that the case?*

Her remark caused me to ponder as I shared it with Trevor, and we talked for hours about this concept. This conversation led to many questions:

- Is marriage about being the perfect match?
- Do some marriages have an advantage over others?
- If we were the perfect match, does that mean we did not fight?
- Does being the perfect match mean that marriage is easy for us while others have a hard time?
- What makes our marriage work?
- What makes any marriage work?

These questions initiated a search for answers. We thought about our marriage—the good times and the bad times. We have been married for more than 40 years and experienced many difficulties in our relationships. But the Bible and our strong spiritual lifestyle have provided the foundation for our marriage. So we studied married couples in the Bible and numerous other sources. We read psychology books and articles and questioned couples in successful marriages. In the end, these sources provided us with rich insights on marital success. The book you are holding is the result of our endeavors.

You might wonder why we use the Bible as the lens for understanding modern marriages. It is our conviction that God created the institution of marriage in the garden of Eden and that He wrote a manual, the Bible, on preserving that relationship. Consequently, this chronicle of human events provides a resource for helping relationships today. We find valuable models and powerful metaphors for the family in the Scriptures. Biblical families and their journeys provide insights for dealing with our contemporary families. As we reflected on problems for marriages today—family feuds, intergenerational conflict, infidelity, betrayal, and domestic violence—we realized that each of these occurred within biblical families. So in this text we draw on biblical marriages to paint the picture and discover important principles; we also use modern psychology to provide additional insights and explanations.

Psychologists have stated that marital success is based on several factors such as healthy expectations, a realistic concept of love, the ability to communicate feelings, an understanding of gender differences, skills in conflict resolution and decision making, and common spiritual goals.[1] These are the factors couples need today to enhance their marriages. None of our research supported the perfect match theory. Unfortunately, many people who get married have the same unrealistic expectations as my young friend. These expectations lead to marital difficulties and cause high divorce rates.

What is the state of the family today? Here are some statistics that provide insight:

- About half of all marriages end in divorce.[2]
- One in three females has been sexually molested.[3]
- Forty percent of couples admit they lie to each other about financial items.[4]
- Sixty percent of men and 40 percent of women are involved in extramarital affairs.[5]

With such problems, some social thinkers have predicted the demise of marriage. This would have dire consequences for the family. Married people live longer,[6] are happier and are more successful in their careers and earn more than their unmarried counterparts.[7] So developing strategies to enhance marriage is necessary for both individual and family well-being.

The dire state of marriages today drives our interest. We have served as family life leaders and facilitators for more than 30 years. We have watched as increasing numbers of couples in our family, our church, and our neighborhood experience divorce. Though both of our parents were married for more than 50 years, our children have few friends who can make a similar boast. As African Americans, we find this particularly troubling. For in the African American community divorce rates are higher than in society at large, and single mothers lead 68 percent of homes.[8] This trend has severe consequences for all communities and for society in general. These statistics increase our passion for helping families and couples.

We are driven not only by concern over general marriage trends, but also by the discovery that most of the states in the USA with the highest divorce rate are in the Bible belt. Except for Nevada, which has the highest rate, many of the states with high divorce rates are in the South.[9] In the Bible belt, couples are perceived to attend church, believe the Bible, and accept its principles—yet their marriages still experience difficulties, ending in discord or even divorce. How do we explain this? Should Christians avoid looking for solutions to marital problems and difficulties in scientific models, psychology approaches, sociological and behavioral constructs, and even educational models?

We believe a Bible-based approach could address the needs of couples throughout the United States—hence this book. Furthermore, because we are marriage and family counselors, in developing this book we combined biblical perspectives with sociological and psychological theory. We also drew upon our own personal experience. This combination of biblical context, psychological applications, and personal experience enabled us to address the complexities of marriage and the unsettled state of families in a postmodern world.

Our study in the Bible of Isaac and Rebekah's marriage provided us with a response to the concept of a perfect match. It was, after all, a marriage that began with prayer. Abraham's servant was commissioned to find the right wife for Isaac, and his prayer was, "O Lord, God of my master Abraham, give me success today, and show kindness to my master Abraham" (Gen. 24:12). God answered his prayer, and Rebekah seemed to be the perfect match for Isaac. Still this couple had difficulties because good marriages do not just happen. Requirements exist even for couples who are the perfect match.

Our personal experience and research has shown us that couples with more difficulties, even infidelity, could survive with the right strategies for marital success. Both David and Bathsheba's marriage and Hosea and Gomer's marriage support the need to develop the right approach to cultivating a marriage. The complexity of successful relationship building requires knowledge of male-female differences, differences in needs, and conflict-resolution skills. This book will address each of these topics.

Each chapter uses a biblical couple to teach a strategy for marital success. The book incorporates primary issues confronting couples in their marriages. Each chapter contains four distinct sections:

1. Begins with a Bible story as context
2. Explores the story and the struggles in this marriage
3. Ends with lessons and strategies from the couples
4. Provides a worksheet that encourages a couple's communication and discussion

For the past twenty years we have conducted workshops for couples and families. We are committed to reducing divorce. Our seminars combine our marriage experience, educational preparation, and Bible principles to provide couples with solutions to withstand the vicissitudes of life. They support the concept of hard work and commitment to each other—not to being a perfect match. We believe all matches have the potential to survive.

We hope you will follow the suggestions and strategies this book provides. Follow-through is essential to success. Trevor and I belong to a gym, and every January the gym is packed with individuals who intend to work on their bodies. They have decided this year will be different. They are going to lose weight and exercise. So in January, we can barely find a parking space. The machines are all full. We have to wait in line to lift the weights. Unfortunately by March, it is back to the old gang. Those who start in January are gone. They have little follow-through.

Making a difference in your marriage requires follow-through; reading this book is not enough. You and your spouse will need to work diligently and consistently to incorporate these factors in your marriage. We hope you will continue to work on your marriage for the rest of your life, not just the next few weeks. We trust you are in this for the long haul.

We have some wishes for you as you read this book and complete the worksheets: Communicate with your spouse more, love each other more, increase your commitment to each other, and grow and be happy with the spouse of your youth. As the Bible says, "May your fountain be blessed, and may you rejoice in the wife of your youth" (Prov. 5:18). This is our wish for you, and our prayer for your marriage.

Unless noted, all scriptural passages come from the New International Version.

Trevor and Edith Fraser
Family life facilitators

www.christianfamilyseminar.org
tfraser10005@comcast.net
efraser10005@comcast.net

CHAPTER 1

Baby, Where Did Our Love Go?

Adam and Eve: Intimacy Lost and Recovered

So the Lord God caused the man to fall into a deep sleep; and while he was sleeping, he took one of the man's ribs and closed up the place with flesh. Then the Lord God made a woman from the rib he had taken out of the man, and he brought her to the man. The man said, "This is now bone of my bones and flesh of my flesh; she shall be called 'woman,' for she was taken out of man." For this reason a man will leave his father and mother and be united to his wife, and they will become one flesh. The man and his wife were both naked, and they felt no shame.

—Genesis 2:21-25

Introduction

I REMEMBER THE first time I saw Trevor. Young and debonair, he was sitting across from me in a Bible study class. I was home after my freshman year at college and wondered who this cute fellow was. He was new to our church, and I was unattached. Unfortunately, I thought he must be married as he was sitting next to a woman who

1

was also new. When introductions were made, I heard great news. They had different last names! He was stationed at Fort Knox and from New York City! My heart skipped a beat. For the rest of the Bible study, we looked at each other and smiled. He smiled at me. I smiled at him. As we exited the room, we had each worked out a strategy to meet personally. That casual meeting more than 42 years ago was the beginning of a great relationship.

Adam and Eve had a similar beginning with just one look. What a way to begin a marriage! The man sees the woman and goes, "Wow!" It was love at first sight. Here is a marriage that God put together. The man and woman had no baggage, no family-of-origin difficulties, and no concern with extramarital affairs. Though the biblical text alludes to leaving mother and father, this couple did not have in-law problems. They really were the perfect match, right?

Yet even for this first couple, marriage was a challenge. It spanned 900 years. During those many years, they experienced many of life's complications: division and distrust, job loss, disappointment, the death of a child, and seeing the children and grandchildren grow up and leave home.

Today, the challenge to maintain a healthy, committed relationship over the life of a marriage is still difficult. According to Wilcox and Nock, the American family has experienced a revolution that involves women working outside the home, with the expectation that men will work more around and in the home. These complications require couples to negotiate on several levels. One is the increased expectation for emotional intimacy in the marriage while still balancing work and home obligations. Wives in the past who experienced intimacy in the marriage were happier even without gender equality.[1] This research suggests that long-lasting marriages have unique struggles, concerns and issues.

Our research found that the longevity of the relationship creates its own demands and that maintaining emotional intimacy is hard work. Recently, Trevor told me we had been so busy for the past three weeks, we had not even kissed! What a difference from that initial look across the room and those early days of constant contact. I was shocked and then recognized that we had not followed our own plans. We had been too busy for each other. Indeed, longevity has its challenges, and this seemed true even for Adam and Eve.

What were their unique challenges? What can modern couples learn from them? How does a marriage survive for many years? These are questions we will explore in this chapter. Adam and Eve faced issues related to emotional intimacy and its loss. One issue that confronted them, resulting in a need to adapt and change, was the role of stages or seasons of marriage. These challenges can prompt the question: Where did the love go?

Adam and Eve's story provides insight on intimacy and a relationship that was dynamic not static.

Adam and Eve: At the Beginning

Unlike any other couple, Adam and Eve were created for each other. They were the perfect match. The Bible introduces this relationship in the first chapter: "Male and female he created them" (Genesis 1:27).

First, God created Adam. Next, God gave Adam a responsibility: to name all of the animals, birds, and beasts. While God recognized Adam needed a helpmate, this responsibility brought Adam to the same conclusion because Adam realized he was alone. So God created Eve. He caused Adam to go to sleep, took a rib from his side and formed the woman, then brought her to him. When Adam saw her, he was ecstatic! He declared her "bone of

3

my bones and flesh of my flesh" (Genesis 2:23). Then he gave her a name—woman.

Their courtship and marriage has several unique features. It began with the first recorded surgery, and God performed it. This was the only time that life comes from a man. Then God, who orchestrated the surgery, performed the marriage. Adam and Eve came to their marriage with no emotional baggage, no extended family, and few outside distractions. Further, the Bible states they were both naked and not ashamed (Genesis 2:25). This nakedness implies a vulnerability to each other and an openness, which is essential for a healthy relationship.

Unlike today, they did not begin the marriage with guardedness and fear of pain. They did not have parents who failed to meet their needs, nor did they have classmates who teased or bullied them. These childhood difficulties often leave individuals with pain, vulnerability, and emotional baggage—all of which they take into the marriage. Adam and Eve did not have these difficulties. They entered their marriage willing to risk being vulnerable and willing to share with each other emotionally, intellectually, and physically. They were not guarded with walls of protection.

Several years ago, we attended the play *Fences* (Alabama Shakespeare Festival, Montgomery) by the Pulitzer Prize-wining playwright August Wilson. We were so enthralled, for the full three hours it took us to drive home we discussed its implication for couples. The play is about Troy Maxson, a man whose personal pain transformed and destroyed many relationships. Troy was always building a fence and had this very famous line: "Fences can be used to keep people in or keep people out."[2]

We have used this line frequently in our counseling. Once we counseled a couple whose relationship was filled with conflict. After a weekend of fighting, they came to our office. During the session, they gave one answer to a question that revealed the power of emotional baggage.

Mary was sharing a remark that her husband Tom made and spoke of how painful it was. He protested, saying she took it the wrong way. She became teary-eyed and said he was just trying to hurt her. I (Edith) asked if she could remember feeling this type of pain before. She again became quiet and teary—and then discussed a time at school when the other kids had called her names and said things that made her feel really bad. The feelings from that event paralleled her feelings over her husband's remark. Tom was shocked. He immediately went over to her and apologized. He had not meant his remark as a put down, and he did not know about her childhood experience.

Similar conditions may be true of your marriage. You may enter the relationship with pain from home—where your needs were not met or where you were emotionally or physically abused. You may enter the marriage with pain from your relationships at school or with other peers. The same is true of your spouse. And, like Tom and Mary, you may be aware of the other's pain. Adam and Eve. however, did not have emotional baggage.

The second unique aspect about Adam and Eve's marriage was the absence of extended family. In a recent conversation, a pastor of a large church bemoaned that mothers were so involved in the marriage of their children. Parents struggle with understanding how to divest their energies from their children's lives. (We will explore this pervasive problem in Chapter 9.) But neither Adam nor Eve had a mother-in-law or father-in-law who opposed their marriage. They had no siblings to contend with. Their marriage came with no history or pressure from extended family.

Finally, this couple had few outside distractions. Neither Adam nor Eve had an outside job; neither Adam nor Eve had bowling team or church responsibilities. They did not have aging parents or adolescent children. They were not compelled to serve on the church board or be an usher.

Like many couples, Trevor and I find ourselves on numerous boards and several committees. We have aging mothers, family responsibilities, and a precious grandson. All these outside responsibilities take time we might otherwise use to enhance our relationship. This was not the problem for Adam and Eve.

In modern life, working together can create additional pressure for some couples. While Adam and Eve worked together in the garden, this did not seem to cause conflict. Instead, there they learned about nature and about each other. An integral emotional linkage and connection held them together. They were similar in background and origins. They had no vast differences. They had many commonalities, which make for a good relationship. They were linked by God at creation, by a shared rib, by proximity as the only humans in the garden, and by love. They were in love and always together.

We do not know how long Adam and Eve lived in this state of marital bliss, but one day they became separated. One Christian writer suggests that Eve wandered unconsciously from Adam's side while working in the Garden,[3] and she found herself near the tree, confronted by a talking serpent. Amazed, Eve was drawn to the phenomenon. Before she realized it, she was first talking with the serpent and then eating the fruit. Either Adam was occupied with something else or he was emotionally distant from her. The Bible implies he was there, but he is not engaged in Eve's conversation the serpent. Thrilled with her discovery, she shares the fruit with him. Whatever occurred between the two, in the end Adam took and ate the fruit. As a result, he changed the course of history—including the chemistry of the marital relationship.

This event transformed the couple, distancing them from each other. The Bible states, "Then the eyes of both of them were opened, and they realized they were naked" (Genesis 3:7). Until then been both had been naked and unashamed. Now they were suddenly ashamed of their nakedness and afraid of God, so they hid. Their conversation with God turned into a blame game, which further distanced them and increased their loss of intimacy. Adam blamed God, talking about "the woman you put here." Then Eve blamed the serpent: "The serpent deceived me, and I ate" (Genesis 3:12-13). This blaming seems so different from Adam's first remarks about Eve—bone of his bone and flesh of his flesh.

What happened to the first couple? What led to the loss of intimacy and the confrontation at the tree? Where did the love go? The Bible doesn't answer specifically, but our understanding of relationships allows us to reflect on some lessons drawn from their experience.

Marital Difficulties for Adam and Eve: Role of Stages in Marriage

Three basic difficulties confronted this biblical couple and transformed their level of connection:

1. Unawareness that marriage is dynamic and not static, that marriage has stages and seasons
2. Loss of intimacy in the marriage by building fences
3. Failure to develop a mutual decision-making process. An exploration of each of these problems reveals their impact on the marriage.

According to Bader and Pearson, most marriages go through stages of development; marriages evolve and change.[4] At each stage has specific tasks for the couple to master before their relationship can transition to the next stage. But during a transition between stages, conflict and division may occur.

The stages are:

- Togetherness
- Reality
- Accommodation
- Transformation

Togetherness

In the first stage of marriage, the couple's task is to understand each other and how they are alike. They try hard to please each other and make an effort to spend time together. Inseparable, Adam and Eve wandered around the garden together. Perhaps they played games like hide and seek. As the only two humans, they had no problems with in-laws, nor did they have problems with Adam wanting to hang out with the boys. They were never apart. When a couple is in this first stage, maintaining the relationship is their primary goal; they will do anything to ensure the survival of the relationship—which they believe means being always together and not being different.[5] These couples are uncomfortable with differences and ignore personal identities to work on developing a couple identity.

We think of Paula and Tony, a couple we counseled—two people deeply in love and so passionately intertwined with each other that they worked together on projects such as remodeling their handyman special home. In their professional lives, they had similar jobs. They were almost always together at various functions and seemed so uniquely matched that their intimate friends would remark they were really close. They attended Paula's church together even though Tony was not a member. He wanted to share the experience. He was committed to his marriage and found it important that they share many wholesome situations regularly. After some effort, they were able to complete the work on their starter home. Such togetherness is typical of this stage. Some couples remain in this stage only a few months, while other couples like Tony and Paul stay in it longer.

What causes a transition from one stage to another? Usually something happens in the relationship. An event triggers a need or desire for a different type of relationship. The couple wants a different pattern of interaction. They focus less on "couple identity" and more on a need to establish an individual identity. In the search for a couple identity, individual needs and desires are less important. As the couple shifts to the next stage, they focus less on how they are alike and look more at how they are different. They find themselves wondering if they can love each other yet have different interests. They begin wondering about how much differentiation is acceptable without threatening the marriage.

Because these are questions most couples ponder, it is likely the first couple did too. When did Adam ask the question? When did Eve ponder the need for differentiation? We do not know. But Adam and Eve began distancing from each other. This suggests that though closely bonded at creation, there came a time when—for whatever reason—they began to be attracted to different events or circumstances. Perhaps Adam and Eve began to disconnect and focus on their own personal identities. They began to go their separate ways. Perhaps Adam was busy with the animals. Maybe he loved to watch them lope through the garden, and their interaction

9

fascinated him. Maybe Eve was concerned with the birds, the trees, and the flowers. There is no biblical explanation for what happened, but we suspect differentiation occurred slowly.

The same phenomenon happens today with recently married couples. Though at first they may spend an extraordinary amount of time together and are enamored with each other, eventually there comes the change and couples move to another stage. Patricia and Gregory Kuhlman call this the reality stage.[6]

Reality

The couple may begin to develop other interests based on their own sense of self. This pattern reflects the couple moving into another stage of marital development. The couple sometimes begins to focus on careers or on buying a house. Perhaps one of them is working two jobs and the other is going to school. For many couples, the arrival of children causes the differentiation and separation. Some begin to feel the spark has left their relationship—a factor some couples often misinterpret and some find frightening.[7] We have seen many couples come into counseling at this stage of marriage than any other. Usually one partner is uncomfortable with the changes.

In Paula and Tony's marriage, change brought discomfort. Since they could not have kids of their own, they decided to adopt. The first child was disabled and required more of Paula's time. The foster care agency had two children from the same home, so it wanted to keep them together. The agency asked Paula and Tony to consider keeping both. They agreed, and this may have been the unraveling of their closely-knit union. Soon Paula had little time for Tony, so he started going to events on his own and working more on activities that excluded Paula. Eventually their relationship became similar to that of their many friends—people living in the same house but not connecting with each other.

When a couple reaches the reality stage, it can be disconcerting. This can be the seed of conflict and confusion, especially because each partner may react differently. One partner often wants to remain in the earlier stage of connectedness and fears the other's need to pursue his or her own issues and identity.[8] One partner may feel free, while the other feels abandoned.

Most marriages go through four stages, but the reality stage is the most treacherous. In contrast to the honeymoon stage, in the reality stage sex becomes routine, and alienation and negativity increase. The spark is gone from the marriage. The couple must do something—have a plan or work hard to address this stage's concerns, one of which is the loss of intimacy. This loss requires couples to renew their relationship, manage the differences, and develop tools for addressing the conflict.

Accommodation

Couples who develop strategies to move from the reality stage transition into the accommodation stage.[10] Here partners learn conflict resolution skills; as in card games, they learn when to "hold them and when to fold them." Some issues are not worth fighting about, a few issues will never be resolved, and others require you to go along with your partner. In the accommodation stage, the couple learns these valuable lessons.

Transformation

The natural progression after successful accommodation is the transformation stage[11] as the couple returns to enjoying the benefits of a marriage, and their intimacy needs are met. The couple has developed a couple identity that allows for an individual identity for each partner. Both the marriage and the partners are transformed by the relationship. Profound intimacy occurs, and the couple shares the ups and downs of marital life.

Understanding the pattern of relationship development raises some interesting questions:

- Does distance always mean a loss of intimacy?
- Does the reality stage mean a couple is not closely bonded?
- Could Adam and Eve have had differences and still been intimate?
- Did Adam's and Eve unique concerns mean a loss of intimacy in the marriage?

These questions lead us to explore two marital difficulties that Adam and Eve and many couples today face: loss of intimacy and lack of a mutual decision-making apparatus.

Marital Difficulty: Loss of Intimacy

The loss of intimacy is one of the major marital problems confronting couples. According to Dr. Rubin, intimacy is the drive for physical union and emotional and intellectual bonding with your spouse.[12] Loss of intimacy refers to the loss of love, lack of attention to your partner's need, and a deficit of affection.

Researchers blame the lack of intimacy more than interpersonal conflict for marital difficulties—since all couples experience interpersonal conflict. Research indicates this loss of affection and validation causes an increase in hostility and conflict. According to Dr. David Ferguson, couples need to maintain intimacy emotionally, physically, and spiritually.[13] Few couples can maintain all three levels of intimacy, but successful transitioning from one stage to another requires these types of intimacy. Early in the marriage, physical intimacy is important; however, in the reality and accommodation stages, one of the primary issues is developing emotional and spiritual intimacy.

Emotional and spiritual intimacy require couples to become vulnerable and open with each other. In our counseling sessions, we often have couples who seem distant from each other and unable to connect. One tool we use to understand this distance is to help the couple develop a metaphor for their relationship. We ask them to describe their distance in physical terms. "Is the distance between you a wall, fence, or door?" These metaphors help us understand the emotional distance between them. One couple said there was a glass wall between them, another couple told us there was a barbed wire fence, and another couple spoke of a high wall built of cement blocks. Each metaphor reveals the lack of emotional and spiritual intimacy in the relationship. This distance causes conflict because of unmet emotional needs.

One pattern that many couples with unmet emotional needs develop is the interactional process of pursuing and distancing.[14] One partner, the pursuer, tends to believe the couple can stay close only by remaining in the earlier honeymoon stage. Pursuers, however, frequently marry someone who needs emotional space—a distancer. John Gray partially depicts this pattern in his discussion about men needing to go into their cave and spend time alone.[15] This cave time is essential for coping with stress. While people typically assume that men need this distance, some females like emotional space too. In the case of our biblical couple, it seems that Eve was the distancer and Adam was the pursuer.

Spouses who are distancers love to pursue their own interests. In their minds, the distance is about pursuing an individual identity and getting their needs met. In the Bible story, it seems that Eve distanced herself and found herself alone at the tree because we hear no conversation involving Adam. If he was present, he was apparently not engaged or aware.

Unfortunately, this pattern has different meanings to each of the partners. While the distancer needs to have emotional space from the pursuer for reflection or pursuing a goal, the pursuer is uncomfortable with that space. The emotional distance makes the pursuer feel abandoned. Instead of working together to find a couple solution, each partner is trying to meet emotional needs individually.[16]

Distancing is not always detrimental to a relationship; people can use it as time for reflection and development. When an individual is stressed, one option is to retreat into the "cave of the mind" and focus on the problem. For some people, problems are best solved alone in the cave. Once the problem is solved, the distancer can come out and share the resolution of the problem with the spouse.

Nevertheless, the story of Adam and Eve conveys that distancing brings risks. Too much or too frequent drifting can lead to a loss of intimacy. This marital difficulty became an important issue for Adam and Eve. A second, related marital difficulty also became evident in Adam and Eve's relationship. This couple lacked the know-how to make major decisions. A quick review of the biblical story supports this observation.

Marital Difficulty: Lack of Mutual Decision-making Apparatus

Once Eve reached the tree and was in conversation with the serpent, she had to make a major decision: eat the fruit or obey God. She was faced with uncertainty. She had to make a choice, but she had never before had to make a major decision. She had no framework for making such a big choice. In a marriage, some decisions can be made unilaterally, but others require the input from both spouses. The decision at the tree was not a time for solo choices. The couple needed to discuss it together, but they had not developed a process for making major decisions. How do couples make major decisions? What is the pattern they need to develop for good decision making?

At the tree, Eve was mesmerized by the serpent. There were at least three options she could have chosen. She could have consulted with her husband, since the decision affected them both. She could have waited and said she need more time to think. Or she could have consulted God since He met with them at the end of each day.

Unfortunately, she did not consult with her husband. She did not deliberate on this decision. She did not receive any input through prayer and study. She did not wait to talk with God. She naively made the decision herself because she believed the serpent. Without a structure to guide her choices, she was vulnerable to the serpent's suggestion.

Couples need a mechanism for decision making in their marriage. This mechanism would help couples settle on which decisions they can make independently and which should they should make as a couple. It would provide structure to help with decision making, reduce vulnerability, and enhance couple communication.

We learned this the hard way. Once we had some extra money but did not discuss how to spend it. I (Edith) assumed we were going to buy an item for the house, such as bedspreads or curtains. Trevor had different thoughts. Rather than discuss how best to use the funds, we independently plotted how to spend this money. Imagine my surprise when the item purchased with the money was a used personal computer. This was not a mutual decision; it was a unilateral decision. Unfortunately, it also was not a good decision, and we still laugh at this computer, which we have never been able to use. At the time, this incident increased tension in the family. Ultimately, it led us to develop a policy for decision making, which we will discuss in the next section.

Lessons for Reflection

We've considered the marriage of Adam and Eve—what happened to the first lovers and their love. So what can we learn from this first couple? How can they provide love and support for marriages today? There are at least four lessons we can learn from this couple:

1. Recognize all marriages have stages and seasons.
2. Work to keep intimacy in the marriage by communicating.
3. Develop an effective strategy for making major decisions.
4. Do not let adversity ruin your marriage.

1. Recognize all marriages have stages and seasons.

Marriages are dynamic, not static. Relationships require that we change because circumstances change—whether one experiences 9/11, Hurricane Katrina, or foreclosure. Such changes affect our relationships. Couples do not remain in the honeymoon stage for fifty years. We become parents, we get older, and we experience grief and loss. Each new factor can affect our marriage and nudge us into different stages in our relationship. Marriages are not static.

In good marriages, couples work together through the various stages. Each stage has its challenges and struggles. Successful progression through the stages requires communication, commitment to each other, and hard work.

A good relationship does not just happen; it takes hard work. Though we recognize that good education doesn't just happen, and that becoming physically fit requires effort, often we think developing good relationships is spontaneous. Instead, a good relationship requires effort and a commitment to each other and the marriage.

Since Adam and Eve's marriage spanned 900 years, it reveals the challenges of marital stages. Think about this couple—they experienced banishment from the garden, increased toil and pain, difficult children, the death of a child, the exile of a child, and generations of children who ignored the patriarchs' advice. None of these difficulties ended their relationship. This first couple continued to grow and develop through the stages of marriages. They learned that all of these tribulations can be resolved if God is the foundation of the marriage. Divorce was not an option for their marriage, and it should not be an option in ours.

Author Elizabeth Marquardt's recent ground-breaking research on divorce reveals that two-thirds of divorces in America occur because the couples drift apart.[17] While these marriages have low levels of conflict, there has been a loss of intimacy. Instead of fighting, these couples just wander apart. Couples allow life's difficulties to divide and separate them, and they fail to support, nurture, and encourage their relationship. Later they they wonder, Where did our love go? These marriages could be saved with counseling, marital attention, and couples' retreats.

Another technique that can help save marriages is to develop a relationship with a mentoring couple. The mentors give the other couple insights and suggestions. They meet regularly, and the mentoring couple is available to assist with problem solving and providing tips from their marital experience. These mentors can help the couple learn to develop the necessary tools for going through the stages of marriage. One of these tools is learning to improve communication.

2. *Develop tools to enhance spiritual intimacy through communication in all stages.*

Couples need to develop ways to improve intimacy in all three areas: spiritual, emotional, and physical. We suggest couples begin with spiritual intimacy—making God an essential component of your day. For Christian couples, this means developing a pattern of worship as a couple. Worship is an essential ingredient in each stage of marriage.

This was important in our marriage. On our wedding night, the first thing we did was to establish spiritual intimacy. I (Trevor) suggested two features that were essential for our marriage. The first was daily worship. I suggested we have worship every day—and that we begin and end the day in prayer. This has been our custom for the past 41 years. The second principle that framed our marriage is found in the Bible: "Let not the sun go down upon your wrath" (Ephesians 4:26 KJV). We have tried to resolve issues before we go to bed, though this principle has been harder to keep.

Worship should frame each day, which means a couple begins the day with prayer and worship together. While mornings are often hectic, couples need to at least begin the day with prayer together.

How do you begin the worship process in the marriage? Here are some suggestions we have found helpful:

- Select a short, inspirational worship thought for reading and discussion. There are numerous devotional books for couples. The readings usually take less than five minutes
- Have couple prayer; it is an intimate time between the couple and God. You can hold hands, or even hug, as you pray.
- Remember each other in prayer throughout the day.
- At the end of the day, come together again for prayer and worship.
- Select a book you both can read and discuss at evening worship. This is a time for couples to reflect on tools to enhance their marital relationships

The end of the chapter lists some books which you might consider reading. There are books that focus on male-female differences, on communication, and on stages and seasons of a marriage—to name a few. Worship not only enhances spiritual intimacy, but also provides tools for improved communication, since worship is a time for talking and connecting.

Emotional intimacy is enhanced by improved communication. At times, distancing will occur in our relationship. It is when we stop talking with each other that distancing becomes a problem. Find time for talking, really talking to each other. Go beyond talking about who will stop at the the grocery store, which team won the game, how your mother is doing, or what is happening in the news. Find time to talk about your relationship and how it is doing. This requires that you delegate time for each other—time to connect and talk about your marriage. Just as your job has weekly or monthly staff meetings, you and your spouse need regularly designated times to talk about your relationship.

Time for reflection, assessment, and planning for the marriage is essential. In the early years of our marriage, we set aside times when we would stop and talk about it. These intimate talks usually occurred on a date night, and one of us would pose the question, "How is our marriage doing? What is going good? What needs to improve?" While these conversations would at times make us uncomfortable, they enhanced our relationship.

Clifford and Joyce Penner suggest this formula for intimacy: 15 minutes a day of really talking and ending with a passionate kiss; one night a week for couples to date, talk, and be affectionate with each other; one day a month for couple time; and one weekend a quarter.[18] Couples need to arrange time for each other, or they will get too busy.

In our marriage, we try to accomplish this in several ways. Daily we have worship, which ends with a kiss. We try to eat at least one meal together and chat. We walk together once a week for about two hours, during which we talk and share with each other. We have a bi-monthly family staff meeting where we discuss finances, scheduling, or other family issues. Finally, we go on a couples retreat at least once a year and usually have an annual vacation together.

All these are ways to arrange couple time together. Still, sometimes we get too busy to find time for each other. Our experience supports that you have to schedule couple time, just as you schedule any other activity. Otherwise, various responsibilities will keep you from having time for each other. If you count on it being occasional or spontaneous, you will give each other only leftover time. It must be intentional.

Unfortunately, too many couples talk only when there is tension. This is not the most effective way to progress through the stages of marriage or to strengthen marital communication. Learning to communicate regularly and effectively reduces arguments and tension. Regularly scheduled conversations create a partnership, companionship, and friendship. Remember, Eve was created to be Adam's companion; a good marriage is based on being each other's companion and soul mate. The story of Adam and Eve is one of partnership with God and with each other.

3. *Develop effective strategy for making major decisions.*

One way to enhance communication and reduce tension is to learn to make major decisions. Adam and Eve did not have an effective strategy for making major decisions; it can create problems for your marriage also.

We remember a young couple, Darryl and Sarah, who were excited about expecting their first child after being married for two years. They had many financial challenges, but had tried to develop a cash-only and pay-as-you-go policy. One day while Sarah was shopping, she saw an unbelievable sale on baby items. They were 50 to 75 percent off, and the sale was ending that day. Sarah was ecstatic to find more than $500 worth of much-needed baby items for only $250. Because it was a sale and she needed to purchase the items that day, she charged everything. She brought the items home and could not wait to share this information with Darryl. Imagine her surprise when he told her to return them all! She was furious, and the couple went to bed without speaking to each other. She felt she had saved the family money. He felt she had violated their cash-only and pay-as-you-go policy. What Darryl and Sarah needed was a policy for making decisions and making major purchases.

How do you develop a policy for decision making? There should be several steps. The couple should meet during a regularly scheduled family meeting and develop a decision-making policy. Begin the meeting with prayer. Decide when unilateral decisions can be made and when dual decisions are necessary. This policy could be applied to expenditures like Darryl and Sarah's, but it also would have been useful for decisions like Adam and Eve's. Any decision that would affect both parties should be a mutual decision.

Mutual decisions will take more effort for discussion and exploration. Your spouse may need time to think about it, so allow for reflection time. While the decision is mutual, it should not be forced on your spouse. Each person's position should be valued and validated. Listen to your spouse's point of view and try to view the situation from his or her perspective. Then mutually decide on a policy that reflects insight from you both.

This policy provides the framework for making future decisions. Thus when confronted with a decision about a purchase, a new job, or a visit by friends, the response would be the same. "I will need to check with my spouse. We decided to have mutual decision making in cases like these, so I will get back to you." In each case, the couple would defer decision making until they can have a family meeting.

In Darryl and Sarah's case, a spending limit for unilateral decision making could be developed. Some couples will decide that any item under $100 could be decided individually, while any amount over that requires a family meeting. Using this model, Sarah would need to call Darryl at work to discuss the sale and try to get a decision. Or she would invite him to meet her at the store and see the great prices for himself. But if the timing was not good for Darryl, this couple may have to forgo the sale and wait for a joint decision on baby clothes.

In mutual decision making you are following the biblical principle to "submit to one another" (Ephesians 5:21). Had Eve and Adam followed this pattern, Eve would have invited Adam to come and talk with the serpent with her. They would have discussed the serpent's offer and together would have made a wiser choice. Ellen White, a Christian writer, states that Adam was not deceived and knew the consequences of his decision.[19] Thus, had he been invited to participate in the discussion, his insight would have resulted in a better decision. The process for decision making needs to be established in a home before one's partner is talking to a serpent in the tree or is in a store with baby clothes on sale.

4. *No matter the harmony or disharmony, all marriages will have adversity and disappointments.*

Adam and Eve teach us that even in a marriage arranged by God with a honeymoon in the Garden of Eden, one should expect adversity and disappointment. While we will explore this concept in later chapters, here are some important factors to remember:

- You and your spouse will approach adversity and disappointments differently. Your gender, family history, culture, and temperament affect how you will face adversity and disappointments.
- The difference in reaction may cause dissension in your relationship. An event that makes you so sad you want to stay home may make your spouse angry enough to want to go out and fight the injustice. Such diametrically different responses can increase tensions in the marriage.

23

In December 1989, I (Edith) got a call that changed my life. My father, after being married for 51 years, had died. Earlier that year, I had invited my parents to come to the college where I teach to share information about growing old gracefully and the role of marriage and elderly. The students were excited, and the session had great interaction. Someone from the school's technology center even taped the class. One of first things I did the day I learned of Dad's death was to get that tape. I took it home and watched it over and over. My husband also wanted to see this tape, so I left it in the VCR for him. Unfortunately, he forgot to remove it, and the class session was accidentally taped over. When I learned the tape of Dad was lost, at first I was sad but then I was furious at my husband. It felt like I had again lost my father. I was angry with Trevor and distant for about six months.

Adversity can have a major impact on a marriage. Difficult times may make you feel more vulnerable and thus increase your need for autonomy and power. These struggles for control will also increase tension in the marriage.

Despite these difficulties, trust and commitment to each other can produce resilience and fortify the relationship. Difficult times can actually increase your intimacy and closeness. This is evident in Adam and Eve's marriage, which survived events that included a son's murder. The survival of this marriage offers important lessons for all couples.

The story of Adam and Eve tells us that marriages can survive as they go through stages when intimacy is disrupted and lost. Making mutual decisions is important for all marriages. Through communication, prayer, and faith, couples can reconnect and restore their relationship. This is a story of hope and promise of a better day for all couples who put their faith in God and in each other.

Suggested Books to Read Together:

Gender Differences

John Gray, 1993, *Men are from Mars, Women are from Venus*

Emerson Eggerrich, 2004, *Love and Respect: The Love She Most Desires, the Respect He Desperately Needs*

William Harley, 2001, *His Needs, Her Needs*

Deborah Tannen, 2001 *You Just Don't Understand: Women and Men in Conversation*

Communication

Doyle Barnett, 1995, 20 *Communication Tips for Couples: A 30-Minute Guide to a Better Relationship Stages/ Seasons of Marriage*

Gary Chapman, 2004, *The Five Love Languages: How to Express Heartfelt Commitment to Your Mate*

Gary Chapman, 2007, *The Four Seasons of Marriage*

Gary Chapman, 1995; H. Norman Wright, 2000, *Communication: Key to your Marriage: A Practical Guide to Creating a Happy Fulfilling Relationship*

Rita Demarri and Sari Harrar, 2006, *7 Stages of Marriage: Laughter, Intimacy and Passion Today, Tomorrow and Forever*

Les Parrot and Leslie Parrot, 1995, *Saving Your Marriage Before it Starts*

WHERE DID OUR LOVE GO?

Personal Reflections

Text: Genesis 2:21-25

1. How would you define intimacy? How would you differentiate between sex and intimacy?

_____

_____

_____

_____

2. What role did intimacy play in your family of origin? Who did you feel you connected to? How did your family's intimacy affect your marriage?

_____

_____

_____

_____

3. Why is true marital intimacy difficult to obtain?

_____

_____

_____

_____

4. Reflect on the stages of marriage. Now reflect on how relevant these stages of development are to your marriage. Which stage best describes your marriage? Which stage would your spouse say best describes your marriage?

_____

_____

_____

_____

5. Discuss with your spouse ways to enhance your marriage and move it to another stage of development.

_____

_____

_____

_____

6. List the strategies you plan to use to enrich and enhance your marriage.

_____

_____

_____

_____

CHAPTER 2

Win, Lose or Draw:
Isaac and Rebekah
Conflict in the Home

Now Isaac had come from Beer Lahai Roi, for he was living in the Negev. He went out to the field one evening to meditate, and as he looked up, he saw camels approaching. Rebekah also looked up and saw Isaac. She got down from her camel and asked the servant, "Who is that man in the field coming to meet us?" "He is my master," the servant answered. So she took her veil and covered herself. Then the servant told Isaac all he had done. Isaac brought her into the tent of his mother Sarah, and he married Rebekah. So she became his wife, and he loved her; and Isaac was comforted after his mother's death.

—Genesis 24:62-67

Introduction

LOVE AT FIRST sight! Hollywood is full of movies about it. Scientists even claim it might be genetic.[1] This is the second couple in the Bible who provide an example of love at first sight! Isaac, the miracle son of an elderly

29

couple, sees Rebekah across the fields and loves her. They meet and quickly get married, and the Bible says he was comforted after his mother's death. Now this sounds like a marriage made in heaven. But the focus of this chapter is on conflict in the home and developing a win-win strategy for handling differences in the marriage.

How could this couple with such a loving beginning teach us about conflict? Is conflict an issue for a couple that is the perfect match? Do all couples experience conflict? What about the husband I met several years ago who said that he and his wife never argue? Is conflict something to avoid? From this one biblical couple, we can learn about all these issues.

Some of the greatest challenges that confronted Isaac and Rebekah—and couples in general— are making difficult decisions mutually, learning to handle the differences in perspectives, and handling conflict.

Research has shown that good communication increases cohesion and intimacy in the marriage, while poor communication can weaken bonds, create mistrust, and encourage contempt.[2] Therefore, developing the tools to have a good argument, learning how to deflect anger, and knowing how to resolve conflict are essential tools for a good marriage. We will look at this biblical example of a couple that experienced conflict even though at the beginning of the relationship they seemed like a perfect match. A little background will enhance our understanding of the dynamics of this couple.

Background and Early Marriage

The story begins with Isaac, the son of Abraham who was ready to get married. He was 40 years old, and his father requested that Eliezer, his faithful servant, go to Ur and find Isaac a wife. In the ancient Near East, the arranging of a marriage was the prerogative and expected role of the parents—so different from our western culture today. But considering our high divorce rate, maybe we could benefit from more parental involvement.

Eliezer focused on his mission and brought great wealth for the prospective bride. On his arrival, he met Rebekah (Genesis 24:62-67), who was Isaac's second cousin. (Marrying a niece or a cousin was a common practice in the ancient Near East.) Eliezer explained his purpose and sealed the deal. He then requested that Rebekah leave immediately. She agreed to go the next day.

Here was a woman who had the strength of character and the faith to go to an unknown country and leave her family, possibly never to see them again. These first steps seem to predict the making of a marriage made in heaven, since the plans and arrangements are God-directed.

Isaac, the miracle son of an elderly couple, saw his bride-to-be across the desert and fell in love. Rebekah knew how to please and take care of Isaac. She was a courteous, kind, friendly, and loving wife to this lonely son. Isaac was the patient, accepting, and peace-loving husband of a refreshingly spontaneous young woman. Rebekah had the making of a good companion, and Isaac had the temperament for a good husband.

This sounds like a love story in which the next line should be that they lived happily ever after. But the Bible is a book of reality, not fantasy. So this couple with the perfect beginning had problems. Again we see that the concept of the perfect match with no problems is a myth. Isaac and Rebekah reveal that even a couple who are the perfect match need basic strategies to preserve the relationship. As the story unfolds, their marriage is challenged in several areas, which we will explore in the next section.

In the early part of their relationship, Isaac and Rebekah were close because Isaac shifted his affections from his mother to his wife, Rebekah (Genesis 24:67). This suggests a relationship with warm feelings of closeness and intimacy. They were childless for twenty years, so the bond must have grown strong between them. On one occasion, Isaac was dishonest with King Abimelech about his relationship with Rebekah, claiming out of fear for his life that she was his sister. He thought the men of the land might "kill me on account of Rebekah, because she is beautiful" (Genesis 26:7). Apparently Rebekah trusted Isaac's scheme of relegating her to the role of his sister when they traveled to Philistine territory. However they were an affectionate couple, and King Abimelech caught them caressing and playing. This display of affection revealed a marriage of love and tenderness.

During their early years, they traveled extensively. Isaac uprooted the family constantly as he dug wells all over Canaan to avoid conflict over water rights (Genesis 26:15-23). There were no complaints from Rebekah about having to move. Despite the environmental stress this couple experienced, they remained committed to each other. They viewed life changes as causes for joy and celebration. But the birth of their children and the subsequent awarding of the birthright became stressors that planted seeds of conflict and disharmony in the home. These seeds took root, grew, and eventually transformed this marriage made in heaven.

Causes of Conflict

Conflict in marriage always seems to occur when several conditions prevail. Research has shown that all marriages have conflict and that the lack of conflict may be even more detrimental to a marriage than conflict. There are some circumstances, events, and situations that will cause conflict for any couple, even the perfect match.

In this story of Isaac and Rebekah, there are obvious seeds that contribute to conflict in their marriage related to the birth of their twins.

> Isaac prayed to the Lord on behalf of his wife, because she was barren. The Lord answered his prayer, and his wife Rebekah became pregnant. The babies jostled each other within her, and she said, "Why is this happening to me?" So she went to inquire of the Lord.
>
> The Lord said to her, 'Two nations are in your womb, and two peoples from within you will be separated; one people will be stronger than the other, and the older will serve the younger.'
>
> When the time came for her to give birth, there were twin boys in her womb. The first to come out was red, and his whole body was like a hairy garment; so they named him Esau. After this, his brother came out, with his hand grasping Esau's heel; so he was named Jacob. Isaac was sixty years old when Rebekah gave birth to them.
>
> —Genesis 25:21-26

The conflict in this marriage had several causes. To begin with, Isaac and Rebekah fought over the children, and each parent selected one son as the favorite. The Bible states: "Isaac, who had a taste for wild game, loved Esau, but Rebekah loved Jacob" (Genesis 25:28). Though Isaac was aware that God selected Jacob to be the leader of the next generation, he was determined to place his favorite son Esau before God's election and to ignore his wife's desire. Rebekah was equally determined that her favorite son Jacob receive the birthright by any means necessary. Isaac and Rebekah attempted to assert their individual will over God's and each other's.

This determination arose from three specific marital problems: 1) not listening, a form of miscommunication; 2) not trusting one's partner; and 3) trying to win the argument or competition. How did these three problems cause division in the marriage?

Miscommunication (not listening)

Something happened in the marriage of Isaac and Rebekah that caused them to not listen to each other. In their earlier relationship, they listened to each other and were even publicly affectionate (Genesis 26:8,9). Eventually Isaac, the pampered only child and man of the house, listened only to himself. Or maybe Rebekah, the charming daughter of a wealthy family, began to think she did not need to listen to Isaac because she knew what God wanted. After all, God had spoken to her, not Isaac. So, the partners did not hear or listen to each other.

When our son was about eight, he and I had an interesting conversation about listening. I (Edith) had asked him to do something, and he did not obey. So I asked him a typical mother question, "Vincent, did you hear me?" His response was revealing. He stated that he heard me, but he was not listening. While this story is funny, this is not good communication. This pattern must have occurred in Isaac and Rebekah's marriage. Adversarial couples frequently have poor communication. Isaac and Rebekah may have heard their spouse's words, but they were really not listening. Instead, they listened to themselves and devised plans that were contrary to each other.

In our marriage, we have found that failing to listen to each other can have dire consequences. A good example of this occurred on the day Kiesha, our daughter, missed her first orchestra recital.

It was her junior year at the Christian high school that Kiesha attended. She had a busy schedule that day. She would be taking her SAT in the morning and playing her flute in an orchestra recital that afternoon. Edith and I both had numerous appointments for the day and planned to meet at the concert. Edith thought she had given me careful instructions to pick up Kiesha after the test and take her to the concert. At two, we both arrived at the concert around the same time. We were able to sit together and waited eagerly for the concert to begin. As proud parents, we clapped as the orchestra entered the auditorium and were especially interested in the flute section. We expected to see our daughter and became worried when she did not appear.

Apprehensive that something had gone wrong backstage, we rushed downstairs after the first piece. It was one our daughter had practiced faithfully for weeks. Anxiously, we asked the director of the flute section for our daughter. Imagine our horror to learn that Kiesha had not arrived at the concert. Edith turned to me and said, "Didn't you pick up Kiesha?" I said, "I thought you did!" The rest of the story is history. We found her back at school in tears. She had missed the first concert of her musical career, all because of poor communication.

Miscommunication had heartbreaking consequences for the marriage of Isaac and Rebekah. It is clear they did not hear each other. They were so angry, they were unable to hear the problem from their spouse's perspective. Why were they unable to hear each other? A closer look reveals deeper, underlying problems that clog the channels of communication. One of these is a lack of trust or distrust.

Lack of Trust/Distrust

For Isaac and Rebekah, the failure to listen or even talk to each other reflected a lack of trust. What are some clues?

We can see this in the bestowal of the birthright, which was bestowed upon the eldest son as an inheritance from the father. It involved preeminence, authority, and the double portion. It also was connected with being a progenitor of the Messiah.[3] Important rights and responsibility were connected to receiving the birthright. When Isaac was ready to bestow the birthright on his eldest son, the issue of distrust was revealed in this marriage. Isaac autonomously made this decision without Rebekah, and she made some decisions that reflected her distrust for her husband.

Isaac was aware that giving the birthright to Esau would upset his wife. So he called his son without discussing this decision with Rebekah. Isaac did not want to talk about this issue with her anymore. He knew this was a subject they could not agree on. He felt it was his decision, and he did not need input from his wife. Isaac worked deceptively to award his favorite son the birthright without his wife's involvement.

Rebekah revealed her distrust in other ways. She had to listen carefully to conversations between Isaac and Esau while waiting for the announcement concerning the bestowal of the birthright. She had to develop an alternative plan as she waited for the discussion between Isaac and Esau. Her spying was so carefully crafted, she was able to put her alternate plan in motion before Esau's arrival back home. This allowed Jacob, her favorite son, to get the birthright (Genesis 27:5-17). For this couple, distrust was disruptive.

Distrust also causes showdowns in modern homes. We can see examples of this distrust when marriage partners do not reveal themselves or when they refuse to be vulnerable in the marriage.

At a men's retreat several years ago, I (Edith) discussed what a woman wants from a man. One thing I suggested was that women want men who were willing to risk being vulnerable and take off the mask. Many of the men were willing to explore what vulnerability in a relationship would involve. But one man said, "You mean, tell a woman what I really feel? Let her know, when I am hurt? No way! If that happens. she will know just how to hurt me." I agreed but shared that relationships cannot develop into richer and deeper ones if we do not take the risk to be vulnerable and open up in an authentic way. To that man, this was not acceptable; he was unwilling to take this type of risk. His relationship did not reflect trust.

When partners build walls or wear masks, they do so for protection. They do not trust their spouses to hold sacred their heart and soul. It seems safer to hide from each other. When there is a mask or wall, difficulties increase in the relationship. How did Isaac and Rebekah begin to lose trust? One factor that leads to distrust is self-focus based on competition.

Competition and Power Struggles

Competition is great in sports, but it can devastate a marriage. Consider Charles and Cathy, who had been married about 10 years. They were in their mid thirties at the time of the marriage. Prior to their marriage, they talked frequently, but once they got married, Cathy complained that Charles had grown silent. He worked hard at several jobs but had little time or effort for her. She did not know what was going on with him or his business. They were both successful in their business life, but not in their marital life because of competition. A win-lose strategy may enhance a business, but not a marriage. During our counseling sessions with Cathy and Charles, their competition was obvious. Each was bright and articulate and spent much of the session trying to win points in the argument and prove each was the smarter. Their relationship was based on winning and being the best—tools that helped them in business but were less useful in their marriage relationship.

Competitive relationships are caused by several factors, including insecurity, self-focus, and a "my way or the highway" attitude. When we are insecure, our sense of identity is based on winning. Being number one is essential to enhance self-esteem, but, as we see in the marriage of Isaac and Rebekah, a self-focus heightens the competitive nature of the relationship. One reflection of self-focus is the feeling that things have to go "my way."

Both Isaac and Rebekah were self-focused. Each wanted the favored child to receive the blessing. Was Rebekah right in wanting Jacob to win? Was Isaac right in wanting Esau to win? Both were right, and both were wrong. Rebekah was right about wanting Jacob to receive the birthright. Isaac was right in wanting to follow the spiritual and social tradition to give the birthright to the older son. But neither was willing to allow God to lead in the process, nor were Isaac and Rebekah willing to submit to each other (Ephesians 5:21). Winning became paramount, more important than God's direction or their relationship. Their attempts to deceive ended in failure. Trust cannot survive in an atmosphere of winners and losers. Isaac and Rebekah developed a win-lose tactic, where one would win and the other would lose. In the end, they both lost.

Most marriage and family specialists recognize that competition and power struggles are an inevitable part of marriage. Marriages are dynamic and changing. As we mentioned in the first chapter, couples begin a marriage connected with idealistic love for each other and at first agree on everything. When couples become more comfortable with each other, disagreements increase, which can lead to a struggle for power. Such power struggles are inevitable and can be an ingredient of a healthy relationship. But they become detrimental when a couple remains locked in a struggle for many years, like Isaac and Rebekah. The power struggle begins to impact all conversations, and the couple disagrees about everything, resulting in a showdown in the home. What happens to a marriage when there is a showdown? The answer is conflict in the home— with all its consequences.

Results of Conflict in the Home

In a marriage, we want a win-win situation. Winners and losers have no place, since the relationship must continue after the argument is over. Just think what happened to Isaac and Rebekah's marriage after the showdown. Who really won and who really lost? Isaac and Rebekah both lost because the son who was deceived resented his lost birthright and began plotting the death of his brother. "Esau held a grudge against Jacob because of the blessing his father had given him. He said to himself, 'The days of mourning for my father are near; then I will kill my brother Jacob'"(Genesis 27:41). As a result, the deceiving son (Jacob) was forced to flee his home and live the life of a fugitive. He never again saw his mother alive. In a sense, Isaac and Rebekah lost both of their children—bringing on themselves pain and disappointment.

In today's environment, this marriage would have ended in divorce in their waning days. Deceit and mistrust brought pain into the relationship, and the marriage made in heaven seemed to be one that ended in hell. They lost all while trying to gain all. Two elderly people, one blind and the other missing her favorite son, were left to live their declining years together—what a sad picture! What a sad end for a marriage made in heaven that started with love at first sight.

Impact of Life Transitions

There is one final element to consider as a condition that contributed to conflict in this biblical home: the disruption in the relationship caused by environmental pressure, life stresses, or transitional points.

The perfect marriage became dysfunctional due to several factors: competition, life changes, and transitional points. The life change due to the birth of the twins became a critical stressor. Research has shown that marital happiness often decreases when children enter the home. The couple may become child-focused instead of focused on each other. Childcare is demanding, so there is less time for each other. Invariably, each parent wants to parent the children the way he or she was parented. But issues from the family we were born into or that raised us frequently cause difficulty in the marriage regarding the role of parents. In Isaac's home of origin, there had also been difficulty over the issue of who received the birthright. Remember, Hagar wanted Ishmael to receive it; Sarah wanted her child of promise, Isaac, to receive it. In both cases, the son of promise was not the oldest son, the traditional recipient of the birthright. (We will explore this phenomenon more in the next chapter.)

Today, stress may come from the birth of a child, a new job, or new work responsibilities, relocation, or dislocation. These stresses can result in conflict and competition, but persistent conflict and competition can be devastating. Just imagine the state in which Isaac and Rebekah found themselves—living in an empty nest with their marriage in shambles!

Lessons from Isaac and Rebekah

What can be learned from this couple of the past? Are there principles that can be used today? After all, conflict and controversy are to be anticipated in all marriages and not just marriages with problems.

1. *Conflict, controversy, and showdowns are inevitable in any marriage.*

In the Bible, conflict occurs over and over in human relationships. First, we must recognize that conflicts are inevitable. No marriages will exist without them. Occasionally, I (Edith) meet couples who proudly boast they have been married for five years or ten years and never have conflict! I find this hard to believe. In fact, I question the couple's truthfulness and their ability to have separate identities.

Expect conflict in your marriage, and when it comes, don't feel devastated and retreat behind a wall of poor communication, mistrust, and self-focus. Avoiding conflict is just as destructive as negative quarrels. Avoidance means not discussing important issues in the marriage, and these issues do not go away. My concerns become like the proverbial elephant in the room or albatross around the neck, influencing every conversation and increasing tension and mistrust. The solution is not avoiding conflict, but rather developing strategies for effective conflict-resolution.

2. *Make plans to fight for your marriage.*

A recent study suggested that of all the factors in relationships, a couple's ability to deal with conflict was the most powerful predictor of marital satisfaction. It's not the absence of conflict that makes a good marriage. All marriages have conflict because marriages are made up of human beings.[4]

41

In homes with high marital satisfaction, the couple recognized they were not competitors but on the same team. So the goal is not to win one's own point, but for the marriage to win. We make plans to fight for the marriage. John Gottman suggests that healthy marriages accentuate the positive and balance negative comments with positive ones.[5] In fact, Gottman suggests that healthy marriages have five times more positive than negative comments.[6]

When you get ready to approach your spouse about a controversial issue, begin the conversation with positives. Complimenting your spouse reflects that you value the relationship. We should always try to appreciate and value our spouse more than we criticize. This requires that we make plans to fight for our marriage and approach our spouse only after we have had time to think—similar to the old rule of counting to ten before you speak. This requires developing rules for a good argument.

3. Follow rules for a good, clean fight

Since conflict is inevitable and even necessary, rules must be learned for having positive instead of negative conflict. Conflict should **never** involve physical assault of any kind, such as hitting, kicking, shoving, or choking. Physical assaults are always inappropriate in marital conflict. Nancy Van Pelt suggests some guidelines for healthy disagreements in a marriage.[7] These guidelines, adapted by the authors, reflect her principles:

> **Pray.** When conflict arises, prior to having a conversation with your spouse, pray an unusual prayer. This may sound trite but it is an essential first step. Pray for yourself, that God will give you the words to say and help you hear clearly. Pray that God will give you

the wisdom to know how to handle this situation. "If any of you lacks wisdom, he [or she] should ask God" (James 1:5).

Choose a mutually accepted time and place. Go to your spouse and ask when is the best time and place to have this conversation. Do not begin the conversation when your spouse walks in the door or while he or she is watching TV, especially a football game or favorite program. Selecting the wrong time makes a difficult conversation worse. "There is a time for everything, and a season for every activity under heaven" (Ecclesiastes 3:1).

Speak the truth in love. In conversation, select your words carefully. While it is important to speak the truth, truth must be encircled with love. The Bible admonishes this in love Ephesians 4:15. One way to accomplish this is to use "I-messages" to take responsibility for your words and thoughts. Instead of saying, "You made me feel this way," say, "I feel this way because." Using I-messages reduces defensiveness and increases communication.

Stay on the subject. Too often couples have kitchen-sink arguments, which mean they discuss everything. If the conversation is about the budget, stay on the subject; do not turn the conversation to an inquiry about coming in late last night. "Do not let any unwholesome talk come out of your mouths, but only what is helpful for building others up according to their needs, that it may benefit those who listen" (Ephesians 4:29). Kitchen-sink arguments do not build up or reflect the needs of each partner equally. Especially for men, since many men prefer compartmentalized discussions, straying from the specific subject increases tensions and difficulty.

When conversation diverts from the primary topic, defensiveness increases. Staying on the subject is a matter of fighting fair. Bringing up past history is unfair and unproductive.[8]

Show respect for each other. Respect is an essential component of good communication. It means to be quick to hear and slow to speak. "Be devoted to one another in brotherly love. Honor [respect] one another above yourselves" (Romans 12:10). During the conversation, listen carefully to your spouse, then observe what he or she says. Once spoken, words cannot be retrieved. "The lips of the righteous nourish many" (Proverbs 10:21). Disrespect does not encourage or enhance a relationship. When one spouse feels disrespected, that partner's needs are not met and he or she is more apt to become angry and try to retaliate. Respect is essential for good communication.

Avoid communication killers. There are words that can heighten the tensions in our conversation or end effective communication. "He who holds his tongue is wise" (Proverbs 10: 19). Therefore, in your conversations avoid the following:

Overgeneralizations which include words like *ever, never,* and *always.* Such words increase disagreement because they accuse and condemn. Besides, your partner can always remember exceptions.

Derogatory names which are used when we call our spouse "an idiot" or "stupid." These are not endearing statements. They are disrespectful and increase negativity in the discussion. It is unfair to call names. "Get rid of all bitterness, rage and anger, brawling and slander, along with every form of malice" (Ephesians. 4:31).

Ridicule and sarcasm, disrespectful attitudes, increase defensiveness and foster retaliation. Avoid making fun of your spouse and saying things like, "Even a baby could do that." When one says, "It doesn't take a rocket scientist to complete this task," the spouse recognizes you have just implied he or she is stupid. These statements increase barriers and emotional distance in the relationship—and are examples of unfair fighting.

Offensive comments about your spouse's family will increase discord rather than enhance marital harmony. Even a child knows that talking about someone's "mama" makes him or her mad. This is the source of many schoolyard fights. We learned that in the kindergarten, and it is still true.

Tears. While we may not be able to manage our tears, do not use them as a tool for manipulation. Talk through the tears; do not allow them to halt conversation. Keep talking as the tears stream down your face. This will provide you more control over your tears.

Silence— if it does not encourage communication. Sometimes silence reflects a need to process the information. But if the person needs time to think, he or she should say so. Internal processors are individuals who need to think deeply about a subject, silently and to oneself. They may think better in silence. But do not retreat behind a wall of silence; it is infuriating for the external processor. Those are people who think out loud, who think about the problem by verbalization. Such people think better when talking it out; they want to process the event verbally. Unfortunately, internal processors and external processors tend to marry each other. In a discussion, partners need to recognize these differences. Rather than being silent, ask for time to think and suggest that you resume the conversation in twenty-four hours. In any case, do not go beyond forty-eight hours.

Quick, angry moves that evoke fear. When you jump up and pace, it can make your partner fearful. If you need to pace while you think, let your spouse know you need to move so you can think. Do not use any threatening gestures. Take a timeout if you need it. Use the timeout to transform your angry thoughts into more rational ones. Yelling, screaming, and threatening tones are never helpful forms of communication. These behaviors eliminate rather than enhance communication; they reduce affection and encourage division in the relationship.

Allow time for your spouse's reaction. Once you have shared your side of the issue, your point of view, *listen*. The most important part of the conversation is hearing and listening to your spouse's response. "Let the wise listen and add to their learning, and let the discerning get guidance"(Proverbs 1:5). "Everyone should be quick to listen, slow to speak and slow to become angry" (James 1:19). One component missing in most couple's communication is the ability to listen. *Empathy* means to look at the issues from the other's viewpoint. Listening empathically means to understand the issue from your spouse's perspective. You already know why you feel that way about the bills being paid, why does your spouse feel differently? What factors, perhaps from his or her childhood, foster this response?

Tom and Mary were in our office; she was really upset about financial insecurity in their marriage. Tom repeatedly assured her that all the bills were being met, but Mary did not seem consoled. Further discussion revealed that Mary was raised in a home where they often went without food. On some occasions, they were even evicted. She never forgot the pain of this poverty and promised herself she would never live with it as an adult. Therefore, financial insecurity carried deeper meaning to her. Listening to your spouse's perspective provides insight into important emotional needs and concerns—and enhances intimacy.

List and evaluate possible solutions and alternatives. All discussions should lead to a solution. Now that we both know the problem, what is the solution? How will we resolve this issue? Together, list all possible solutions and be creative—list everything both of you can think of. Do not eliminate any alternative or put down any suggestion. During this step consider all options, for evaluation will come later. Evaluation too early stops the process. For brainstorming to be effective, you need creativity. Clearly consider any alternative solution, since what you have done in the past is not working.

We use this method in our personal finances. Trevor was paying the bills and became concerned about the number of checks I was writing but not recording in the checkbook. The resulting increase in bounced checks and overdraft fees led to increased tension in our relationship. When we followed the process we outlined and listed numerous options, we developed the method we now use. Trevor manages the family account. We pool our resources in that account, but we also keep a separate account for me where we deposit the money for the food bill and my allowance. This strategy has stood the test of over 20 years. It provided me with my own credit history; it also reduced the number of insufficient-funds checks and overdrafts. This process reduced the tension in our marriage.

Choose and implement the best alternatives. Now you are ready to select the best option and method to implement the solution. Together go over each alternative and list the pros and cons. Discuss alternatives based on what is realistic for you. Finally, select the best choice for both persons. Discuss the best way to implement this option and when you plan to implement it. A timeline is essential. Also, discuss who will have primary responsibility to carry out the plan. These are essential components for making a change.

End the "clean fight" with couple prayer. Once you have a plan to resolve the conflict, you end your discussion with couple prayer. Couple prayer is an intimate time and can include holding hands or hugging as you pray. End your couple prayer with a kiss. This is the time to bring you as a couple back together. To kiss and make up is one of the best steps to ending the showdown and developing a truce in your marriage. While conflict is inevitable, there are some things you can do to enhance your marriage. This includes increasing dependence in each other.

4. Develop trust-building activities in your marriage.

One way to enrich your marriage is to develop activities that will enhance and increase your time together. Some of these activities include

- Have couple prayer and couple worship daily (begin and end the day with prayer for each other).
- Arrange daily and weekly connecting times.
- Go on a least one marriage-enrichment weekend a year.
- Read self-help books together and discussing them to enrich your marriage.

5. Recognize transition points and stressful times when they occur, and use these times to renegotiate.

Be alert to transition points and choose to talk more at these times. After the birth of a child, the death of a parent, a change in jobs—these are times for increased talking, not times to shut down. These times require that we change the routine or find different times for couple prayer or weekly dates.

Transition requires that we renegotiate instead of retreat from each other or to continue as if there had been no change. These are times to talk about our pain, our struggles, and our difficulties and then recognize the effect of the change on the marriage. We have found that each time we moved, we had to renegotiate. We have moved twelve times and lived in seven states. Each of these moves had an impact on our relationship. Usually these moves involved changes in our employment status. We needed to talk more, since job changes frequently require more time away from the home. We had two children; this required renegotiation. We have had numerous family members to live with us: siblings, grandmother, parents, nieces, and nephews. Each of these additions required that we renegotiate and adapt.

In conclusion, Isaac and Rebekah's marriage provides insight into making the marriage an option for growth and development. It suggests that marital success is not predictable, but requires that couples work hard to develop strategies for success. It suggests tools for loving each other enough to fight for the marriage—and not to avoid conflict. Finally, it offers these lessons for approaching conflict in the marriage:

1. Conflict, controversy, and showdowns are inevitable in any marriage.
2. Make plans to fight for your marriage.
3. Follow rules for a good clean fight.
4. Develop trust-building activities in your marriage.
5. Recognize transition points and stressful times when they occur and use these times to renegotiate.

WIN, LOSE, OR DRAW
Personal Reflections

Text: Genesis 24:62-67

1. Reflect for a moment on conflict as you experienced it as a child. How was conflict handled in your home? What was the philosophy about conflict you learned?

_____

_____

_____

_____

2. How has the message you learned about conflict in your home of origin affected your marriage?

_____

_____

_____

_____

3. Now reflect on your spouse and his or her family. How do you think conflict was handled in that family? How has the message your spouse learned affected conflict in your marriage?

_____

_____

_____

_____

4. What do you believe are acceptable behaviors for *you* in an argument? What are some things that are unacceptable for *you* in an argument?

_____

_____

_____

_____

5. What are acceptable behaviors for *your spouse* in an argument? What are some things that are unacceptable for *your spouse* in an argument? Ask your spouse these same questions.

_____

_____

_____

_____

6. Develop an acceptable protocol using some of the information you learned in this chapter. Feel free to make adaptations that are appropriate for your marriage.

_____

_____

_____

_____

7. Develop some plans for trust-building activities in your marriage (dates, family meetings, marriage enrichment weekend) and list them below. Be specific. When do you plan to begin these activities?

_____

_____

_____

_____

CHAPTER 3

Chips Don't Fall Far from the Block, or Chips off the Block

Jacob, Leah, and Rachel: Blended Family with Generational Concerns

Some time later Joseph was told, "Your father is ill." So he took his two sons Manasseh and Ephraim along with him.

—Genesis 48:1

And Joseph took both of them, Ephraim on his right toward Israel's left hand and Manasseh on his left toward Israel's right hand, and brought them close to him. But Israel reached out his right hand and put it on Ephraim's head, though he was the younger, and crossing his arms, he put his left hand on Manasseh's head, even though Manasseh was the firstborn. ...

When Joseph saw his father placing his right hand on Ephraim's head he was displeased; so he took hold of his father's hand to move it from Ephraim's head to Manasseh's head. Joseph said to him, "No, my father, this one is the firstborn; put your right hand on his head."

But his father refused and said, "I know, my son, I know. He too will become a people, and he too will become great. Nevertheless, his younger brother will be greater than he, and his descendants will become a group of nations."

—Genesis 48:13-19

Introduction

WE CAN STILL remember them, though the series was on TV in the 70s. There was Greg, Marcia, Peter, Jan, Bobby, and Cindy plus Mom and Dad. Who are they? *The Brady Bunch*! Blended families are still on TV today with the real-life blended families of Bruce Jenner and Kris Kardashian Jenner who between them have ten children and are featured on E![1] The Rev. Edson Gilmore of Jason Lee United Methodist Church in North Salem acknowledged his family was blended; there was his mother's three daughters, his father's two sons, and the six children they had together.[2]

The Bible is filled with blended families. These infamous families are strikingly different from the *Brady Bunch*. Perhaps, they are more like Jenner's! Did the *Brady Bunch* provide a model for us to follow? According to Ron Deal, "The Brady Bunch lied!" Blended families do not have it so easy. What is the best strategy for blended families? How can the Bible and ancient couples help us with a modern problem?

Focusing on the family of Jacob and his wives, Leah and Rachael, provides some insight. It is quite profound that families in the twenty-first century have similar struggles as this ancient biblical family. In this century, there has been an increase in blended families. "One out of every three Americans today is a stepparent, stepchild, stepsibling or some member of a step family… there are more than 11 million remarried households in the US."[4] A blended family or a stepfamily is "a primary kinship group whose

56

members are joined as a result of second or subsequent marriages."[5]

Using this definition, it is clear that the family of Jacob, Leah, and Rachel was a *blended* family revealing some of the challenges: *favoritism, boundaries, family of origin issues, and division.* We will explore each of these issues in this chapter.

A quick explanation of some of these terms seems essential. Just as countries have borders that are invisible unless there is a specific delineation, each blended family also has personal borders or boundaries. Not only does the family have personal space—a specific area in which most people are not allowed to enter without permission—the family itself has boundaries. These indiscernible lines of demarcation separate an individual, couple, or family system from the outside surroundings.[6] Family boundaries control information flow and the type and quality of interaction. They also establish identity. A boundary could be compared to a fence; a fence is meant to communicate ownership of land, protect and defend geographic space, and keep intruders away.

Derrick and Eve had been married for six years. The couple came to the office because Derrick was upset that Eve told her mother and sisters everything that happened in their home. They didn't have any secrets. Eve, however, felt that what she shared were not important issues; she complained that Derrick just didn't want her to spend any time with her family. This was a couple struggling with boundary issues. These issues become even more complicated in a blended family.

All individuals are products of the social context, the family in which one is raised. Social scientists prefer to call it *family of origin.*[7] Thus, the family has a major impact on many aspects of life. In reflecting on Derrick and Eve, their different families influenced how information and was shared and with whom it was shared. Derrick was an only child in a family with very little interaction with other members of the extended family. Derrick's family had many family secrets that were seldom discussed; they were hidden and rarely disclosed. On the other hand, Eve was from a gregarious, large family with very few family secrets—a "tell-all family." We can understand how family of origin circumstances play out in ways that create conflict and boundary issues. Derrick wanted to keep it. Eve wanted to be expressive and free.

The institution of marriage is a window to the world that frames our feelings and shapes worldview. I (Trevor) remember as a child growing up in a Jamaican home. This upbringing affected many aspects of my life. The foods I eat, such as rice and peas, callaloo, and plantain reflect my family heritage. My family affected the orderly approach I continued in my household today. My mother was really neat, and her neatness influences me today. On the other hand, my father influenced me by his use of witticism to explain everyday life. My father was always quick to express witticisms to explain the way things were or the way people would react. For those who would be critical of others, he would say, "People who live in glass houses should not throw stones." When one might waste or disdain food, he would comment, "You don't miss the water till the well runs dry." If children did something reminiscent of their parents, he would say, "Chips don't fall far from the block." A similar phrase is used by Edith's southern culture, "An apple doesn't fall far from the tree." These kind of sayings were prevalent in our home. The family of origin influences has a major impact on our life.

We will explore each of these psychological concepts (boundaries, family of origin, blended family) through Abraham's to Joseph's family. To understand the influence of family of origin requires an overview of the family of Abraham, Isaac, Jacob, and Joseph. It reveals a number of unresolved family issues surrounding birthright and favoritism—issues that have emotional impact for several generations. This family has lessons for today's family to learn.

Family Historical Review

This biblical family's history begins with Abraham and Sarah, who were married for many years without any children. Tired of waiting for the son of promise from Sarah, Abraham had a child by Hagar, Sarah's servant. This son's name was Ishmael. When Abraham was 100 years old and Sarah was 90 years, they had their son Isaac. He was to be the son of promise and the one who would carry the family name.

Isaac was single until the age of forty, when he married Rebekah his second cousin. This couple had a relationship that might be described as a "marriage made in heaven" (chapter 2). Their marriage was God-led and God-directed (Genesis 24). They were married for more than twenty years with no children. Isaac implored the Lord for a child, and the result was twin boys, Jacob and Esau. Jacob was the younger twin son born to Isaac and Rebekah.

As an adult, Jacob connived with his mother to steal the birthright from his brother. As a result, Jacob was forced to flee to his mother's homeland. He ran for his life in the wilderness and went to a land he knows nothing about. It is in this land that Jacob, Rachel, and Leah began their story. (See Genogram page 81.)

Generational Similarities

To understand the role of the family, reflect on all three generations depicted in the genogram. What similarities are noted in this ancient biblical family? There were many similarities among Abraham, Isaac, and Jacob.

1. *All three had a personal encounter with God that was transformative:*

Abraham talked with God numerous times (Genesis 12:1-4; 13:14-17; 17:1-22; 18; 21:12-14; 22:2) and had many visions, dreams, and face-to-face conversations with God. Isaac, like his father, also had direct encounters with God (Genesis 25:21; 26:2-6). During his encounters, Isaac entreated the Lord for children when his wife was infertile, and he also listened when the Lord admonished him not to go to Egypt. Jacob also had many encounters with God and even wrestled with God (Genesis 28:13-16; 31:3; 32:24-31; 35:1-4, 10-13; 46:3-6). God directed Jacob's path, told him where to go and when to leave. God changed his name after a night of struggle.

Sometimes God changed their names after the encounters. For example, God changed *Abram* to *Abraham* and *Jacob* to *Israel*. Often these encounters provided them with their mission statement and their lifelong goals. Each of these three had transformative encounters with God.

2. *An important similarity that affected family dynamics is the display of favoritism.*

Each of these men had a favorite son; we can see that favoritism creates jealousy. Abraham's family was divided after the birth of Isaac because Sarah felt that Ishmael, the son of Hagar the slave, mocked her son-of-promise Isaac. The results were tensions and conflict that ended when Ishmael and his mother were sent into the wilderness (Gen. 21:9-19). Thus the seed of contention was introduced hat would plague this family for four generations.

60

For Isaac, the issues of favorite son revolved around his choice of Esau, his firstborn. The Bible states, "And Isaac loved Esau, because he did eat of his venison" (Gen. 25:28 KJV). His wife Rebekah loved Jacob better. This resulted in Jacob conspiring with his mother to steal the birthright from Esau—and Jacob being forced to flee for his life. Once again, favoritism produced separation and division in this family.

You would think that Jacob would have learned from his family the consequences of favoritism. But this pattern continued because Jacob had a favorite wife who bore him his favorite sons, Joseph and Benjamin. In Genesis 37:3, we read, "Jacob [Israel] loved Joseph more than any of his other children" (NLT). This is astonishing, since Jacob had 12 sons, in addition to daughters. Although the history of this family should have taught Jacob that having a favorite is detrimental to family security and family relationships, Jacob still selected Joseph as his favorite—and even gave him a coat of many colors. The results of favoritism are still the same. There were tensions, conflicts, and confusion, which resulted in separation and division. Joseph the favorite son was sold into the wilderness. The result of favoritism harmed this family once again. The chip didn't fall far from the block.

3. *Another generational pattern involved the recipient of the birthright.*

In all three families, the favorite son was not the oldest son. Nevertheless, the favorite son received the birthright. This favoritism caused struggles between sons over who should get it. At times, this struggle involved two generations—and it may be argued the struggle has passed down to the present generation.

While Ishmael was Abraham's oldest son and customarily would have received the birthright, Ishmael was sent away and Isaac was designated the heir apparent (Genesis 21:10-13). A similar scenario occurs in the life of Esau and Jacob. While Esau was the older twin, the birthright went to Jacob. Finally, when Jacob neared the end of his life and called his twelve sons together, Reuben the firstborn did not receive the blessing. Instead, Joseph received the greater blessings from his father (Genesis 49:22-26).

The issues of favoritism and the birthright led this family to periods of distrust, difficulties, and disappointment. It led to separation and division in the family. Abraham had to send Hagar and Ishmael away. Isaac and Rebekah had to send Jacob away after his deception, and Joseph's brothers sold him away. *Once again the chip didn't fall far from the block*. Like father, like son. We may even say that these younger sons experienced some separation anxiety, and that the eleven other brothers continued to distrust Joseph reaction to them after their father's death.

4. *The final similarity between these three men, deals with dishonesty, integrity, and family secrets.*

At some point in their experience, all three men exhibited dishonest tendencies. Abraham (Genesis 12:11-13, 20:1-5) and Isaac (Genesis 26: 6,7) were both dishonest about the identity of their wives. They claimed their wives were their sisters. While Sarah may have been Abraham's half-sister (Genesis 20:12), Rebekah was Isaac's second cousin. Jacob was dishonest to his father when he pretended to be Esau (Genesis 27:18-26).

The pattern of deception that persisted within the family may have reflected some family secret of preferences with mother against father. This alignment reflects something that happens in many families—and is also a boundary issue. For example, Joyce and her mother were very close. They had always been close; her mother would sometimes come into her bedroom at night, and they would talk for long hours. Joyce's father seemed to resent this closeness, but Joyce loved it. At times she and her dad would have disagreements, and she knew she could always go to her mother who would change the punishment or side with her. Joyce and her mother were on the same team. The mother-daughter duo often slept together. This inordinate closeness is another example of misalignment or improper balance. Alignment problems can happen in any family, but are accentuated in blended families.

The dishonesty in this biblical family continued in the next generation. Jacob's sons were dishonest with him when they failed to report the actual cause of Joseph's disappearance—another example of a family secret. Instead of being honest, the brothers blamed his disappearance on a wild beast (Genesis 37:33,34). This family secret was maintained for many years. How did these boys keep the truth from their father for fifteen or twenty years? The chip doesn't fall far from the block.

Family secrets are detrimental and cause conflict in many families. Peg and Sal had been married for many years when Sal's mother died. He and his older sister, Barbara, worked on the arrangements, and she confessed she had a family secret she needed to share. Barbara told Sal she was not his sister; instead she was his mother. This news was devastating for Sal especially when he discovered who his biological father was. These revelations caused Sal to begin a process of self-understanding, which resulted in increased tensions in his marriage—resulting in a subsequent divorce. Family secrets about historical events such as rape, incest, or suicide can be toxic for couples and families.

Family secrets were present in the family of Jacob, Leah, and Rachael—and the difficulties had lifelong consequences for this family. Tensions resulted in pressures, and the pressures caused family dysfunction and dissension. Favoritism and the negative consequences of tension in these marriages resulted in a family characterized by jealousy, disagreement, and division. These are important issues to explore for blended families.

Jacob's Marriages

A quick review of the story begins with Jacob fleeing from his home and traveling to his mother's home in the land of Haran. Upon arrival in Haran, he met Rachael at the well, much like Eliazer had met Rebekah many years earlier. This meeting united Jacob with his mother's people and reveals that Rachael, whom he finds beautiful and attractive, is his cousin. Soon he began to work for his Uncle Laban and requests Rachael as payment. The Bible says he "served seven years to get Rachel, but they seemed like only a few days to him because of his love for her" (Genesis 29:20).

Laban gathered the men and then had a feast for the wedding, but he sent Leah to Jacob that night instead of Rachael. Jacob must have been thrilled in his tent after seven years of waiting because he had finally gotten the woman of his dreams. When he woke up and, in the light of the morning, looked into the face of his bride he saw Leah—Rachael's sister with "weak eyes" (Genesis 29:17), not his beloved Rachael. Thus the pattern of deceit, dishonesty, and fraud continued; Jacob, the trickster, was tricked.

Jacob confronted his father-in-law and Uncle, Laban, who offered him an "option." Laban promised him Rachael after one week—if he would work for him for seven more years. Jacob accepted the deal and got Rachael a week later. The Bible states that he loved Rachael more than Leah (Genesis 29:30). The seeds for conflict and dysfunction were sown in this family.

In the next chapter, one sees the sisters fighting over who will sleep with Jacob, then the sisters fought over whose handmaid would sleep with Jacob (Genesis 30). At the end of chapter 30, Jacob had eleven sons and at least one daughter by four different women. The sisters were fighting each other and even involving the children. Conflict and confusion were prevalent in this family. This family manifested all the characteristics of a dysfunctional family.

Dysfunctional families are characterized by unstable, rigid, or chaotic family patterns.[8] There is little support for the developmental needs of individual members. Typical problems for dysfunctional families include:

- problems with inclusion—deciding who belongs in the family.
- problems with boundary issues—deciding who resolves which issues.
- problems in alignment, which relate to choosing sides and settling allegiances.
- problems in the ability of individuals to carry out their function of being husband, wife, or child.

We see all these dysfunctional behaviors in this biblical family.

This family had problems with deciding who belonged in the family since it is a complicated, polygamous family. There was definite confusion about the role of Bilhah and Zilphah since their mistresses claimed their children from Jacob as their own. The relationship between the sisters was fraught with confusion over inclusion. Leah accused her sister on one occasion of usurping her position as wife: "Wasn't it enough that you took away my husband? Will you take my son's mandrakes too?" (Genesis 30:15) This example also shows problems with boundaries and alignment for the family; Rachael bargained for the mandrakes by offering for Jacob to sleep that night with Leah. When Jacob returned home, Leah informed him, "You must come and sleep with me tonight. ... I have paid for you with some mandrakes that my son found " (Genesis 30:16 NLV). Jacob complies.

There is no sense that this family had developed a problem-solving method and clear line for decision making. The sisters were in a battle, and every other member of the family seemed to have been inconsequential in their battle. Rachael explained this process when she states: "I have struggled hard with my sister, and I'm winning!" (Genesis 30:8 NLV). This is a family with secrets: The sons never revealed the real cause of Joseph's disappearance, so Jacob is led to believe he was killed by wild beasts. Another secret in this family occurs after Reuben sleeps with Bilhah, his father's concubine and his aunt's maidservant (Genesis 35:22). This is really an incestuous relationship. Conflict and strife in the family form the context for the eventual selling of Joseph into slavery in Egypt. Family deception continued, and it provides a potent illustration about generational issues.

How can a polygamous family bring help to blended families today? Some sociologists believe that in America there exists serial monogamy. Recently a woman walked into the office requesting marital help. She was having difficulty, but wanted to save this marriage. It was her third husband! When couples are married two, three, or four times, they are confronted with challenges similar to that of this polygamous biblical family. This is a powerful story with some compelling lessons for mothers and fathers, husbands and wives in the twenty-first century

Challenges Learned From Jacob, Leah, And Rachael

The first challenge we can learn from this family is the power of family of origin. Parents are their children's first windows to the world; they influence the development of norms, relationships, standards, and even selection of partners. Think about when you use words or statements that you have heard from a parent. Or remember activities that your family valued during your childhood, which you have put into practice in the family as an adult. Such is the power of the family of origin. Reflect on that role as a parent, think about food preference—even the approach to marital roles and responsibilities. Each reveals the power of the family origin. Here are some examples of the power of the family influences.

In a family life workshop, a woman was discussing the power of parents on her interactions. She explained that her mother loved buying and collecting shoes—but that her father thought this was frivolous. So her mother developed the habit of purchasing shoes and hiding them from her husband. The mother would collude with her daughter in the secret. The woman admitted growing up believing men did not like women to purchase too many shoes since her father had only a few basic shoes. When this woman got married, she continued this belief and tradition. She would purchase shoes and hide them from her husband. Imagine her surprise after six years of marriage to discover that her husband did not care if she purchased shoes! She had for six years used a message from her family of origin to frame her interactions with her husband. Generational messages can affect a marriage.

Consider Alice, raised in a home with a demanding father who would come home angry at times and be silent. When this happened, it became the responsibility of the entire family—mother and children—to make him happy. They would bring him his shoes and something to drink. The entire energy of the family system was focused on making him happy. Alice grew up and married Ted. When Ted arrived home silent, remembering her father, Alice knew what to do. She did everything to placate him and make him happy. She brought his shoes and fluttered around him to remove his anger, but to no avail. In fact, the tensions increased; he became more angry. Finally after several years of tension, she discovered that for Ted, silence meant "Leave me alone. I need some me time." Imagine the devastating effect her family of origin messages had on this new family system. *Generational issues can have a devastating effect on a family system.*

Generational messages can affect the role of neatness (some may use a euphemism such as *flexible*) in the home. Trevor comes from a home where dishes are never left in the sink, where individuals clean the kitchen while cooking so that when the meal is complete, the kitchen is spotless. I come from a home that was more flexible about dishes in the sink and cleaning the kitchen while cooking. In my family of origin, leaving clothes on the floor would not signal chaos or a lack of marital commitment.

These two different family orientations increased conflict in the relationship, especially if one spouse viewed the orientation as an indication of marital commitment. When a spouse states, "If you love me, you would not leave dishes in the sink or clothes on the floor or leave the toilet seat up," then family orientation is used as an indicator of love or commitment. Whether a couple's home is orderly or disorderly can be influenced by messages received from one's family of origin—and are not usually indications of marital love.

Finally, communication patterns and the role of affection and touching are frequently the result of family messages. In the home of origin, as you observe parents interacting with you and the external world, you develop a mental picture concerning acceptable forms of communication in relationships.

As I (Edith) reflect on communication patterns in my home, I remember that confrontation, intense feelings, and disagreements were discouraged. When one disagreed, the result was often silence, and one would return to the issue several days later in a calmer frame of mind. But in Trevor's Caribbean family, the tolerance level for confrontation, intense feelings, and disagreements was quite high. Intense, evocative, emotional discussions would continue until some form of resolution occurred. Within hours of ending the conversation, all were laughing and talking just as they had prior to the discussion. These were two different approaches to marital and family communication, and they influenced the communication patterns in our marriage. Although our family of origin patterns differed, neither was right or wrong—just different.

Families also give messages about affection and touching. Josh came from a loving, touchy-feeling family. Family members greet each other with hugs and kisses. He met Sarah in college, and they began dating. Eventually, Josh asked her to marry him.

While he recognized that Sarah was not as affectionate as he was, Josh did not recognize it as a family of origin issue. Soon after their marriage, he had an opportunity to spend time with her family, and he noticed the difference. Her family, while very nice, displayed little open affection. Josh and Sarah soon found this difference to be a point of contention. Sarah would repeatedly state that she was just not that type of person, and that love could be shown in other ways. In fact, Sarah admitted to feeling uncomfortable with too much hugging. Josh understood the difference but longed for a spouse who was more affectionate. Once again, family of origin differences has a major influence on marital relationships. In blended families, these factors are complicated by the addition of a previous relationship with a different set of rules and expectations that can influence the interaction between the spouses.

The second challenge we learn from this biblical family is that when dysfunction is ignored, division in the home will persist. In this biblical family, the wives argued, the children argued with each other, and at one point the boys even fought the people of the land. Dysfunction became the pattern in this family. The family of Jacob, Rachael, and Leah was fraught with conflict and discord. Imagine the impact of these disputes on the children.

One example of this occurs in Genesis 34:13. Raised in a home where deception occurred frequently, the sons of Jacob deceived the Shechemites and proposed to form an alliance through circumcision. While the men were healing from the surgery, the son's of Jacob came into the village and killed all the men for defiling their sister. When their father reproved them for their actions, they felt justified in their behavior. In a real sense, Jacob was known as the original deceiver. The lives of his adult children show they were raised with dysfunction, deceit, and discord.

In counseling individuals with a particular dysfunction, we often see this pattern in their behavior. Men raised with abusive fathers often grow up to become abusive. It is true that hurt people hurt others. This dysfunctional pattern became their normal way of communicating, and these men continue the pattern of dysfunctional, abusive communication. Research shows that a man who saw violence between his parents is three times more likely to beat his own spouse. Unless there are intentional efforts to change the patterns, family of origin issues can be repeated for generations.[10]

The third challenge we learn from this family—unique to blended family due to misalignment—involves the reduction of the sense of "we-ness." In this biblical blended family, there was a clear demarcation between Leah and Rachael and between their children. This dysfunctional alignment and favoritism—a common problem for blended families—increased the family's dysfunction. A couple should handle difficulties in the relationship between them as parents, alone. Parents should not involve their children in the discussion, and they should present a united front. This is true for any marriage, but especially for blended families. By involving the children, as Leah did with her sons, division in the family increases. Clearly, the division between the adults in Jacob's family complicated the parent-child relationship and exacerbated the relationship between children. Each wife competed for Jacob's attention. It became a win-lose strategy, which is ineffective in family life.

While overtly polygamous family systems are unusual in the US, many sociologists believe we have do have serial monogamy, and blended families are one of the fastest growing family systems. Couples in a blended family struggle with alignment issues. For example, should the wife put her husband and that relationship first—or should she put the parent-child relationship first. While this alignment issue can occur with other couples, it is fraught with complications in the blended family.

Martha had been a single mom of three children: Keven, 13; Dejuan, 10; and Latrell, 8; for seven years before she

71

married Mike. The children liked Mike, but resented the reduced time they had with their mother. This brought tension to their home. Further, Martha's oldest, Kevin, did not feel that he had to listen to Mike since he was accustomed to being the "man" in the home. He felt bitter about the new, sterner parent and the loss of authority with the younger children, who now looked to Mike as the authority figure. The parent-child relationship was affected by the fact that Kevin's biological father, although not in the home, was involved with his son and did not feel Kevin had to obey Mike. This further complicated the parent-child alignment in the home.

The question that arises is how can one overcome powerful and dysfunctional family of origin messages?

Overcoming Family of Origin Dysfunction

1. Recognize the power of God.

"I can do all things through Christ which strengtheneth me" (Philippians 4:13 KJV). To some degree, everyone has family of origin issues from the first Adam. All have sinned and come short of the glory of God (Romans 3:23). But "If God be for us, who can be against us? " (Romans 8:31 KJV).

This recognition will cause a change in attitude. This psychological change will cause a change in one's behavior that can have a positive impact on one's marriage. Too often in a marriage, we focus on the spouse changing. Partners cannot change their spouses, but they can change themselves! They need to recognize areas of dysfunction that need changing.

Once we recognize that—along with the power of God—we need to critically assess and acknowledge our family of origin messages and issues. Here are some typical issues that must be overcome: being too critical of your spouse, being too permissive as a parent, or playing favorites in the family. In a marriage, the couple should work together as a team. The parent-child relationship should not take precedence over the couple relationship, except in extreme cases like physical or sexual abuse. One's spouse and the couple relationship—even in a blended family—is the most important relationship. Unless there is abuse, it comes before the parent-child relationship.

Once couples have critically assessed and acknowledged their family of origin messages and issues, they can submit these areas to God. This is best accomplished through prayer and Bible study. Individuals must allow God to transform and change them. Don't focus on your spouse, but ask God's help in making changes. Submit this problem verbally to God, then allow God to transform these areas. Sometimes one might have a prayer partner who will pray with you about the concern and hold you accountable for working consistently on this area. You are now ready for the next step.

2. *Realize God can use your dysfunction and disadvantage as the means to overcome obstacles.*

Look at Joseph's life again—he was the favorite son who was sold into bondage because of the family division. While the actual reasons were kept a secret, these dysfunctional situations allowed Joseph to save the family. God used these events as a means of escape. God can still use dysfunction to help families reconnect. God does not take away the dysfunction, but uses it as a means for overcoming. "And He said unto me, my grace is sufficient for thee; for my strength is made perfect in weakness. Most gladly therefore will I rather glory in my infirmities, that the power of Christ may rest upon me" (2 Corinthians 12:9 KJV). God will take our negative and dysfunctional parts and use them for our growth. The secret is that we must recognize the dysfunctional parts and turn them over to Jesus.

God says he will use our disadvantages as a way of escape. God has promised that he will "with the temptation also make a way to escape, that ye may be able to bear it"(1 Corinthians 10:13 KJV). Do not become disconnected from the Power Source. Joseph did not allow his early experience in Egypt—in prison and in slavery—to hinder his relationship with God. Joseph stayed connected to God, the source of his power. With God's help, you can turn family dysfunction into a positive.

3. Review Family Messages.

We must review our family messages, then accept or reject them. Recognize that while some family messages are not sinful, they are detrimental. Review family messages to see if they are true, honest, and reflective of one's present circumstances. Paul says, "When I was a child, I spake as a child, I understood as a child, I thought as a child: but when I became a man, I put away childish things" (1 Corinthians 13:11 KJV).

Sometimes we need to discard, reframe, and forget some messages we received as a child. In a workshop for couples, a woman shared that her aunt said that men generally do not want their wives to have a good time when they are visiting family without them. The woman accepted this advice, so she always told her husband she was not having a good time. When the husband attempted to understand why she was so unhappy with her family; she shared the belief she had learned from her aunt. He was astonished, as this did not reflect his feelings. She needed to discard this message, though it had been perpetuated among the women in her family.

Other messages from the family might define marital roles, including statements like: "A real man doesn't wash dishes" or "A woman works better with children" or "Only a man can pay the bills." Women may be told, "Keep a little money aside—don't let your husband know how much money you have" or "Do not depend on any man." These messages from the family of origin can hurt the marriage.

Other messages are more detrimental to one's esteem, such as the one I (Edith) received as a child. I had a cousin who told me I would never amount to anything. This was a very negative message. But I did not need to let that message be the determining factor in my life. Negative messages, which affect your self-esteem, can shape your relationship with your spouse. All married persons need to review old messages, assess their worth for themselves and their marriage, and ignore or discount messages that do not support their marital goals.

4. *Seek godly mentors who can provide alternative ways of correcting your dysfunction.*

The Bible is full of examples of the power of mentoring. Consider Abraham and Lot, Elijah and Elisha, Paul and Timothy. Paul charges Timothy to "Cling to your faith in Christ, and keep your conscience clear" (1 Timothy 1:19 NLT). He tells Timothy not to abandon his faith. Godly mentoring is encouraging and supportive—yet will still admonish.

Many couples, especially blended families, could benefit from a godly mentoring couple. These are people who can assist couples as they navigate the murky waters of marriage. Such couples should reflect a commitment to God, a commitment to each other, and an ability to support and work with others. These are couples who have had years of successful marriage and radiate love for each. Research has shown that mentoring couples can be helpful to young couples and new marriages.

How do you find such mentors? Submit the need to the Lord and pray for guidance, then look around your church for godly mentors, couples who will facilitate your growth. Look for couples who meet these criteria:

- have had a successful marriage for at least ten years.
- are involved in the marriage ministry of your church.
- are willing to be open and honest with you.
- have a strong spiritual commitment.

We (Trevor and Edith) still seek advice from godly couples who have been married longer than we have. We feel their experience can help our relationship. We also have several couples who contact us on a regular basis to enhance their relationship. Some of them actually say, "We need to come in for a tune-up." Like cars, all marriages can benefit from periodic tune-ups. Growth can occur if you reflect on the meaning of the dysfunction and look for God's lesson for you. God wants to transform you for good. Let God, circumstances, and godly mentors transform you and your marriage.

5. Take time and allow the growth process to occur.

Remember, God does not heal marriage problems or personal dysfunctions instantaneously. The marriage of Jacob, Leah, and Rachel had difficulties for many years. The pain caused by the sisters's competition probably began in their home of origin and did not disappear immediately. Nor did the division caused by favoring Joseph disappear at once. It is believed that Joseph lived in Egypt for at least fifteen years before he became prime minister. Healing takes time. God used Joseph's experience in Potipher's house, and in prison, as times for growth and healing to occur. These were times of preparation for his future position. Since the healing process was not instantaneous, Joseph needed all these experiences to enhance and encourage his growth. After all, all things work together for our good (Romans 8:28). God does not promise instantaneous healing. Let God take husbands and wives through the healing process. Finally, there are some additional lessons from this family that apply only to blended families or stepfamilies.

6. *Remember a blended family or a stepfamily is different from a two-parent biological family.*

Don't assume that traditional family behavior will work in stepfamilies. Stepfamilies are qualitatively different from biological families.[11] Enhance your stepfamily development:

- **Avoid the divide-and-conquer strategy between children.**[12] The family of Jacob, Rachel, and Leah used the divide-and-conquer policy, and it was detrimental for the family system. Avoid a "my children and your children" approach, as it causes division. Parents should collaboratively develop a stance for working with the children. If you find this is difficult to work on together, seek godly mentors or counselors to help in the situation.
- **Avoid favoritism in the home.**[13] Abraham loved Isaac, Isaac loved Esau, and Jacob loved Joseph. This family was fractured by favoritism. Such an approach is one of the hazards of blended families. Since these families are based on previous family relationships and previous attachments, the temptation of

favoritism is more prevalent. Favoritism supports the "divide-and-conquer" strategy and increases the possibility of division and separation in the family.

- **Develop your own traditions and rituals.** In a blended family, you are combining two different homes with two different traditions. Each family comes to the marriage with different approaches to problem solving, different ways of celebrating holidays, different religious expressions, and different family rituals. Rituals are usually designed to "mark and facilitate family developmental transitions and changes."[14] They are important to clarify family policy, values, and prescriptions. For example, graduation ceremonies are important rituals that reflect the completion of one level of academic achievement. Families react differently to these occasions; some families view graduations as very significant and will travel extensively to these events. In our family tradition (Edith and Trevor), graduations are very important and as many as fifty family members may attend. Other families may be content with just sending a check. When two families are combined in a blended or stepfamily, rituals must be developed for *this* family unit. Mealtime habits, religious expressions, and holiday celebrations must be developed. Stepfamilies need their own rituals—not those from the family of origin or previous marriages. Rituals solidify family identity, clarify family relationships, and reduce family tensions.

- **Be prepared to negotiate differences between the various households in which children are a part.**[15] For many children in blended families, visitation on weekend, holidays, and summers are normal. Making the change between two different households can be confusing and disorienting. Both parents need to work together for the child. Parents should look for ways to reduce the confusion and tension for the child—and avoid increased stress over various rules, rituals, and patterns. This will require parents to be flexible, respect differences, and work in partnership with the other home. Working together as a team, rather than as adversaries, can help reduce dysfunction in a blended home. Families that cannot work together might consider professional assistance to aid the process.

- **Recognize that the parental bond may predate the couple bond, yet protect the couple relationships.** The challenge of a blended home is to stay true to couple relationship without making the children feel obsolete. The marriage relationship must be supported and valued; but this new arrangement must also respect the old parenting bond. Make all effort to keep children from feeling they are being replaced or are insignificant now that the parent has a new spouse.

7. *Remember, there is hope for those who follow God.*

While it is true that the chip doesn't fall far from the block or apple far from the tree, family of origin is not a destiny. Family myths do not need to control your life. God is still in control. God wants to be the Block, the Chief Cornerstone in your life. God wants human beings to be modeled after him, not just one's family of origin.

God wants us to transform into his image. How can one be like Jesus?

- Allow God to review and revise family dysfunctional messages.
- Allow God to rewrite the family messages and script.
- Approach Jesus, the Tree of Life, and allow the Chief Cornerstone to be the Block from which the chips of your life emanate.

While families are our windows to the world, God wants to expand our window and enhance our vision. As we allow God to lead our lives, they become transformed. This transformation will have a powerful effect on our marriage, our children, and our home.

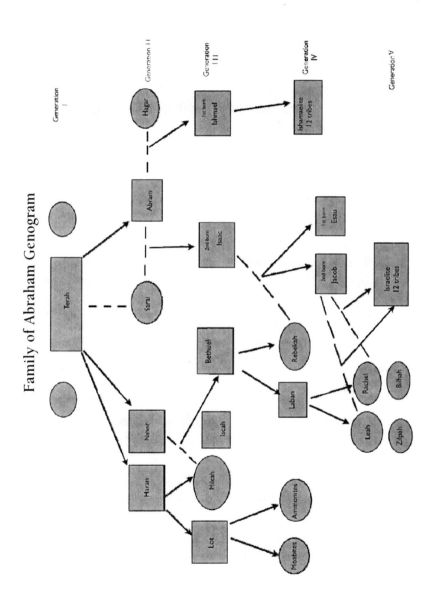

Family of Abraham Genogram

CHIPS DON'T FALL FAR FROM THE BLOCK
Personal Reflections

Text: Genesis 12-36

1. Reflect for a moment on some patterns in your family. What are some family patterns that have been transferred from generation to generation?

   _____

   _____

   _____

   _____

2. What are some family patterns that your spouse has transferred from generation to generation?

   _____

   _____

   _____

   _____

3. How have these family patterns affected your marital relationship? How might God address these patterns?

   _____

   _____

   _____

   _____

4. Do you recognize any family patterns that were dysfunctional? What are they? How do they affect your marriage?

_____

_____

_____

_____

5. How might you specifically address these areas of dysfunction? How do you plan to overcome the dysfunction that you bring into your marital relationship from your family of origin?

_____

_____

_____

_____

6. If you are in a blended family, what are some unique challenges of this type of family? How have previous relationships impacted your marriage?

_____

_____

_____

_____

CHAPTER 4

Betrayal and Disappointment
David And Bathsheba

In the spring, at the time when kings go off to war, David sent Joab out with the king's men and the whole Israelite army. They destroyed the Ammonites and besieged Rabbah. But David remained in Jerusalem.

One evening David got up from his bed and walked around on the roof of the palace. From the roof he saw a woman bathing. The woman was very beautiful, and David sent someone to find out about her. The man said, "Isn't this Bathsheba, the daughter of Eliam and the wife of Uriah the Hittite?" Then David sent messengers to get her. She came to him, and he slept with her. (She had purified herself from her uncleanness.) Then she went back home. The woman conceived and sent word to David, saying, "I am pregnant."

—2 Samuel 11:1-5

Introduction

HE WAS THE most powerful leader in the world. He had just won a landslide victory in the election in 1994.

He was charming. His wife was seen as a partner, and his daughter was viewed fondly. A wonderful speaker, a popular president—but then the rumors started. There were rumors about an affair with a 25-year-old White House intern. Rumors were rampant, including talk of a blue dress and reports from another employee for the government. Soon it was the only news on television, radio, and the Internet. When confronted, President Bill Clinton stated, "I did not have sexual relationships with that woman." He later famously responded to the question about whether they had sex: "It depends upon your definition of sex." He was the world's most powerful leader, and still he was the victim of scandal and impeached. The president was not alone; we could explore the life of famous preachers (Jimmy Swaggart, Jim Bakker, and Ted Haggard), top congressional leaders (Newt Gingrich), former governors (James McGreevey, Elliot Spitzer, David Patterson, and Mark Sanford) or even famous athletes (Magic Johnson, Kobe Bryant, Rick Pitino, and Tiger Woods).

We could also compare these men to a famous king in the Bible—David. Like King David, all these men were involved in one of the most devastating yet prevalent affronts to marital happiness —infidelity or the extramarital affair. In his landmark research, Kinsey's data indicates that *one* out of every two husbands engaged in sex with an outside partner before the age of forty, and *one-fourth* of the wives in this study had extramarital experience by the time they reached age forty.[1] Recent research reveals that infidelity is increasing. Peggy Vaughan, author of *The Monogamy Myth* states:

> Conservative estimates are that 60 percent of men and 40 percent of women will have an extramarital affair. These figures are even more significant when we consider the total number of marriages involved—since it is unlikely

that all the men and women having affairs happen to be married to each other. If even half of the women having affairs (or 20 percent) are married to men not included in the 60 percent having affairs then at least one partner will have an affair in approximately 80 percent of all marriages.[2]

Thus infidelity is a significant marital stressor. Among women it is increasing rapidly and almost equals the rate for men.

The issue of infidelity is a historical concern as extramarital affairs are one of the sins mentioned in the Ten Commandments. One would be extremely idealistic to think infidelity is absent from Christian homes today. It is not! Usually, infidelity involves only one partner as the philanderer, while the other partner remains unaware. Infidelity is a marital tragedy, since it can mean the dissolution of the marriage. The numerous incidents of infidelity force us to confront the myth of monogamy.

The prominence of this problem makes it an important one to explore with Christian couples in the twenty-first century. Several questions arise as we explore this issue:

- What are the factors that make infidelity so commonplace?
- What are some of the causes of marital infidelity?
- What effects does infidelity have on the marriage relationship?
- Can a marriage recover from infidelity?

These are a few questions to explore in the biblical marriage of David and Bathsheba. However, before we discuss these questions, we must explore the context of their marriage. It began with infidelity, deceit, and murder.

Unlike Adam and Eve or Isaac and Rebekah, God did not bring this couple together. This couple's marriage was not the result of courtship or a relationship like Jacob and Rachael's. David did not have to work seven years to get Bathsheba. While David was attracted to Bathsheba's beauty, their marriage was not the result of a beauty contest like Esther and Ahasureus, the heathen king we discuss in a later chapter. This was a marriage with a sinister beginning of betrayal, adultery, and deceit.

Interestingly, in many novels or movies, adultery and betrayal are portrayed as glamorous. Society does not view infidelity negatively. In the movie *Dr Zhavago* or the *English Patient*, extramarital relationships are depicted as great love affairs. The love of the adulterous couple is romanticized and seems to transcend time and space. These couples risk all to be with each other. Love, as these movies depict, seems more exciting because it is the forbidden fruit. These fictionalized accounts imply that marital affairs derive from irrepressible passion. Love that risks all for just a moment of pleasure! However, is an affair really about passionate, uncontrollable love? What are the roots or basis for marital affairs?

Like all human behavior, an affair cannot be explained by one factor. An affair involves complex emotions and has negative consequences, and this biblical story provides a unique depiction of the elements of an illicit love affair. The Bible effectively conveys the long-term effects of an affair and provides powerful lessons and warnings for couples today.

David and Bathsheba's Affair

A review of this story shows that affairs don't just happen; there are steps in the process. For married people today in a society where infidelity is increasing, it's relevant to examine these steps in the process of infidelity and betrayal as this story portrays. The story begins: "In the spring, at the time when kings go off to war " (2 Samuel 11:1). But David, the warrior king, did not go to battle this year. For some reason he was not busy with his usual task of war. Without his usual routine as king, he was inactive and his defense mechanisms were down. Thus, the stage was set for the steps in the progression to infidelity. We will explore five steps in the progression of an affair:

1. Being vulnerable.
2. Creating sexual fantasies.
3. Initial seeking for the person.
4. Pursing the person.
5. Having a sexual encounter.

Step one—Being in a vulnerable time period.

This can be a time when one is relaxed, unguarded, and at the height of career development. This can be a dangerous time because it increases susceptibility to marital infidelity.

At a stage of his life when his defense mechanisms were down, David preferred a life of ease and contentment. He was relaxed. For David, these were times of increased danger for infidelity in the marriage. When one is at the height of power—receiving honor and acclaim and living a life of ease—can be a time of danger for infidelity. This could be paralleled with the infidelity of the popular former president of the United States. Like David, President Bill Clinton was vulnerable when he felt strong and secure against his political enemies; he let his guard down. A time of increased vulnerability could be when one is at the height of success—or it when one's marriage is having major difficulties.

At this time of relaxation and reduced stress, at this time with a change in schedule, at this transitional time, David could not sleep. The Bible says he arose from his bed. Perhaps, he was sleeping too much, or perhaps he was bored. The precipitating factors are not known, but David arose from his bed and went on the roof. He was probably arising from his midday siesta. He was well rested, feeling confident and competent. As David went to the roof, his eyes began to wander.

While there is no inherent danger in being idle—though many mothers have said, "An idle mind is the devil's workshop"—being idle was dangerous for David. Still, everyone who looks does not follow through to adultery. During the 1976 presidential campaign, Jimmy Carter was quoted in *Playboy* as saying, "I have committed adultery in my heart numerous times."[3] President Carter was referring to his eyes wandering, looking, and desiring mentally. A look does not always lead to marital infidelity, but it does increase one's susceptibility. This was true for David. He was just looking, and his gaze fell on a woman who was very beautiful and was taking a bath. This gave David an exquisite view of all her beauty. Now David must have looked for some time at this sight. This sight did several things to David, which initiated the process to marital infidelity. What were these things? He began to have sexual fantasies about this woman. He began to imagine himself in an adulterous relationship with her.

Step two—Creating a sexual fantasy can lead to adultery.

While in the mind, sexual fantasies can also involve activities like pornography. For David, as for many others, adultery began in the mind, *first*. Jesus recognized this when he stated, "But I say unto you, that whosoever looketh on a woman to lust after her hath committed adultery with her already in his heart" (Matthew 5:28 KJV). A look does not mean, however, that one will have an affair. Reflect on the words of President Carter, who professed to be innocent of any marital infidelity. If a look always led to an affair, the rate of marital infidelity would be higher than fifty percent.

While this is a dangerous time, the gazing spouse still has power of choice at this time. In this biblical story, David could *have stopped* here. This man after God's own heart could have found a way of escape. He did not have to engage in marital infidelity; it seems David did not listen to his inner voice. God always sends the Holy Spirit through the still small voice to warn of danger and to provide an alternative way. David heard the internal and external warnings but ignored them. He was following the pattern of those who have thrill affairs. They are looking for the excitement of sex with someone new.[4] So he moved on to the next step, a more precarious progression.

Step three—Inquiring/investigating to obtain information about the person.

David wanted to find out more about Bathsheba. A modern analogy would be to get her phone number or email. When the spouse takes this step, it is harder but not impossible to extricate oneself from the affair. In this case, David received external warnings to obstruct his descent into marital infidelity. Listen to the warning from the servants, "Isn't this Bathsheba, the daughter of Eliam and the wife of Uriah the Hittite" (2 Samuel 11:3)? Since David was the king, the servants could not say to him, "God would not want you to take Uriah's wife in an adulterous liaison." They could not say, "King David, to have such a relationship would be a sin." So what did they say? She is the daughter of one of your trusted and mighty men of arms and the granddaughter of Ahithophel, your well-known counselor.[5] Furthermore, this comment revealed that she was married. She was the wife of Uriah. This was meant to be a subtle warning to the king, but he did not heed this warning. David chose not to listen.

While David was on dangerous ground, he still had the power of choice. After all, David had many wives (at least eight) and many concubines. It is curious why he did not go to one of them at this time of temptation. It seems one of the attractions of an affair is a sexual relationship with someone new and forbidden. So instead of going to any of his wives or concubines, he sent for Bathsheba, Uriah's wife. This led to step four.

Step four—Pursuing the person

David sent for Bathsheba. This step was the point of no return because when he saw her in person, the sexual tensions between them increased, and he allowed himself to become involved in marital infidelity.

As family counselors, we have worked with many couples whose marriage was ruined by a marital indiscretion. Frequently, the philanderer admits to discerning the mounting sexual tension between himself or herself and the lover—prior to the sexual relationship. The sexual tension between the two increases until it reaches a crucial point. The relationship reaches a point of no return, and a sexual encounter seems inevitable when both individuals sense the mounting sexual tensions between them. This is a risky time. Both feel powerless to leave. The sexual desires demand consummation of their relationship. "I have got to have him!" "I have got to have her!" At this step, the couple sees only one way out of this situation—*a sexual relationship*. Sometimes the erring partner feels compelled to proceed and prove his manhood or her womanhood, as the following examples illustrates:

Jeff had worked for several years with Sally, and frequently the coworkers were involved with sexual bantering and discussion. They talked about their sexual abilities and bragged about their sexual prowess with partners. The sexual tension between Jeff and Sally began to increase. Finally, one day Sally brought a key to work; it was for a motel room. She told Jeff, "Here is the key, and I am tired of hearing you brag about your sexual prowess, if you are so great, prove it. Put up or shut up." Jeff was in a predicament; he was a married Christian, but he did not want to lose face in front of all of his co-workers. What was he to do? Prove he was the man or prove he was not a man. Jeff went to the motel room that night to prove his manhood, and this led him into an adulterous relationship with Sally that lasted for several years. For many adulterers, this stage ends with a sense of the inevitable. One must proceed. There is a feeling of *fait accompli*. This leads them naturally onto step five.

Step Five—Having an actual sexual encounter

Why, when one is married and can have sex, is an affair necessary? Why did David who had all these other wives, need to look at another man's wife? This reflects the complex emotional dimensions of an affair. Despite what one might see in the movies, an affair is not primarily about love, nor is it just about sex. No one reason can explain this complex relationship. Peggy Vaughan, whose husband had an affair for seven years, has speculated that there are many forces that foster an affair. One force pulls the philanderer toward an affair because of sexual desire, novelty, curiosity, and excitement. There are also enticing internal forces, like the desire to escape problems in a marriage, fill gaps in marriage, and prove one's worth.[6] Finally, societal pressures glamorize the affair in movies, soap operas, and even in discussion of public figures. Thus, the philanderer feels pulled toward the affair and supported by society. Peggy Vaughan's experience could provide insight for understanding ancient affairs and modern ones, too. These are some of the primary reasons provided for the affair:

Reasons for an Affair

Lust

The partners want to see what a sexual encounter would be like with another person. How will it be different from sex with their husband or wife? What would sex be like with someone so beautiful or handsome or tall or short or exciting? Lust is about passion—a longing for the forbidden and a craving for someone who is not accessible and belongs to someone else.

Excitement

An affair can also involve the sheer exhilaration of sneaking around and hiding. The thrill of doing something precarious, something forbidden, something that is unacceptable becomes exhilarating and even titillating. The couple has to arrange clandestine meeting places and speak in codes. They have to concoct not only a secret name when they check into the hotel but also stories to cover their tracks. Like actors and actresses, they have to pretend and deceive in their own private play. For some couples, it is the excitement of the affair that is attractive. It makes them feel vibrant and alive. It might help them capture some of the excitement of their first love.

No Commitment

An affair means no commitment. One does not have to make the bed or clean the closet. Promises to the other person are not necessary. One can come and go into his or her life at any time. If there are any tensions between parties, they just drop this relationship. There are no obligations. There are no bills, no children, no house payments or responsibilities. Adulterers can give what they want to the relationship—when they want to give and how they want to give. Or they could choose not to give at all. They can leave the relationship whenever because there is no commitment. For some, this is one of the attractions of an affair.

Doing the Forbidden

There is a certain attraction to breaking the rules: doing what is not acceptable. Like Eve of old, tasting the one prohibited fruit makes it attractive. The one relationship that is denied is enhanced by the denial. Uriah's wife suddenly becomes the world's most beautiful woman. No other woman will do. "Get her for me." The attraction is the fact that she is forbidden. She is off-limits. Thus, like David, one must taste the forbidden fruit. Like Samson, the one relationship God has not permitted is the one he has to have. It seems to be a daring act of bravery.

Self-esteem Booster

For many, an affair may be an attempt to boost failing self-esteem. He wants me more than his wife. Or now I have two women (or men) who love me. They both are available at my beck and call. Now I have two people vying for my affections. The affair is an attempt to bolster one's faltering self-esteem and prove one is valuable and worthwhile. The affair proves one is not too old to get a partner. The affair provides both participants with a boost to their failing sense of self.

Just a quick caveat: One of the most vulnerable persons to an affair as an ego booster is someone recovering from a devastating divorce. The divorcee may need validation to prove his or her sexual appeal or to get some sense of appreciation. An affair may prove the divorcee still has it. It may prove he or she is still lovable and valuable. It may prove one is still sexually attractive and able to perform.

Reworking Unresolved early Childhood Memories

Most people enter adulthood with pain, unresolved relational dilemmas, and unmet needs from the family of origin. In marriage, the expectation is that such a relationship will help address and resolve that baggage. One believes that the spouse will assist in the reworking of relational pains, unresolved needs, and disillusionment from childhood. However, all too frequently, the marital partner is busy dealing with his or her own baggage, which leaves little room to assist with the resolution of the spouse's childhood pains.

In some marriages, the couples are able to meet their disparate needs simultaneously. When this happens, marriage is a powerfully healing balm. In other marriages, both partners bring so much pain and limited capacity to address unresolved relational conflicts that no one's needs are met.

George was abandoned by his mother and lived with his grandmother, who eventually became unable to take care of him. George spent many years in the foster care system. But George was a good student who was able to improve his economic situation by attending and graduating college.

While in college, he met Camille, who came from a two-parent family that seemed healthier. While her parents were happily married, economic security was always a problem. Camille's father often was unemployed or underemployed. Camille entered the marriage needing economic security and expecting a loving husband. George entered the marriage with many needs and no model for a good marriage. When he was unable to provide the economic security expected, George began to suspect that Camille was seeking security in other relationships. Unmet needs can lead to an affair. When the needs are not met in the marriage, the pain intensifies, and the unresolved attachments and affections become worse.

The straying partner may use affairs as an attempt to compel additional attention from the spouse and to help resolve his or her own childhood issues. The affair could force the other partner to admit something must be wrong and perhaps to foster a home environment that will be more responsive to the needs of the straying partner. Ironically, the affair is used to force attention to the marriage and to the needs of the straying partner.

Finally, an affair may be an attempt to:

Escape from Working on Marital Relationships

Marriage is hard work, and both partners must make a commitment to the process. It requires taking time to communicate. It requires denying one's needs and meeting the needs of the partner. It requires working on issues and problems related to communication patterns, personal responsibility, and boundaries.

Some of the questions prompted by marital issues are: "Do I have to change my ways and approaches to make this marriage work? If so, how much changing will I need to do?" "How separate can we become and still feel married?" "Can I hang out with the boys ?" "Can I play bridge with the girls?" A marriage requires working on developing a strategy for problem resolution. Each of these concerns increases tensions in the relationship and requires the partner to work on these concerns together—while still handling other personal concerns and stressors of life at the office and in the community.

Sometimes a partner is unwilling to maintain the commitment to problem resolution. He or she would rather find a relationship with no obligation and no requirements. A relationship that makes no emotional demands is an escape from the marriage. It provides a listening ear of a partner who can bolster the ego, it provides support in home conflicts, it provides understanding yet brings no obligation. The affair addresses needs that are unmet. It provides an outlet for emotions unexpressed and allows the straying partner to work on unresolved childhood issues. These are some of the reasons for an affair.

One may become involved in an affair for several reasons. David had some of these needs. Perhaps he needed a boost for his self-esteem, or maybe he was interested in doing the forbidden. Maybe he just wanted a no-commitment relationship or to experience sex with such a beautiful woman. Which one bests explains David's situations? We don't know the answer. But David was involved in an affair; he had an adulterous relationship with Bathsheba— a married woman. This relationship was initiated by David and—as with many affairs—had a sexual focus.

Consequences of an Affair

Once one has the sexual encounter, like David, he or she is really in trouble. Now comes the dilemma of what to do about the relationship—continue it or end it. If one continues, how can the affair be hidden? This was not a concern for David. He thought he was finished with his sexual tryst until Bathsheba said, "I am pregnant." Then he began the cover-up, which ended in David arranging the murder of her husband. Then David and Bathsheba were united in a "quickie marriage." But you cannot cover up sin forever. "Be sure your sin will find you out" (Numbers 32:23 KJV). So David found that there are consequences for sin.

Let's review some of the consequences for David's great sin. First, Bathsheba and David's child, the child of an adulterous relationship, died. David grieved the baby's illness and death (2 Samuel 12:16-19). Not long after, incest occurred in David's house when Amnon slept with Tamar (2 Samuel 13). Amnon's rape and subsequent rejection of Tamar resulted in Amnon's death at the hand of Absalom, his stepbrother. Then Absalom fled Jerusalem fearing the consequences of the murder. Joab arranged Absalom's reconciliation with his father, David (2 Samuel 14). Absalom returned—and began an armed insurrection to steal his father's throne (2 Samuel 15-18). So Absalom divided the nation, began a civil war, and committed sexual sins with his father's concubines. Finally, Joab killed Absalom against David's express command. What a litany of consequences for one moment of sexual indiscretion! What a lot to happen to one family!

Sin has its consequences. David was unable to chastise his sons when they committed sins; he seemed incapacitated by his own guilt. How can you really reprimand someone when you are guilty of major indiscretions? As a parent you are powerless to chastise your children. A pastor recently told me of a father who was upset with his son because the son was disrespectful to him. The pastor confronted this young man in front of his father and was shocked at the son's response. "How can I respect this man who disrespected my mother by having an ongoing affair since I was twelve years old?" The father could not deny it and was upset with his son's knowledge of it. Like David, there was no counter-response, only remorse. What a tragedy! What family pain. Incest! Homicide! Insurrection! Civil war! Murder!

Throughout all these events, David remained a man of sorrow. Crying at the death of three of his sons. His sorrow is revealed in the books of Psalms (Psalms 3, 9, 38, 51, 86). Somehow David recognized their deaths as the consequence of his adultery and homicide. He recognized that this was his fault, and sin had its penalty. What a powerful lesson for this ancient monarch to learn.

Lessons from the Affair

This monarch and this couple have lessons that are enduring for the twenty-first century. These lessons are essential for us to review:

Be careful of any one of these steps:

Step one: When one is in a vulnerable time period.

Step two: When one begins to have sexual fantasies about someone other than one's spouse that lead to adultery in the mind and heart.

Step three: When one inquires and investigates to obtain information about the person (such as a phone number or email address).

Step four: When one pursues the person (begins eating meals secretly with the person).

Step five: When one seeks an actual sexual encounter.

Be careful especially of steps two to four. The sin is not in being tempted, but in the yielding to the temptation.

Learn to listen to the still, small voice—one's conscience; it is God's warning sign.

When you find you are getting too close to someone of the opposite sex who is not your spouse, God will send a warning. *Listen*. At times, God uses the emotional system to provide warnings, such as when a person begins to feel uncomfortable because of rising sexual tensions. Most affairs begin as emotional affairs before there is any sexual interaction. After the emotional affair begins, sexual fantasies about this person increase. The feelings become less platonic. *Listen,* before your emotions and sexual tensions drown out God's still small voice. Learn to listen to the inner voice and then obey.

Be aware of emotions; they serve as a warning sign to what is happening inside and warn of danger.

When one begins to feel inappropriate things for a boss, fellow employee, friend, or colleague, watch out. When a driver sees the flashing red lights and hear the bell at a train track, what do those sights and sounds mean? A train is coming, beware—yet every year people are killed because they do not heed those warnings. Emotions are an internal warning system. Some Christians are uncomfortable with emotions because of mixed messages about them. However, emotions inform us of internal struggles, emotional conflicts, and unsafe liaisons.

When God is sending a warning, "Flee fornication, evil lust, and temptations" (See 1 Corinthians 6:18).

We must follow the "Joseph principle." Joseph found himself in a situation that could have become adulterous. Potiphar's wife pursued him. Today this would be called sexual harassment. In Genesis 39:10 we read, "She spoke to Joseph day after day." She was at step four. She was in hot pursuit of Joseph. How was this young man able to say No? He used the Word of God as his armor to defend himself against the temptation. He also tried to reduce the time they could be together alone. He knew this was dangerous. He tried to avoid Mrs. Potipher, but the day came when they were alone in the house—and she grabbed him. What did Joseph do? Did he say, "Well I tried; I guess I am caught now." No! The Bible says he fled. Joseph was a slave, yet he did not yield. This course of action still provides a plan for today. *Flee and don't get entrapped.* Do not let feelings impede your flight! Go! Feelings should not determine your obedience to God. Feelings should not determine your fidelity to your spouse. Keep your commitment to God and your marriage vows.

Finally, develop strategies to work on if you find the marriage is not emotionally satisfying.

This leads to another warning, which is not from this story but necessary. When having marital difficulties, be careful in choosing a counselor. Don't share marital problems with someone of the opposite sex who is primarily a colleague, friend, or acquaintance. This can be dangerous. Sometimes the sharing begins innocently—then more and more of the marital difficulties are shared with the other person. This allows that person into the sacred circle to hear intimacies that should be shared only with a marital partner or a professional counselor. The boundaries become blurred, and one becomes more vulnerable in the interactions with this colleague, friend, or acquaintance.

This can create a precarious situation. While Christians should be kind and listen to others, perhaps someone with major marital problems needs to see a counselor and not a colleague. Instead of giving up on the marriage, decide to work harder on the marriage. Consider marriage counseling. There are many counselors who can provide tools to enhance your marriage. Many churches sponsor couples retreats, or you can find one on the Internet. Finally, read a book together such as *His Needs, Her Needs* by William Harley. Develop a proactive stance; do something to improve your marriage.

Final Reflections

There are still a few remaining questions about infidelity. *Can there be infidelity when the marriage is going well?* Yes, some partners may need to work on some unresolved issues. David had many wives including Abigail (1 Samuel 25), who were probably good wives for him, but he still became involved in an affair.

Is there any hope for marriages after infidelity? Yes, this is another lesson from David and Bathsheba. While God did not arrange their marriage, still He blessed their marriage. Though the child of adultery died, the next son survived, and he became the heir apparent and eventually the king—the wise king—Solomon. Bathsheba proved herself to be a courageous queen. Just read how she and Nathan, now allies, defended the kingdom for Solomon in 1 Kings 1:11-28. This marriage was blessed. Indeed, God can make something wonderful happen after adultery. In this case, the adultery led to marriage. For marriages today, adultery does not have to end the marriage. Couples confronted with adultery will need to begin the healing process and seek counseling. Some factors are necessary for an affair to end. Unlike David, one cannot marry the lover *and keep* the spouse. As a Christians, one *must* end the affair and take the following steps, adapted from Dr. William Harley:[7]

- Confess the affair to your spouse.
- Determine never to see or communicate with the "lover" again.
- Expect some withdrawal after this decision.
- Rebuild the marriage on a strong spiritual foundation.
- Work on marital restoration in counseling or some other active engagement; a marriage cannot just return to normal.
- Address issues of the offended spouse related to forgiveness and resentment.
- Learn to meet one's spouse's emotional needs.
- Spend time together, eat meals together, go out on dates weekly, and rekindle the relationship with quality time together.
- Develop the habit of total honesty.
- Follow biblical principles of relationship.

While an affair is devastating to a marriage, the marriage can survive. In *The Monogamy Myth*, Peggy Vaughan explores the emotional damage of her husband's affair. She decided that her love for her husband, her commitment, and the eighteen years they had been together required her to fight for her marriage. So many couples have survived an affair, including: Hillary and Bill Clinton, Martin and Coretta King, David and Michelle Patterson, and even Franklin and Eleanor Roosevelt. The marriage can survive and thrive. Remember, God can do exceedingly abundantly above all that we can ask or think if we put our trust in him. That is the lesson of David and Bathsheba. Marriages can survive any assault—even adultery—*when God is in the midst.*

BETRAYAL AND DISAPPOINTMENT

Personal Reflections

Text: 2 Samuel 11:1-5

1. How might you incorporate the following aspects mentioned in this chapter into your marriage: meeting emotional needs of your spouse, spending time together, and honesty? Be specific and develop some specific plans.

_____

_____

_____

_____

2. Reflect on the other solutions suggested in this chapter. How might you make your marriage adultery-proof? Discuss this solution with your spouse and make a decision to incorporate these concepts in your marriage.

_____

_____

_____

_____

3. How do you explain the infidelity of David? Which reason cited do you feel was most important and why?

_____

_____

_____

_____

4. While betrayal and disappointment can involve infidelity, how might one be unfaithful to his or her spouse without infidelity? Give specific examples.

_____

_____

_____

5. As you reflect on your marriage, how have you been unfaithful in your relationship? Which reason cited best explains your choice to look outside the marriage for happiness and satisfaction?

_____

_____

_____

6. What consequences have your marriage experienced as a result of your "infidelity"?

_____

_____

_____

CHAPTER 5

Loving When It Is Hard To Love

Hosea and Gomer: The Story of Forgiveness

When the Lord began to speak through Hosea, the Lord said to him, "Go, take to yourself an adulterous wife and children of unfaithfulness, because the land is guilty of the vilest adultery in departing from the Lord." So he married Gomer daughter of Diblaim, and she conceived and bore him a son.

Then the Lord said to Hosea, "Call him Jezreel, because I will soon punish the house of Jehu for the massacre at Jezreel, and I will put an end to the kingdom of Israel. In that day I will break Israel's bow in the Valley of Jezreel."

Gomer conceived again and gave birth to a daughter. Then the Lord said to Hosea, "Call her Lo-Ruhamah, for I will no longer show love to the house of Israel, that I should at all forgive them. Yet I will show love to the house of Judah; and I will save them—not by bow, sword or battle, or by horses and horsemen, but by the Lord their God."

After she had weaned Lo-Ruhamah, Gomer had another son. Then the Lord said, "Call him Lo-Ammi, for you are not my people, and I am not your God."

—Hosea 1:2-9

Introduction

I T WAS THE wedding of the century. She was a sixteenth cousin of the royal family, and her brother was the godson of the queen. She was shy but interested in helping others. The public was captivated by her beauty and charm. He was second in line for the King of England. No expense was spared in the wedding. A congregation of 2,500 gathered beneath the soaring dome of the cathedral to witness the ceremony, which was televised to a worldwide audience of 750 million. Eleven years later, however, the fairytale wedding became a nightmare. Stories of affairs by both Princess Di and Prince Charles appeared in the tabloids. The revelations shocked the adoring public. It was hard to believe the storybook marriage was ending in an affair—or multiple affairs.[1]

How does one love after an affair? Why didn't his marriage survive the affair? Many other couples do survive, as we saw in the last chapter.

What makes for an effective marriage? Too frequently, a couple is categorized as potentially successful or unsuccessful because of external factors. Each marriage has a life of its own. Sometimes relationships that appear stable can be volatile—and marriages that seem to have great potential are unstable. Consider the recent marriage of Prince Charles to Camille Parker. While not nearly as ideal and romantic as the headline marriage to Diane, it seems more stable.

Why do some marriages last after an affair and others end? What are the determining factors? One important aspect for Christians is to invite divine leadership and accept providence. How willing are we as individuals to allow God to direct the unfolding of our relationships?

This chapter focuses on the marriage of Hosea and Gomer and explores the pain of affairs and the power of forgiveness. This marriage seemed doomed from the start. Hosea and Gomer had a marriage that many doubted would succeed; surprisingly, it survived against all odds. God did the directing while Hosea and Gomer did the listening. Hosea and Gomer's marriage started out challenging and complicated. It was built on difficulty, differences, distress, and duplicity. Yet we can learn valuable lessons from this marriage,

Challenges of Hosea and Gomer's Relationship

This story unfolds with God commanding Hosea to get a wife from the worst part of town, a woman with a sordid past. Though she was from the worst part of society, God told Hosea to marry her. Needless to say, many theologians have problems with this story. Some suggest that this is not a *literal* story but a dream. Others suggest this is a parable or allegory. This has a lot of credence since the context of the book of Hosea addresses the relationship of Israel to God. The bulk of the book emphasizes the spiritual adultery that Israel commits, the persistent idolatry with other nations.[2] Still, commentaries including the *Seventh-day Adventist Bible Commentary* strongly suggest it is a literal story.[3]

This story provides valuable lessons about a difficult marriage that can be saved. However, if we take the view that it is a literal story, we must explore some disturbing consequences and some perplexing questions. How could a righteous God suggest that Hosea marry a prostitute? Why would God make such a request? On a more personal level, if I were Hosea, would I obey this command?

The Bible commentary offers several speculative explanations for God's request. First, Gomer was not a prostitute at the time of her marriage, yet came from a family of prostitutes. Second, God never asks us to do anything that is not for our good. Third, God was merely providing permission; Gomer was someone Hosea already loved[4]. Let us look briefly at all three scenarios.

First Scenario

Gomer was *not* a prostitute at the time of the marriage, yet she came from a family of prostitutes. From this perspective, it is possible that Gomer was a "good kid" from a bad home situation. Thus, Hosea was commanded by God to rescue this young woman and make her a part of a spiritual family. The plan was to expose her to a better spiritual community and use this marriage covenant as a means for her salvation. Through living an orderly and consistent life with God as the center, Gomer could be transformed by these three factors: the presence of God, the protection of home, and the power of love.

Second Scenario

This alternative scenario is based on the assumption that "God never asks us to do anything that is not for our good." From this perspective, Gomer was a prostitute when Hosea married her. Yet God asked Hosea to marry her anyway. In this scenario, it seems that while Hosea was asked by God to marry a woman who had a sordid and salacious heritage, God saw her as *redeemable*. Perhaps she was struggling with *change* in her life and God wanted to provide her with an alternative lifestyle. She also became part of an object lesson from God to Hosea and Israel. Seeing Israel as redeemable, God used this marriage as an example of his love to adulterous Israel. God wanted to give Hosea living proof of his relationship with humanity. In this scenario, the marriage is essentially about redemption and maintaining a covenant. God may have intended something very special for Hosea when he reached out to restore Gomer. This marriage would be a constant reminder of God's forgiveness.[5]

Third Scenario

This final scenario is based on the premise that God was merely providing a *permissive* command, for Gomer was someone Hosea already loved. This scenario is possibly the saddest. It did not matter if she was a prostitute or if she came from a family of prostitutes, Hosea loved her! When God told him to marry her, Hosea was probably thrilled because she pleased him.[6] Hosea was not concerned about her sordid past or whether she had an STD. Gomer was the woman he loved. Possibly Hosea thought, *all she needs is love,* so he loved her. Perhaps he loved her with a *covering* love; maybe he loved her with a *clinging* love; maybe he even loved her with a *controlling* love. His covering love meant he would not allow her to do things that other wives did; he feared she would return to her former life. So he limited her trips to the market by going to the market himself. His clinging love would mean he was always with her in the house, at church, always by her side. He was uncomfortable allowing her out of his sight. His controlling love provided advice and direction in every aspect of her life, such as her dress, diet, speech, and cleaning.

Reasons for Marital Difficulty

While we cannot know which scenario accurately depicts Hosea and Gomer's situation, each ends the same way. Something happened to this marriage that resulted in Gomer leaving Hosea and seeking other lovers. There are numerous reasons for an affair, including dissatisfaction with the relationship, dissension between partners, dissolution of love in the relationship, or disintegration of the marriage bond. There are also personal problems that contribute to marital difficulty: emotional emptiness, need for sexual variety, inability to resist new sexual opportunity, alcohol or drug addiction, revenge toward a partner who had an affair, or even evolving values such as a belief that monogamy isn't natural.[7]

The impact of an affair on a marriage is devastating. The loss of trust and damage to self-esteem result in only thirty-five percent of marriages surviving after an affair. One factor that contributes to the breakup is the intense emotional attachment. Affairs are not just physical connections; they are emotional. With the increase of working women, many affairs happen in the workplace.[8]

The reasons for Gomer's affair are likely complex. Perhaps one or both parties caused the disruptions that led to Gomer's downfall. Hosea was accustomed to condemning sin and rebuking evil. So perhaps Hosea condemned her sins at home and rebuked her for her behavior. Possibly he complained about the way Gomer fixed the bread and figs; perhaps the women in her household did not cook nor teach Gomer to cook. Or perhaps he rebuked her for the way she dressed. In her family, the women wore lots of jewelry and make-up, like most "professional women," but now that she was married to a preacher, he wanted her to alter her wardrobe and appearance to suit her status as a preacher's wife. Something happened in their relationship that triggered her desire to return to her family of origin and her family's profession—causing her to want more excitement, leave Hosea's austere home, go to the streets, and become a common prostitute.

Or perhaps the problem was Gomer. She found Hosea's love too confining and longed for her old life with its autonomy and independence. She yearned for a life of freedom, making her own choices and being her own woman.

She may have even longed for multiple partners. Possibly Hosea was not an experienced lover; he did not know all the sexual enticements that her previous experiences had taught her. When she compared him with those other lovers, Hosea was unexciting; he was not the man she wanted. So eventually Gomer yearned for more excitement in her life than just worshiping and studying the Bible. Something caused her to leave Hosea's home and the children and stray to her former lifestyle. The Bible states she was enticed by the sensation of other lovers (Hosea 2:5).

Research supports Gomer's apparent enticement with sensation. "Several studies have shown an association between sexual satisfaction and overall relationship satisfaction in marriage. More specifically, husbands and wives who say they are sexually satisfied in their marriage are also likely to report high levels of overall satisfaction with their relationship."[10] Sexual dissatisfaction could be the difficulty that occurred in this marriage because Gomer was sexually experienced. Research by Joan Kahn and Kathryn London suggests, "Women who were sexually active prior to marriage faced a considerably higher risk of marital disruption than women who were virgin brides." Gomer's previous sexual experience put her at higher risk for marital disruption.

It could be that her love of her old life was so powerful, Gomer was drawn by it even though Hosea had provided for her needs and though she was concerned for the children. The biblical reference in Hosea 2:4,5 suggests that Gomer was always going back to her old ways and that God depicts her behavior as how Israel treated Him. Some have speculated that only the first child was Hosea's because the Bible intimates that Gomer conceived and bore a daughter (Hosea 1:6) and later a son (Hosea 1:8). In fact, chapter two clearly speaks of children of whoredom, so there is evidence that these children are the results of her philandering.

What an embarrassment Hosea must have felt! He had married this woman God directed him to marry. He is dutifully performing his task as a prophet; however, Gomer begins to seek love and pleasure outside their marital relationship. She has affair after affair. If that is not painful enough, she leaves Hosea for someone else—or maybe just to be a prostitute—and leaves him with the children. Some of the children are not even his, but children from her adulterous lifestyle (Hosea 1:2,3; 3:1-3).

Hosea must have been in pain as he struggled to deal with this loss, raise the children, and perform the task of a prophet. Eventually, despite the pain and difficulty, he was better able to handle the separation. The children stopped asking about their mom and even looking for her. Life was all settled, and they could go on. It is at this time that Hosea got another message from God.

> The Lord said to me, "Go, show your love to your wife again, though she is loved by another and is an adulteress. Love her as the Lord loves the Israelites, though they turn to other gods and love the sacred raisin cakes." So I bought her for fifteen shekels of silver and about a homer and a lethek of barley. Then I told her, "You are to live with me many days; you must not be a prostitute or be intimate with any man, and I will live with you."
> —Hosea 3:1-2
> (*A lethek is a measure or weight used in the ancient near east to show balances.*)

Hosea must have been bombarded by many feelings at this message. He must have felt sad, to some degree angry, and certainly traumatized. The battle of shame and the feeling of a damaged ego would have been prominent in his internal struggle. When God told him to go and seek Gomer, Hosea probably did not want to. Hosea must have had many misgivings. What was to be the nature of their future relationship? Was he expected to trust her again following so many betrayals? Could he love a woman who had abandoned him for others? How could he walk in the council with other men after such a humiliating situation? Although Hosea had all these feelings, we see the outcome of his emotional turmoil. He obeys God. The only way he could obey God despite his misgivings and pain was his relationship with God.

Hosea's pain caused him to struggle inside with his feelings and God's requirements. To follow God's requirements, he had to reconcile with Gomer. However, no one reaches this level of reconciliation without a struggle. Hosea's experience provides an object lesson for everyone. It is a lesson of forgiveness—the lesson of loving when it is hard to love. This is one of the hardest virtues to apply in a relationship, especially after adultery.

Hosea had to experience some process to be able to say, "I know what you have done, but I still love you. I still think of you as significant in my life. I care about you. I will be with you." How could Hosea reach this decision? How could he forgive? Forgiveness is a process, and Hosea had to go through some stages of forgiveness to reach this level of reconciliation.

The Process of Forgiving and Healing

What is the normal process of forgiveness? Research and personal experience reveal the following steps.

First, Hosea had to honestly recognize and experience the pain. What feelings did Hosea have? Along with the pain from a loss of trust and grieving the loss of a spouse, he experienced a variety of emotions. Pain produces feelings of betrayal and disappointment. There are other reactions after the disappointment such as the *hurting* or, as some would say, heartache. All this involves emotional pain, disappointment, deception, and sadness because Hosea made himself vulnerable to Gomer. He removed his defensive wall, and the consequences were negative. These consequences made him angry, and he may have begun to hate Gomer. He could have hated himself for being vulnerable. Sometimes people even hate God for allowing the experience of so much pain.[11]

This is a precarious position since often in this *hating,* people get stuck and stay angry and become embittered for the rest of their lives. At this part of the process, Hosea may not have wanted to forgive; he wanted revenge. However, according to Dr. Frederick Luskin, after we are able to articulate the feelings, we need to talk about our situation and our pain with a trusted confidante.[12] To begin to risk sharing our scars and pain with others and our heavenly Father is an essential component of the healing process.

For Hosea, this must have involved realizing that hating hurts. It left him bitter and gave Gomer too much power over his life. It stirred up excessive anxiety and stress. Hating is overwhelming, so there is a need to seek healing. Now Hosea was ready to begin to heal and forgive himself for being vulnerable.

Healing yourself takes time; it is a process. According to Lewis Smedes, the first step is to rediscover the humanity of the person who hurt us. "As we start on the miracle of forgiving, we begin to see our enemy through a cleaner lens, less smudged by hate. We begin to see a real person."[13] Too frequently, the pain, hurt, disappointment, and anger blind us. The Gomers of our life become monsters, villains, animals, or cheats. In the moment of pain, all we can see is the transgression. We cannot remember the good times. However, the first step in the forgiveness process requires the return to humanity.

In my (Edith) counseling with adults who as children were abused by their parents, I frequently hear of parents being described as monsters, wicked, evil or satanic in the adult children's recollections. As the adult child retells the narrative, a change in his or her perception of the parent from evil to sick—or from satanic to misguided or mentally ill—always signals the beginning of healing. As adult children rediscover the humanity in their parents, they begin the healing process.

Hosea had to come to this same conclusion; he had to recognize Gomer's humanity, remember her troubled background and use it as a lens for understanding her. Forgiveness is not about condoning the action, it is about recognizing "that the primary distress is coming from the hurt feelings, thoughts and physical upset you are experiencing now, not what offended you or hurt you."[14] There is a new perspective of the person who hurt you. You see him or her in a new light and with a new spiritual lens. Only God can give us the spiritual lens to forgive. Once Hosea recognized Gomer's humanity, he was ready for the next step.

In the second step, Hosea had to surrender his right to get even. It was natural for Hosea to want revenge. It was natural for him to want to get back at her and make her feel his pain. However, if Hosea was going to forgive, he had to give up this right. He had to give up vengeance, which is "our own pleasure of seeing someone who hurt us getting it back and then some."[15] Too often, we believed that giving up vengeance is giving up justice. But these are two different activities, as supported by this text: "The Lord is slow to anger, abounding in love and forgiving sin and rebellion. Yet he does not leave the guilty unpunished" (Numbers 14:18). Justice can bring closure, but vengeance never does.

Hosea also had to revise his feelings toward Gomer. This required that he begin to bless her. What does this mean? Blessing required Hosea to give up his negative wishes and desires for Gomer and begin to wish good things for her. It meant he actively prayed for God to help her. This was not easy at first, but Hosea had to come to this place before he could go and get Gomer. He had to believe that reconciliation was possible.

Some people may never reach this stage. That is what is so powerful about the story of Hosea and Gomer; it is the story of *both* forgiveness and reconciliation, which leads us to the final stage in the process.

The final stage is the "coming together." This is when Hosea picked himself up, dusted off himself, and—though it was painful—invited Gomer back into the house. He had to reach out to her with honesty and lovingkindness. Gomer also had a part in the reconciliation, because Hosea could not force her to return. He could only offer forgiveness and let Gomer accept or reject it. In this situation, reconciliation occurred—but that is not always the case. Whether forgiveness is received or rejected, one can still be healed without reconciliation.[16] This was equally true for Hosea; he did not have to choose this route.

Hosea did not have to forgive, but he did. He could have said, "Why should I forgive? I have not been promiscuous, I can't forgive. I have not been unfaithful. It isn't fair. I did not leave her, she left me; I am not to blame. She has been two-timing." But what were his options if Hosea chose otherwise?

There are only a few options if you choose not to forgive. Let's consider them briefly.

Approaches to resolving pain

1. *I'll forget it!*[17]

Is this possible? The mind is like a computer without the delete button. All information is retained. So how do we forget it? One option is to repress unpleasant feelings or memories, but psychologists argue that repressed memories still have an impact. Frequently unpleasant situations go into our long-term memory, so they are not really forgotten. Instead, individuals use a tremendous amount of emotional energy to suppress feelings of hurt or try to repress painful memories. Forgetting is not an effective tool. Unresolved pain has an impact. It either affects us emotionally or it simmers under the surface and affects us unconsciously:

Sarah came to my (Edith's) office for counseling because she was extremely promiscuous. She was attending a Christian institution and appeared to be adhering to all of its policies. However, Sarah knew she was living a lie. Most of her relationships developed into sexual ones. In fact, most of her relationships were casual and involved only sexual interactions. She was deeply disappointed in herself. She would promise herself to discontinue these casual sexual escapades; but the next time she was out with a fellow, the same activity occurred.

During the course of our counseling, she revealed a history of sexual abuse. Sarah had experienced this abuse at a very young age. Initially, she did not even remember the event. Nevertheless, the repressed memory had a major impact on her relationships with men. Even though repressed, her sense of self-worth and devaluation from the abuse affected all her relationships with men. So while it is easy to simply say, "I'll forget it," this choice can still have consequences.

Bob and Mary had been in a mentor-mentee relationship for some time. Bob was a professor at a small college and encouraged Mary to do her best. She finished college and entered graduate school with Bob's help. Even when she began her career, they kept in touch. Bob became instrumental in helping Mary work on her doctorate and obtain a position at her alma mater. Unfortunately, working together led to an incident in which Bob felt betrayed by Mary. He told himself, just forget it, I will just ignore her and pretend this never happened. However, each time he saw Mary, he remembered the incident, felt the pain of betrayal and became incensed. Forgetting the pain, which accompanies an incident, is not easy.

2. *Another alternative is: I'll get my revenge.*[18]

Clara and Calvin were married to each other. Clara resented Calvin telling her how to drive, so she would refuse to take the wheel when they went on trips. This was fine with Calvin; he would not have to deal with her reckless driving. Once he was extremely tired, but Clara would not offer to drive. So Calvin got in the car and attempted to drive home. He dozed off, caused a serious accident they barely survived.

How does this work? Can you ever get enough revenge to satisfy your longing? Should revenge come with interest? If your spouse has hurt you, should repayment include five percent interest? Is five percent interest enough, or should it be ten percent interest for an affair? Should an affair like Gomer's, which resulted in prostitution and public shame, require more repayment? How do you get revenge when someone has an extramarital affair? Go out and have an affair yourself? How many affairs are necessary to repay your hurt? One? Two? Three? Princess Di had an affair with her riding instructor;was this sufficient to repay Prince Charles for his ongoing affair with Camille Parker?[19]

What do extramarital affairs cost in emotional and psychological pain? Reflect for a moment on the example we just considered of Bob and Mary. What should Bob do to repay Mary? Should he look for a way to create a similar opportunity to betray Mary—one in which she gets pain. How would Bob measure the pain? How much pain would he need to inflict? And if you get your revenge; does it really remove your pain? Remember, revenge is not a human responsibility. It is not in our job description. Vengeance is not our responsibility but the Lord's. "It is mine to avenge; I will repay" (Deuteronomy 32:35). "Do not take revenge, my friends, but leave room for God's wrath" (Romans 12:19). So while revenge is an option, it is not a viable one.

3. I'll forgive them for what they have done-

This the only best option. Here are some reasons to forgive as suggested by Lewis B. Smedes.[20] Forgiveness provides some positive results personally. To be fair, you have to forgive since forgiveness gives you back control of your life. The memories of the incident and the personal hurt no longer control you. Now you can see the person, talk with the person, and talk about the person without unbelievable pain or anger. Frequently, individuals hesitate to forgive because of a fear of being tolerant of sin. However, we can forgive fairly without tolerance of sin. Forgiveness does not condone sin. When an evil act occurs, justice must be done, but God would have you forgive the person—not the activity. Darold Bigger was a religion teacher at a Christian college when his 25-year-old daughter was raped and murdered on Father's Day, 1996. He exemplifies forgiveness:

I've always dreaded what I would do if someone hurt my girls. A man of ample temper and doffed determination, I've hoped strong friends would surround me at such a time to prevent me from doing something I would long regret.

But these feelings didn't come. There was no clenched teeth rage at Anthony, Shannon's killer: no seething passion for revenge. This wasn't my choice, mind you. It was a gift! I was surprised by grace!

My real faith crisis came months later.... Seeing him for the first time did not help. Not being able to detect any hint of sorrow or regret hardened me.... When he appealed his guilty pleas and wished to have his sentenced reduced trying to get out of what he had confessed to doing, it was too much for me.... This journey has shown me how deeply sinful I am.[21]

How could Darold and Barbara Bigger forgive? Darold heard a sermon about Jesus' command to "love one another" (John 13:34,35). The message was a turning point for Darold Bigger. While he could not imagine loving Anthony, he knew anger and resentment were deadly. He realized he could do nothing to let go of his anger and resentment. The answer was God. He felt the grace of God fill his life as he remembered this verse: "But God demonstrates his own love for us in this: While we were still sinners, Christ died for us" (Romans 5:8).[22]

So Darold and Barbara Bigger's resentment was healed, and they forgave the person—not the deed. God does not expect you to excuse adultery, murder, rape, or other such heinous acts, but he does expect you to forgive the person.

Steps to Forgiveness in Your Marriage

The challenge one faces in a marriage involves how to forgive like Hosea. This is the crucial lesson from Hosea and Gomer for couples today. Yes, *forgiveness is hard!* Yet "with God, all things are possible" (Matthew 19:26). This is a challenge God wants couples to take seriously. Here are some specific suggestions that may prove helpful in your marriage:

1. Ask God to lead you in the process.

Begin the forgiveness process with prayer to God. "This is the confidence we have in approaching God: that if we ask anything according to his will, he hears us" (1 John 5:14). God wants us only to ask, and He has promised to lead us all the way. "In your unfailing love you will lead the people you have redeemed" (Exodus 15:13). Forgiveness is not always humanly possible; it is a gift from God. Darold Bigger could not have forgiven Anthony for such a reprehensible deed on his own; God had to lead him all the way in the process of forgiving.

Begin to pray for your spouse and yourself. Call your spouse's name in prayer. Pray that God will lead and direct in your spouse's life. This prayer is essential. Then pray for yourself. In this prayer, request the power to let go of the anger. Pray for the power to let go of the pain and pray for the grace of God to replace the anger and the pain with his love. You need the indwelling of the Spirit of God.

2. Be specific in your prayer.

Use verbs, not just nouns, to explain the specific activity or concrete deeds necessary for forgiveness. Verbs are action words. So in your prayers use action words to develop a specific plan for the forgiveness process. For example, "*Remove* the anger I feel toward Sally for criticizing me in public." This describes the action needed for forgiveness. This type of statement is better than a general request

123

like, "Help me be more forgiving." That is neither specific, action-oriented, nor does it provide an action plan. Make specific action words an integral component of prayer, such as, "I need your direction in speaking clearly to my wife" or "Help me to know how to be sensitive to her needs."

3. Be patient. It takes time.

Healing from an emotional wound is not instantaneous. It takes time. While there are instant potatoes, instant messaging, and instant coffee, there is no instant healing and forgiveness. Reflect for a moment on the physical domain to understand this. If you break a bone, do you expect an instant cure? While God can instantly mend your broken leg, he usually allows the healing to take place over time. According to medical friends, these things must occur for your leg to heal: You must stabilize the limb, maintain the stability (keep the limb in the cast), and make sure it gets oxygenation. The blood needs to flow to the limb, and nutrition needs to get to the site. The entire healing process takes four to six weeks.

Just as physical healing takes time, so do emotional healing and forgiveness. In the physical realm, the time depends on severity of injury. A triple bypass, which is a major surgery, takes more time to heal than a broken leg. The healing process from a triple bypass may take up to six months. The more severe the injury, the longer the healing process. The same is true in the emotional domain. Therefore an injury from a spouse that involves embarrassment from unkind words might heal faster than an injury from an affair. While each causes emotional pain, the severity of the pain is different. Since healing takes time, be patient with yourself in the forgiveness process.

4. *Prime the pump—say it before you believe it.*

Sometimes you need to say the words of forgiveness aloud, even before the process is complete. The connection between them is complex, but our thoughts influence, regulate, and affect our feelings. Thoughts can even transform feelings. In a sense, this self-talk is transformative. Arrange a meeting with your spouse after you have prayed and are beginning the forgiveness process. Tell him or her about your prayer for the marriage and for him or her. Acknowledge your wrong and say the words of forgiveness. For example, say, "I was wrong for overreacting at the party. I know that made you feel uncomfortable, and I also forgive you for the harsh words you spoke in public."

The Bible states, "For as he thinketh in his heart, so is he" (Proverbs 23:7 KJV). Your thoughts have power to help you to forgive and heal. It is important that your statement be conciliatory. Admitting you are wrong first, prevents sounding self-righteous or condemnatory. If you cannot sound compassionate and caring and cannot offer grace with love, then do not follow this step. Instead follow the step below.

5. *Be silent if you need to, don't say anything:*

If you are unable to say the words with sincerity, then *do not say anything*. Yet, there are times when having a conversation will be more destructive. These are the times when "silence is golden" and when words would add fuel to the fire and cause more dissension. If you cannot have honest conversation, then "be silent." Wait for a more opportune time to speak. In Ecclesiastes 3:7, we read there is "a time to be silent and a time to speak." If you reflect on the hurtful incident and find you cannot prime the pump and cannot speak without rancor, then perhaps you should keep silent until later. Keep silent while you work on the internal battle to resolve your pain and hurt.

6. *Learn to forgive yourself.*

Frequently, self-forgiveness is an essential part of forgiving others. Stop the derogatory self-talk and put-downs! When you are in pain from an emotional hurt or disappointment, you often become angry or upset with yourself. Why? You see the pain as a lack of ability or deficiency. You wonder, "How could I be so stupid?" or "Why did I let myself be vulnerable?" or "That was naïve" or "Only I would fall for that story." You may find yourself in the midst of an internal battle that involves intense tongue-lashing. You are really displeased with yourself.

Now is the time to be gentle to yourself. While this may not have been your wisest decision, reflect for a moment on your motive. What led you to make this decision? Consider what you were trying to accomplish. Give yourself the benefit of the doubt. Be as considerate to yourself as you are with others. Perhaps you made an honest mistake. You are not perfect. You did not mean for this to become a negative. After reflection, forgive yourself as you would someone else. Be compassionate with yourself.

7. *Remember, forgiveness is God's invention, and He says try it; you will like it.*[23]

God began the forgiveness process in Eden. He forgave Adam and Eve, and he has been in the forgiveness business ever since. God is always ready to forgive us: "You are forgiving and good, O Lord, abounding in love to all who call to you" (Psalm 86:5). He wants us to enjoy the pleasure that comes from forgiving hearts. In fact, his forgiveness is dependent upon our ability to forgive. Matthew 6:14

states, "For if you forgive men when they sin against you, your heavenly Father will also forgive you." (See also Mark 11:25, Luke 11:4.) God wants us to benefit from the power of forgiveness, but his forgiveness is conditioned upon our ability to forgive others. God invites us to forgive and even provides a stimulus by offering us forgiveness first. God says try forgiveness; you will like it!

Inappropriate Forgiveness

Just as there are appropriate steps in the process of forgiveness, there are also things to avoid doing. Here are some inappropriate methods of forgiving:

Do not forgive too quickly. Frequently Christians recognize the importance of forgiveness and even God's expectation to forgive. So they may rush to forgive someone because of the biblical expectation. This quick forgiveness occurs at the expense of self. If your spouse says an unkind word, you can forgive him or her the next morning. But if your spouse has an affair or leaves you for another individual as Gomer did, that kind of forgiveness takes time. To rush and forgive may reflect not forgiveness—but denial or ignoring the pain and hurt. In Hosea's case, a quick forgiveness could have been a way to avoid discussing the difficulty that adultery had caused the marriage. Saying a quick "I forgive you," and then never again discussing the incident is not genuine forgiveness, as we see with John and his wife.

John and his wife were devastated by the death of their daughter. She had been brutally beaten to death by her husband and discovered the next day by their young son. At the funeral, John said, "I forgive the young man," then refused to talk about the event again. Why should he discuss it? John had forgiven him, and he did not need to talk about it or think about it again. He refused to discuss the event with his wife, would not go to counseling, or even admit to any emotional pain. This denial had long-term negative consequences to his marriage, his health, and his career.

Covering up pain does not make it go away. An Ethiopian proverb states, "He who conceals his disease cannot expect to be cured." We cover or ignore our pain only at great personal emotional expense. The pain still exists, and often affects us physically as well as emotionally.

Do not wait too long; the reverse is equally damaging. Holding on to the hurt and pain for long periods has negative consequences. It becomes too hard to give up the pain because it has becomes a part of you. "If we wait too long to forgive, our rage settles in and claims squatter's rights to our souls."[24] When you nurse the pain, caress the hurt, and cuddle the disappointment, you incorporate them into your psyche. The hurt, pain, and disappointment become a part of your emotional structure, permanently.

The consequence of nursing the pain is that it becomes the center of your conversation; you talk about the incident all the time. You discuss the situation as if it was an ongoing process, and you linger on the event. These factors get absorbed into the fabric of your life. People who can discuss only hurts and pains are unpleasant to be around; friends begin to leave because no one wants to discuss the subject.

Waiting too long is debilitating emotionally and physically. I (Edith) remember when a painful event was all I talked about. Soon I noticed people avoided talking with me. I noticed that when I began the conversation, my friends began to glaze over. This also happened to April. She had suffered a great injustice; her husband left her for another woman. It was a very public affair, divorce, and remarriage. April was devastated. Six years later, the power of the infidelity was still evident. She discussed it with her neighbors, she shared it when she went bowling, and she talked about it with each new guy she dated. She had been hurt, and she wanted her ex-husband to suffer as much as she had. She waited too long.

Do not wait too long. Hosea could not hold onto pain and successfully restore his marriage.

Do not wait for repentance from the other person[25]

Forgiveness is not just for your spouse; forgiveness is for you. If you wait until your spouse recognizes the wrong he or she has done, you may wait forever. You need to forgive as soon as possible. Everyone has the right to self-determination. Your spouse can choose to say I am sorry or can continue to believe that he or she is right. Either way, you need to forgive them so you can be released from your pain, hurt, and disappointment. Hosea did not wait until Gomer said she was sorry. He went to her. He made the first step. Once God has revealed to you the need, you must follow that lead like Hosea.

Do not demand or expect a Hollywood ending[26]

In the best of all worlds, when you say, "I am sorry and I forgive you. I want to make amends," your spouse might apologize. But in reality, you may be rebuffed. Gomer could have said I do not want to come with you, but Hosea still needed to forgive.

I (Edith) can remember an occasion when I said I was sorry and the response was, "I don't believe you. You say it too frequently and glibly." My apology was rebuffed. There are no guarantees that your forgiveness will be accepted. You must extend it because forgiveness is not just a duty, but an ought of opportunity. Look at forgiveness as a gift that God allows us to share in his experience. God forgives and invites us to do the same. God can help us to forgive and make it a transformative experience.

Conclusion

Hosea was asked to forgive an adulterer and a whore, yet God led him successfully through that process. What about your relationship? What areas need forgiveness and reconciliation? What is God asking you to forgive? Is it something *small*? You must learn to differentiate between actions that require forgiveness, and those that warrant magnanimity.

Some actions do not merit forgiveness, such as leaving toilet seats up at night or forgetting to put your clothes in the hamper, or taking up most of the space in the closet. These are just some of life's little irritations. We must be willing to put up with them. These are not items to forgive but items to tolerate as members of the human family. Life's irritations call us to show generosity of spirit.

Is it something *bigger* like cruel words or insensitivity to your needs? Perhaps it is the use of sex as a bargaining chip? Perhaps it is even something emotionally devastating, such as betrayal or adultery? Hosea has shown us the power of unconditional love—the role of forgiveness in marriage.

Hosea and Gomer's relationship was one that most people predicted would not work. The partners were not "the perfect match." Their marriage was fraught with difficulties from the beginning. Yet because of unconditional love, this marriage flourished as the years went by, while the relationship between Isaac and Rebekah started perfectly and ended with family disintegration. The difference lies in forgiveness and unconditional love. These two attributes made Hosea and Gomer's marriage, which seemed to be made in hell, become a marriage made in heaven.

Loving When It Is Hard To Love
Personal Reflections

Text: Hosea 1-3

1. How do you differentiate in your marriage between actions that require magnanimity and those that require forgiveness? Cite some examples of each.

_____

_____

_____

_____

2. Reflect for a moment on the role of forgiveness in your home of origin. Was forgiveness encouraged, discouraged, or ignored? How did this position frame your feelings about forgiveness?

_____

_____

_____

_____

3. List some actions in your marriage that require forgiveness from you to your spouse. Where are you in the process of forgiveness? How do you plan to offer forgiveness to your spouse?

_____

_____

_____

_____

4. Are there some actions you need to be forgiven for? Where do you think your spouse is in the process of forgiveness? What actions could you take to encourage the forgiveness process in your relationship?

_____

_____

_____

_____

5. What are the spiritual lessons from Hosea and Gomer for your marriage?

_____

_____

_____

_____

6. Reflect on the marriage of Isaac and Rebekah, the marriage made in heaven. Compare it with the marriage of Hosea and Gomer. What are some strengths you learn from this comparison?

_____

_____

_____

_____

7. How important are the actual words *I am sorry*? Is it possible to give gifts and provide increased encouragement and positive strokes instead of actually using the words *I am sorry?*

_____

_____

_____

_____

CHAPTER 6

The Challenge of a Blended Marriage
Facing Marriage In The 21st Century

But after Xerxes' anger had subsided, he began thinking about Vashti and what she had done and the decree he had made. So his personal attendants suggested, "Let us search the empire to find beautiful young virgins for the king. Let the king appoint agents in each province to bring these beautiful young women into the royal harem at the fortress of Susa. Hegai, the king's eunuch in charge of the harem, will see that they are all given beauty treatments. After that, the young woman who most pleases the king will be made queen instead of Vashti." This advice was very appealing to the king, so he put the plan into effect.

—Esther 2:1-4 NLT

On the third day of the fast, Esther put on her royal robes and entered the inner court of the palace, just across from the king's hall. The king was sitting on his royal throne, facing the entrance. When he saw Queen Esther standing there in the inner court, he welcomed her and held out the gold scepter to her. So Esther approached and touched

the end of the scepter. Then the king asked her, "What do you want, Queen Esther? What is your request? I will give it to you, even if it is half the kingdom!" And Esther replied, "If it please the king, let the king and Haman come today to a banquet I have prepared for the king."
—Esther 5:1-4 NLT

Introduction

S HE WAS THE daughter and the granddaughter of a minister. As a daughter of the south, she attended a historically black college and became a civil rights activist. She was the first black woman admitted to the mississippi bar. He was Jewish, raised in a liberal family in Minnesota, the son of a lawyer who belonged to that state's progressive Democratic-Farmer-Labor Party. Peter Edelman left Minneapolis to attend Harvard University and Harvard Law School.

He then was picked to clerk for U.S. Supreme Court Justice Felix Frankfurter. Early in his career, Edelman was exposed to poverty and injustice in the Watts neighborhood in Los Angeles.

In Mississippi these two individuals—one white, one black—one Baptist, one Jewish— met and married. For more than 30 years, this couple has confronted the challenges of being different, religiously and racially. Marion Wright Edelmen has distinguished herself as the founder of the Children's Defense Fund; her husband, Peter Edelman, is a Georgetown Law School professor and a noted scholar. Both are friends of presidents and recipients of numerous national and international awards and honors. Despite this success, Marion Wright Edelman has admitted that their differences in religion and race have caused challenges to their marriage.[1]

This modern power couple provides some insight into the challenges that confronted Esther and Xerxes. Let's reflect on this biblical couple in the book of Esther. What do we know about them and their marriage?

A six-month party with men drinking, a king requesting a public showing of his wife (soon to become his ex), a divorce, and a beauty contest. All these events resulted in a crisis of trust for Esther and Xerxes before they married. However, this marriage is even more complex when it comes to decision making, for each came from a different ethnic and religious background. What happens when people from other cultures and religions get married? How does this affect the decision-making process? In this chapter, we will look at all of these challenges to marriage. First, let's review some facts about marriages today.

Interracial marriages are increasing in America. In 1970, interracial marriages represented 0.7 percent of all marriages. That rose to 2.0 percent in 1980 and 2.2 percent in 1992. With the introduction of the mixed-race category, the 2000 census revealed interracial marriages to be somewhat more widespread. With 2,669,558 interracial marriages recorded, that comprises 4.9 percent of all marriages.[2]

There is also an increase in interreligious or interfaith marriages.[3] An interfaith marriage is a union in which the two spouses, like the Edelmans, follow different religious traditions. Inter-religious/faith could be any combination of religions (Hindu and Christian), different branches of a religion (Baptist and Methodist or Sunni and Shiite), or even different commitments to a common religious community. This would occur when two Catholics marry, and one goes to mass daily while the other goes only once a year. It is estimated in the US that at least "60 percent of Catholics between the ages of 18 to 38 are married to non-Catholics, and 50 percent of recent Jewish marriages are to non-Jews."[4]

The percentages may be similar in other faith traditions. While statistics on interfaith marriages are hard to come by, spiritual leaders believe the numbers are growing.

Although interracial and interreligious marriages are increasing, these challenges are not new. Edith and I come from the same religious tradition, but from two different ethnicities, so we recognize the unique challenges these relationships present. As we find in the Bible, Esther and Xerxes' marriage captures the complexities of these marriages. Let's review this ancient marriage to understand the context of their relationship.

Unfortunately, Esther and Xerxes are seldom viewed as a couple. Esther is one of two women who gives her name to a book in the Bible, yet this book is also the story of an intriguing marriage— one with an unusual almost storybook beginning. It is not a marriage arranged by God, but it was in God's providence. The marriage began because of a crisis, and it was later confronted by a crisis.

Courtship and Marriage

Like many good stories, theirs has two distinct strands that soon weave together. One strand deals with King Xerxes (*Ahasuerus* in Hebrew). This Persian king ruled as far as India to the east and Egypt to the west. He had been king for three years and decided it was time to celebrate. Now this was no ordinary party; the Bible says it lasted for six months, then he held a special seven-day banquet. Imagine a six-month party! It provided an opportunity for Xerxes to display the opulence and grandeur of his kingdom. The banquet, the grand finale of the six-month party, was even more impressive. It seems to have been seven days of non-stop frivolity. "By the king's command each guest was allowed to drink in his own way, for the king instructed

all the wine stewards to serve each man what he wished"
(Esther 1:8). It was a great party time for the noble men in
the kingdom, with unlimited drinking and debauchery.

There were two parties going on at the same time. In the
Middle East at that time and even today, men and women
entertained in separate quarters. Therefore, Queen Vashti
entertained the women in her quarters while the men
attended a separate party. At the end of seven days, the story
of Xerxes takes a unique turn. After a week of drinking
and carousing with the noblemen, Xerxes seems to have
wanted to "show off for the boys." The king recognized that
only one beautiful object remained to be displayed—his
queen Vashti. So, he called for her to come out with her
royal crown, in her royal gown, and show herself to his
noblemen.

This request provoked a crisis because Vashti refused
to display herself. We do not know her reason. Modesty is
important in the Middle East, where women veil themselves
before men, so possibly Vashti felt it was wrong for a wife
to expose herself in this manner. Perhaps it was because
of the men's drinking. Perhaps it was a feminist stance by
this queen who thought it was below her dignity to display
herself in such a manner. If Vashti came from a wealthy
family, this display would not reflect her status and dignity.
Perhaps Vashti knew her husband and thought that obeying
this request would embarrass herself and Xerxes when he
was sober.[5] Or maybe as the hostess of her own party, she
could not leave her guest unattended.

Regardless of the reason, her refusal caused a marital
and a government crisis. It angered the king and embarrassed him in front of the other noblemen. This act of civil
disobedience, this act of women's liberation, created a
problem for the king. His wife did not obey him in front of
other men. Unfortunately Vashti and Xerxes did not have

a mechanism for solving major problems when this crisis occurred in their marriage.

The other men wondered if Vashti's act would affect other wives in the kingdom as well. Perhaps they feared that a refusal to cook or clean would be next! So the men conspired to make an example of Vashti, so no other wife would follow her model.

> This very day the Persian and Median women of the nobility who have heard about the queen's conduct will respond to all the king's nobles in the same way. There will be no end of disrespect and discord.
> —Esther 1:18

The men's response was swift and harsh. They suggested: Banish the queen and divorce her. The king immediately agreed and issued a royal degree, which could not be repealed. Thus one strand of the story deals with Xerxes, Queen Vashti, and the demise of their marriage. The downfall of this marriage reflected an inability to handle a crisis in the marriage.

The parallel strand of the narrative involves an orphaned Jewish girl named Esther from the tribe of Benjamin. Her parents had died and she, as an only child, was adopted by her cousin, Mordecai. Her cousin worked as a butler in the King's palace and loved Esther dearly. The Bible says Esther was lovely in form and feature. Living with her cousin seemed to have made her content.

The parallel strands in this narrative intertwine as the search for a substitute queen begins. Esther 2:1 reads, "Later when the anger of King Xerxes subsided, he remembered Vashti." A time came when the king, despite his harem, thought about his beautiful queen and missed her. He wanted someone he loved and respected. He wanted someone who could meet other needs besides his physical needs, and he had no one to replace Vashti. Once again, his wise men, the same ones who suggested that he banish and divorce Vashti, came forward and suggested he hold a beauty contest to get a new queen. They did not want him to bring Vashti back! So the king commanded that all of the beautiful virgin girls of the kingdom come to the citadel for a beauty pageant. It was a Miss Persia beauty contest, and the winner would be crowned queen—not just for a day but forever.

One of the young virgins was Esther—our Jewish orphan girl. Her route to becoming queen reveals something about her character. One of Esther's primary attributes was that she was charming. We see this in her ability to connect with Hegai, the custodian of women. Not only her exterior beauty, but also her captivating personality attracted this government official. She had an inner beauty that came from her relationship with God. She was able to bond with Hegai, a pivotal component of her preparation to become queen. She also stayed connected with her family—her cousin Mordecai who made daily visits.

Another strength Esther revealed was her willingness to listen to wise counsel. When Mordecai suggested she not reveal her religion, she followed his instructions. Later, we learn that she was a very bright and courageous woman. These characteristics were framed by her deep spirituality and loyalty to the God of her people. This strand of the story shows us a beautiful woman with charm, brilliance, and spiritual commitment. Thus the stage is set for the rest of the story: about a crisis in the marriage of the beautiful, charming, smart, and spiritual queen and the proud, loving, but fickle king.

The two strands of the story intertwine when King Xerxes, after almost four years alone, searched for a new queen using a beauty contest. Esther, one of the participants, had been preparing for a year. This contest allowed the proud, powerful, pompous king looking for a queen to meet a beautiful, brilliant, and charming Jewish orphan girl. The stage was set for a Hollywood ending, and perhaps a Hollywood beginning.

Esther walked into the room, and the sight of this sensuous, beautiful, and dignified woman mesmerized Xerxes. In a moment, he forgot about Vashti. The Bible says he looked at Esther and loved her more than all the other women. For Xerxes, it was love at first sight. He must have felt like Adam after he awoke, saw Eve, and said, Wow! "This is now bone of my bones, and flesh of my flesh" (Gen. 2:23 KJV). Perhaps he was like Isaac, who after he saw Rebekah, "was comforted after his mother's death" (Gen. 24:67). After Xerxes saw Esther, he was comforted after the loss of Vashti. But love does not mean that obvious difficulties would be removed from this marriage. These included:

1. Xerxes was a divorcee who had divorced his wife for a minor infraction, because of a poor decision-making capacity (Esther 1:12-15).
2. This was an interfaith marriage. He was not a Jew, and she was Jewish. This couple was not equally yoked as the Bible would define it. "Do not be yoked together with unbelievers. For what do righteousness and wickedness have in common? Or what fellowship can light have with darkness" (2 Corinthians 6:14).
3. Their ethnic identities were different; he was Persian, and she was Israelite.
4. He loved to party, get drunk, and hang out with the fellows (Esther 1:4-6).
5. He was unpredictable (Esther 2:1).

How this couple managed these difficulties in the midst of a crisis reveals much about the character of Esther and Xerxes.

Challenges of Differences in Marriage: Faith, Race, or Culture

Interracial and interfaith marriages have unique challenges involving conflicting views on morality, ethics, theology, worldview, and family traditions. These may influence many of a couple's decisions, wants, priorities, and needs.[6] For example, how many children should they have or how should they raise the children? Will the children receive religious training or attend parochial school? These questions confront interfaith marriages. Finances can be another challenge as the couple faces questions like whether to give ten percent of their income to the church, since tithing is not a tradition in all faiths.[7]

Marion Wright Edelman reflects on the many challenges cause by the differences between her and Peter.[8] She discusses their ethnic and racial differences and concludes that the most difficult area for their marital adjustment involved religious differences. Many of these issues related to religious traditions and child rearing (for example, whether to have a bar mitzvah). Esther and Xerxes faced additional challenges since the external community did not support marriages between different ethnic groups. Such couples must confront stereotypes, negativity, and stares. Couples in marriages across ethnic groups must address differences in child rearing and holiday celebrations, as well as unsupportive laws.

"Stanford University sociologist Michael Rosenfeld calculates that more than seven percent of America's 59 million married couples in 2005 were interracial, compared to less than 2 percent in 1970."[8] Rebecca Kahlenberg says these marriages have higher conflict and divorce rates. Why? One factor involves differences in speaking style. Some cultures have a style that is highly involved, allows for disruptions, and may be comfortable with conflict.[10]

In our intercultural marriage, we noticed this difference. In my (Trevor's) family, confrontation and conflict were acceptable and valued. We often saw our parents vehemently disagree about some item. It was not unusual for the family "discussion" to involve every member of the family with loud voices and lots of gesturing. We were an animated family.

On the other hand, in my (Edith's) family, I seldom saw my parents argue, and we were not comfortable with conflict. Instead, issues would simmer. Snide remarks would be made, and eventually the disagreement would require the injured parties sit down alone and discuss the event.

Martha was a white Christian American woman who married Hamed, an Egyptian Muslim. While they had much that was different, they had much in common. Both were teachers, loved children, and shared a love for adventure. From this union came two children. When their children were teens, Martha and Hamed decided to spend a year in Egypt. Unfortunately, their eldest son, Mohammed, became sick and died. In keeping with the tradition in the Islamic religion and culture, he was buried within 24 hours, but Martha was not allowed to attend. This cultural practice increased her depression and grief at the loss of her son. Their daughter was expected to conform to traditional Muslim attire and rules that were unlike those she experienced in America.

Their story reflects some of the challenges such marriages experience in the area of child rearing and gender roles. These cultural practices complicate decision making in a crisis or transition, and they are pivotal points of conflict for interracial and intercultural marriages in the US today.[11]

Impending Crisis

The stage was set for Esther and Xerxes as the two strands of their story intertwined and moved toward a finale. The stress on their marriage was heightened by the limited time for interaction, their different religions, and an impending crisis. All relationships will experience a crisis from which they cannot escape. For some couples, it might be a crisis of *finances*. For others, it might be a crisis of time or commitment. For some couples, like Isaac and Rebekah, *children* may bring a crisis. For some, it is a crisis of *infidelity*. Regardless the cause, they will have a marital crisis. A crisis requires that spouses trust each other to make decisions that are good for each partner and the marriage.

For Esther and Xerxes, the crisis occurred after four years of marriage.[12] It came when Haman, the king's prime minister, persuaded the king to kill all of the Jews. Esther did not know about the decree, so when Mordecai came to Esther in sackcloth and ashes, she was surprised to hear of the decree. He requested that Esther go to the king and save herself and her people.

Trust is a pivotal component of a good marriage. During their four years of marriage, Xerxes had learned he could trust Esther. Early in their marriage, she had warned him with information from Mordecai about plot to take his life. This warning saved his life (Esther 2:19-23). But Esther did not know if she could trust Xerxes, especially as she reflected on his treatment of Vashti. Could she trust him to accept her if she came to him unbidden? Could she trust him to love her if he really knew she was Jewish? Could she trust him to save her and her people from his trusted prime minister?

These questions frame the crisis of trust for this couple. The way Esther and Xerxes handled this crisis offer lessons for marriages in the twenty-first century. Here are the seven steps to resolving a crisis in your marriage.

1. Confront the crisis.
2. Take action, accept responsibility.
3. Use it as a time to grow.
4. Fast and pray.
5. Develop a plan.
6. Recognize the importance of timing and setting.
7. Implement your plan carefully and prayerfully.

Confront the Crisis

When Esther heard that her cousin was in sackcloth and ashes, she sent him some clothes, but Mordecai refused them. Custom prevented Esther from going to Mordecai, so she sent an intermediary to discover the trouble. The intermediary brought back news of the decree, a copy of the edict, and a request from Mordecai that Esther go before the king and "beg for mercy and plead with him for her people" (Esther 4:8). Esther resisted this idea. She wanted to avoid the struggle and pretend the situation did not involve her. She wanted to sit on the sidelines and not deal with this crisis. But Mordecai told her that she could not avoid the crisis. *When a crisis occurs in the relationship, one must confront the crisis.*

Too frequently in marriages, couples may have a response similar to Esther's. A couple in a financial crisis may try to ignore it. Some methods such couples will use to avoid the crisis include not talking with bill collectors or refusing to open bills when the mail comes.

Luther and Mary had been married for two years. Each brought debt to the marriage. During these two years, their debt increased significantly as Luther went through an eight-month period of unemployment. Their debt ballooned to over $20,000. Soon debt collectors were calling regularly, and warnings came in the mail daily. Luther and Mary developed the habit of not answering the phone calls except from family members, and they neatly stacked the warnings unopened in a corner. Like Esther, their first response was to try to ignore the crisis. Unfortunately, ignoring bills does not remove the debt and may even prolong the indebtedness.

Another example of not dealing with a crisis without confrontation occurred in Jeff and Carla's marriage. They had been married for several years when Jeff would begin to disappear overnight or for weekends. Carla never knew when it would happen, and he did not contact her while he was gone. Jeff would return calmly with a limited explanation for his absence. Carla was confused but did not want Jeff to get upset. She thought that if she just ignored the occasional absences, Jeff would eventually stop disappearing. Like Esther, her first response was to try to ignore the crisis. Unfortunately, ignoring an absent spouse does not foster marital commitment. When one spouse receives frequent phone calls from someone of the opposite sex, the evidence implies infidelity. But sometimes the injured spouse ignores the disappearances and phone calls and pretends that "no news is good news." Blaming the other person is viewed as easier than confronting the spouse. Again, like Esther, the initial response is to try to ignore the crisis.

Frequently, instead of confronting the crisis, we do other things: eating more, working more, socializing with friends, or even spiritualizing the problem by going to church and praying. These approaches do not address the problem. However, Esther and Xerxes teach that we cannot successful avoid a crisis. This leads to the second lesson from this biblical couple.

Make A Decision To Take Action, Accept Responsibility

When a crisis occurs in the relationship, the couple must do something. A crisis confronts us with choices: to act or remain silent; to do nothing or take an action; to accept responsibility for the solution or sit passively by and let others accept responsibility. This was the dilemma that confronted Esther. She knew what had happened previously. When Vashti faced a crisis, her decision making led to her being deposed as queen. Both Vashti and Xerxes made unilateral decisions that destroyed the marriage. Esther knew this would not work to save her people or herself. She feared her husband's reaction, since it had been thirty days since she last went before the king. The king had not called her, and custom required her as a woman to wait for his invitation.

Esther feared for her life. She did not *want* to do anything, but she *had to* make a decision—and to do nothing was a decision. If a couple chooses not to open the bills, the decision has been made not to pay them. If the husband ignores the calls from a spouse's extramarital lover, then the decision has been made to allow the relationship to continue. *Passivity is a decision!* It is not action, nor is it taking responsibility, but passivity is a decision.

Too frequently, passivity and an inability to make decisions are based on a lack of values. "It is not hard to make decisions when you know what your values are."[13] If Esther trusted God, if she allowed God to lead, then she must take action. To take action required that she be like Daniel and purpose in her heart to act. Mordecai warned Esther that

148

she must make a choice. He warned her that like Joshua of old, she must choose whom she must serve: God or man (Joshua 24:15). Furthermore, Mordecai warned her that she might have come to the royal position for such a time as this (Esther 4:14). God wanted to teach Esther a painful but necessary lesson. It was a message that involved growth. Which leads to the third step this biblical couple took.

Use the Crisis as a Time to Grow

Recognize that the crisis, the struggle, the pain, can be an opportunity to learn and grow. Haman, the prime minister, meant the decree for evil, but God used it for good. God had a lesson for Esther and her husband to learn. She was about to have a faith encounter with God that would transform her marital relationship and strengthen it. A time of marital crisis can be a time to grow, a time to learn about yourself, your spouse, and God. A crisis is a time of reflection and introspection when you question yourself and God. This time of soul-searching can lead to growth.

Pain and growth often occur simultaneously. The Bible overflows with stories of growth after a crisis. After Adam and Eve ate the fruit, they had to grow and become more intimate in their marriage. As we will see in Chapter 7, after a series of losses challenged Mr. and Mrs. Job's marriage, the results were growth and restoration in their relationship with each other and with God. Consider even David and Bathsheba, who experienced a crisis at the death of their child, but grew closer and became the parents of future King Solomon. A crisis provides an opportunity for a faith venture with God. It can be a time of marital growth in ways unimaginable.

In our marriage, we have had many crises. Once we had tremendous financial loss due to an unwise investment and flooding on our property. A time of loss is *not* a time to assess blame and make accusations. Yes, poor decision making occurred, but in the midst of a crisis, blame throwing does not help resolve the issue. So we focused on finding solutions to get us out of the problem. It became a time for real dependence on God. In retrospect, God led us through this time of difficulty. Couples can experience significant growth only if they use the crisis as a time for increased contact with God and each other. Esther's life reveals the need at these times to increase interaction with God through fasting and praying—the fourth step to handling marital crisis.

Fast and Pray

Esther turned to God before she acted. Times of crisis require spiritual connection, spiritual reflection and spiritual intervention. Esther requested that Mordecai and her people fast and pray with her. She fasted and prayed herself. This time of introspection provides spiritual and physical cleansing. Esther needed to cleanse her life of excess baggage. Perhaps as an orphan, she struggled with issues of self-esteem. Perhaps as a woman, she doubted her ability to save her people. Perhaps she had misgivings about God's direction in her life. Fasting and praying provided her with time to commune with God and gain assurance of God's love for her. She was able to discern that God was a Father who valued and loved her. She was able to recognize that God had a plan for her; her misgivings about God's direction were reduced. Praying provided her with the chance to confess her sins. As she prayed, God provided her with a *vision*—a way out of her dilemma.

Fasting and praying often results in a vision, a plan. In my (Edith's) life, when confronted with a crisis in our marriage that requires decision making, I pray for Trevor and myself. I pray that God will give me the words to say and help Trevor to hear. I pray that I will find the best way to share the dilemma and that we will come up with a mutually acceptable solution. Prayer changes you, it changes your spouse, and it changes the outlook on the situation. The best reaction to a time of fasting and praying is the ability to develop a God-directed plan; this is the next important lesson we can learn from this couple.

Develop a Plan

God will lead you to a plan, just as he led Esther. God, who had the plan of salvation from the foundation of the earth, will encourage your development of a plan. Esther's God-led plan involved going to see the king. Reflecting on her first encounter with the king, she knew it was important to appeal to his senses. So she went to him dressed magnificently. She knew what he would like, so perhaps she even wore that dress that had enticed him four years earlier. Next, Esther planned to feed the king all his favorite foods. In her plan, she invited not only the king but also Haman, her accuser.

Esther knew that to get out of a crisis, she needed a carefully crafted plan. She recognized that one gets more with honey than vinegar. So she developed a plan that would appeal to the king, a plan that would entice and not rebuff, a plan that would elicit support—not result in her being dethroned like Vashti. In essence, Esther developed a plan that would woo her husband to see her predicament. Fasting and praying led to a plan that reached her husband by using his love language, a plan that recognized his needs and met them.

In his book *Five Love Languages*, Dr. Gary Chapman suggests that one must talk to a spouse in a language that meets his or her needs. According to Chapman, these languages may include words of affirmation, quality time, receiving gifts, acts of service, and physical touch.[14] Perhaps for Xerxes, receiving gifts was significant. Thus Esther developed a plan that used his love language and met his needs. A critical component of applying a good plan is timing, which leads to the sixth step.

Recognize the Importance of Timing and Setting

Esther asked her people to fast for three days before she went to see the king. She wanted to make sure she went at the *right time*. When she spoke to the king, she did not express her concerns in the open court. She instead just invited him to dinner because she realized some things needed to be discussed in private. As a couple, avoid discussing your problems and concerns in open court.

Aisha and Mark were attending a party. After Aisha made some derogatory remarks about Mark in front of the others, everyone got quiet. They did not know what to say. Mark had two options: Let Aisha know his feelings right away in the midst of the party or ignore the remarks and discuss it later. Mark chose to discuss it later. On the way home, he shared his feelings with Aisha. He told her how embarrassed he was by her remarks. In the privacy of their car and later at home, they discussed the situation and developed a solution to avoid it in the future.

Esther knew that timing was an important principle for making a good decision. Therefore, she went to see the king only to invite him to a first meal. After that meal, Xerxes felt content and pleased. She had given him the gifts of a meal, her presence, and her conversation. He asked what she wanted—and even promised half his kingdom, again conveying the importance of gifts to him. But Esther demurred; she still did not tell him the reason for the meeting. Instead, she continued to execute her plan. She sweetly invited both Xerxes and Haman back the next day.

Some of the best decisions making takes time, do not rush the plan. Recently as Edith and I were at a couple's retreat sharing these principles, a young lady questioned the concept of taking time. She said how stressful it was for her to wait. In fact, she mentioned that if she waited more than "five hours, the stress would kill her." In our marriage, we have found we sometimes need to wait several days before we can resolve an issue. We encourage couples not to wait more than seventy-two hours. Some issues take even longer to resolve. Esther was able to persuade her husband to save her people and herself because she waited.

Waiting is necessary and essential. In your marriage, you can learn a lot from this concept of timing and planning. For this important discussion, Esther chose a time after the meal when her husband was relaxed and feeling good, rather than stressed. She knew timing was important. If your spouse is watching Monday night football, this is not a good time to share a significant concern. Neither are the Super Bowl or the World Cup good times. If the baby is crying or just broke a dish, this is not a good time to share a significant concern. For some women, neither is the middle of Oprah Winfrey nor a favorite TV show a good time.

Choose a *mutually acceptable* time and place. Ask your spouse if this is a good time for a discussion. If not, ask for a time that would be better. You need to choose a time within forty-eight to seventy-two hours. Discipline yourself to follow these steps carefully and prayerfully. This may mean not rushing to share it because of your need for catharsis. You may have to delay gratification and wait until God shows a better way. It means waiting on God to show

His will, so you can follow. Then execute your plan: the seventh and final step.

Implement Your Plan Carefully and Prayerfully

Once she shared her concerns with him, King Xerxes and Esther were prepared to work together to implement a plan. Esther followed a God-directed plan; she and the king developed a decision to save her people—including making her uncle Mordecai the prime minister. Their marriage was strengthened by this decision-making process. God was glorified. Not only was Haman destroyed, but his plot to annihilate God's people was also thwarted.

Something good came out of the crisis. However, you must be willing to recognize God's leadership and allow God to change the circumstance. You must find yourself in God's will and say, like Zechariah of old, "'Not by might nor by power, but by my Spirit,' says the Lord Almighty" (Zechariah 4:6). Reflect on these seven steps and use them carefully in your decision-making process in your marriage.

Their decision-making process resulted in Esther becoming a confidant for Xerxes in handling her people, and he developed a deeper appreciation for her based not only on her beauty, but also on her personality. The same can be true for couples today. Developing problem-solving tools to handle a crisis is essential for marital success and preserving a healthy relationship. However, problem solving is complicated by differences in religion and ethnicity.

What does this couple teach about maintaining successful, healthy relationships despite major differences? Esther and Xerxes were very different in many ways: age, religion, ethnicity, culture and class, but they used these differences not as sources of frustration but as a cause to celebrate. This couple treated differences as an asset and not a liability. Here is some guidance from the marriage of Esther and Xerxes about the role of marital differences and their impact on the relationship. Clearly, Esther was aware of the differences and used her knowledge of her husband's culture to frame her approach. We see her successful negotiation of these differences in her ability to handle the crisis and to work with her husband afterward and save her people.

Numerous authors suggest strategies for successful marriages when the couples differ ethnically, racially, educationally, religiously, or culturally.[15] Four of these suggestions include

1. Learning about your partners culture, race, ethnicity, or religion.
2. Negotiating and renegotiating differences.
3. Communicating with in-laws.
4. Being tolerant.

Become a cultural explorer; learn about your partner's culture, race, or religion. This may include visiting your spouse's home country, going to his or her church, and trying different foods. Prior to marrying into my husband's large, friendly, Jamaican family, I had never heard or tasted fried plantain, ackee and codfish, callaloo, or bami. I decided to learn about these foods and appreciate them. I looked at the opportunity to try these dishes with excitement. Some I learned to love and cook, such as plantain or rice and peas. Others I tried and decided they were not for me, such as boiled bananas or turn meal.

Successful marriages of couples who are different require an appreciation for the other's culture and an acceptance of both of your traditions into the family. On the other hand, Trevor learned to love collard greens. Most of our special meals include greens and rice and peas. We have combined foods from both cultures.

Learn to negotiate and renegotiate differences.

This includes negotiating differences in conversation styles and gender roles. If one partner has a highly involved and conflictual communication pattern, and the other has a passive, calm pattern of communication, learn to understand the differences and develop a style that incorporates both cultural patterns. As a couple, seize the opportunity to build a new tradition. Develop a negotiation style that fits both in the marriage. Trevor's family's had a direct and combative discussion style, and Edith's family's a more subtle and indirect style. Trevor and I developed new traditions in communication; we do not have the conflictual style of his family, and we also try to avoid the subtle, indirect style of mine. We actually set aside time to address issues or concerns in our marriage. This works for us.

Communicate with in-laws.

Many cultures see marriages as occurring between two families. We know of one Hindu family who actually accompanied their son and his wife on their honeymoon. While the bride was dismayed at this prospect, the family saw this as an opportunity for family meals and times of togetherness. Your in-laws can help you understand the cultural differences. Not long after our marriage, I (Edith) requested that my mother-in-law send recipes that were Trevor's favorites. She taught me a lot about the Jamaican culture and their foods. In-laws can facilitate your cultural exploration and explain the differences, so see your in-laws as potential friends, not potential enemies.

Be Tolerant.

Tolerance requires that one become broad-minded, understanding, and able to see the marriage from another perspective. It means one is open-minded and not operating from an ethnocentric point of view. The cultural or ethnic perspective with which you were raised is not the only lens, or the correct one, for every crisis. "There is more than one way to skin a cat." Develop an attitude that appreciates differences and celebrates them.

Finally, successful interracial, intercultural, or inter-religious marriages require optimism. Expect the best. Esther expected positive results from her discussion with Xerxes, and she got them. She approached her husband with a plan and a willingness to let God lead. When God is in the plan, there is a reason to be optimistic. "God, who is able, through his mighty power at work within us, to accomplish infinitely more than we might ask or think" (Ephesians 3:20 NLT) will lead you through marital difficulties.

While marital differences influence problem solving in a marriage, differences need not doom the marriage. Like Esther and Xerxes, a couple must be willing to work a plan and celebrate the differences. *Viva la difference!* These characteristics are the foundation for marital success.

It is our prayer that you will develop problem-solving tools that will enhance your marriage despite your differences. May all of the crises and differences in your marriage be a foundation for success, as they were for Esther and Xerxes.

FACING MARRIAGE IN THE 21st CENTURY
Personal Reflections

Text: Esther 2:1-4, 5:1-4

1. Reflect for a moment on a crisis in your relationship. How do you and your spouse traditionally handle a crisis?

    _____

    _____

    _____

    _____

2. As you review your strategy for handling crises, explore how you learned this strategy?

    _____

    _____

    _____

    _____

3. How might you incorporate Esther's strategy into your marriage? What if your spouse does not agree that this is the best strategy?

    _____

    _____

    _____

    _____

4. Review, 1 Samuel 25:2-38. What lessons can you learn from Abigail's resolution of a marital crisis? Is her strategy applicable today?

_____

_____

_____

_____

5. What are some of the unique challenges of blended families?

_____

_____

_____

_____

6. How have you worked to resolve these challenges? What are some new strategies listed in this book you might try?

_____

_____

_____

_____

CHAPTER 7

Marriage for the Tough Times
Marriage in Tough Times

In the land of Uz there lived a man whose name was Job. This man was blameless and upright; he feared God and shunned evil. He had seven sons and three daughters, and he owned seven thousand sheep, three thousand camels, five hundred yoke of oxen and five hundred donkeys, and had a large number of servants. He was the greatest man among all the people of the East. His sons used to take turns holding feasts in their homes, and they would invite their three sisters to eat and drink with them. When a period of feasting had run its course, Job would send and have them purified. Early in the morning he would sacrifice a burnt offering for each of them, thinking, "Perhaps my children have sinned and cursed God in their hearts." This was Job's regular custom.

—Job 1:1-5

Introduction

G EORGE AND JOY had decided to go play bingo. It had been a long time since they had been able to go out.

Around 10 o'clock, George was called out. A man said, "Just go home. Something terrible. Please just go home" What a message for parents to get. So George and Joy rushed home; there were police everywhere. When the police came out to talk with her, Joy said she knew something was wrong. No one could look at them, and no one seemed able to talk. But the inactivity in the house indicated something was terribly wrong. Joy's immediate response was, "They're all dead, aren't they."

All of her four children who were home had been brutally shot and killed. This included, Stephen, 14; Gregory 12; Tonya, 4; and Stacy, 2, who was sucking a bottle at the time of her death. Guns that belonged to George had been used to shoot all of the children. Stacy had been shot three times; Tonya was shot four times. Greg, who tried to escape, was shot four times, and Stephen, under the couch, was shot once at the base of his neck.

Three weeks later, on October 5, 1977, George and Joy lost another child, 17-year-old Stephanie, who died from ovarian cancer. Living in poverty with their children dead, George and Joy had experienced a series of catastrophes that could have ended any marriage.[1] When a couple is confronted with such difficulties, it is often called a Jobian or Job-like experience.

The book of Job is probably the oldest written book of the Old Testament. Its main character has the dubious distinction of being called "righteous" by God. Here was a man on whom God was willing to stake His own reputation. Job was blessed with wealth, physical health, many children, a good partner, and many friends. He was respected in his community.

Job probably expected happiness and peace all his days. God said he was upright and a man of integrity. While the book makes little reference to his wife, it is likely that she too was a respected person of integrity.

Statistics for marital dissolutions are high; almost 50 percent of marriages do not survive. These statistics are complicated by adversity and difficulty that can devastate marital relationships. The death of a child deeply affects a marriage; in fact twelve percent of marriages where a death occurs end in divorce.

In the *Reader's Digest*'s Marriage in America Survey, forty-seven percent of respondents said that a layoff or job loss was a major challenge in their relationships; about half described the experience as negative.[2] Chronic illness also affects the quality of the relationship between partners.

The marriage of Mr. and Mrs. Job had all of these possibilities. Dr. Gary Chapman calls these difficult times the winter season of your marriage. So we must explore the biblical lessons for surviving in the tough times. While many of the marriages we have considered had tough times, no marriage in the Bible faced and survived tough times like Job and his wife.[3]

Historical Review

Let us quickly review the adversity that confronted Mr. and Mrs. Job so we can have the context to understand this marriage. Job and his wife had owned extensive property: "seven thousand sheep, three thousand camels, five hundred yoke of oxen and five hundred donkeys" (Job 1:3). When translated into today's finances, he had more than $8,489,080 in stock and bonds, along with many servants.

Once adversity struck, the first area affected was financial loss. Mr. and Mrs. Job lost all their financial holdings. It was like the stock market crash of the 1929s, the Enron debacle of 2002, the sub prime financial fiasco that wrecked Bear Stearns in March 2008, and the Bernie Madoff ponzi scheme, which took some $50 billion of people's retirement accounts and ruined many nonprofit organizations and charities. In each of these catastrophes, millions or billions of dollars were lost, and the economic catastrophes spilled over into relationships.

Right after the financial loss, all Job's children were killed. Few people lose all their children at once.

For the past twenty years, I (Edith) have been involved with parents who have had their children die tragically. I have worked with MADD (Mothers Against Drunk Driving), POMC (Parents Of Murdered Children), and other organizations. Each experience revealed the long-term impact of the death of a child on the family. However, I have never worked with any family who had more than two children killed. I have worked with several parents whose only child died—and the depth of their loss seemed insurmountable.

Mr. and Mrs. Job were confronted with the death of all their adult children at one time, an unbelievable calamity. This type of loss would cause them to feel numb. Yet this was not the end of their tragedy. Job was also confronted with a chronic illness. For Mrs. Job, that was the last straw. Feeling hopeless and overwhelmed, she insisted that her husband curse God and die.

Job and his wife went from being a wealthy, well-respected duo with ten great children to an impoverished, childless pair disdained by friends. What a devastating experience! What a downfall for this team! Their situation was further complicated by Job's illness, his wife's disdain, and his friends' criticism. How does one understand the marital stressors on this marriage?

Marital Stressors

This couple came under intense pressure. The Bible specifically states that Satan assaulted Job's home. Let's assess the difficulties that couples confront today that mirrors these problems.

First, financial disaster. Job lost everything. Today the number one cause of marital discord is financial difficulty. When couples cannot meet their expenses, it affects their relationship. Forty-three percent of married couples argue over money issues—the major reason couples fight.

> "Money is one of the many reasons that a marriage can break up, especially if times of financial distress have continued over a lengthy period of time. In fact, financial stress appears to be the cause of about 80 percent of all divorces. This goes to show just how stressful financial trouble can be for a couple who both are affected by it."[4]

Consider the failed marriage of Casey and Galina Serin. These would-be real estate moguls went from being real estate investors to a couple with five houses being foreclosed. They used their credit cards and fraud to amass a debt between $200,000 and $500,000. They divorced because of their debts.[5] A major financial loss can devastate a marriage and can lead to suicide, homicide, or divorce.

Even without major financial loss, money still impacts the couple. Sometimes finances reflect a power struggle in the marriage. When finances become a battleground—it's "your money" and "my money," there is marital discord and difficulty.

One challenge many couples confront is their attitude about money and money management. In some homes, money was saved and frugality was important. In other homes, money was spent and purchasing was important. When a saver marries a spender, you can expect discord and difficulty.

Darryl and Destiny were young and in love when they got married. Darryl was a technological whiz and Destiny, a nurse. They loved doing things together. But once they got married, differences appeared in their money management attitudes. Darryl loved to purchase the latest gadget. Whenever he made any more money through overtime or special projects, since it was "his" money, he spent it before he got home. Destiny was a saver and wanted to develop a plan for family purchases. At first, she tried explaining to Darryl the importance of saving. He would listen politely, but the next time he had extra money, he continued to spend. Soon this issue became a point of major conflict. Darryl felt he should be able to spend his extra money without any consultation. Destiny felt they should develop a list of priorities for family purchases. "How many big screen TV's does a family need?" she asked. This issue had a major impact on their marriage.

One critical area of conflict for couples is dividing the bill payment responsibilities. Couples struggle over having a joint account, separate accounts, or a combination of joint and separate. They must decide the best money management plans for their marriage.

While financial difficulties are a major marital challenge, Job experienced even greater difficulties, which we will explore. In Job's situation, Satan next attacked the children; all their children died in one day. From my (Edith's) experience with Compassionate Friends, Mothers Against Drunk Drivers, and Parents of Murdered Children, I learned some valuable lessons about the effect of the death of a child.

After a child's death, a couple's satisfaction with their marriage decreases greatly. Why is that so? Men and women grieve differently. Often men become more involved with work and other tasks to avoid dealing with their grief; they do not want to talk about it. Women often want to cry and talk about the loss and how it feels for them. These different reactions cause misunderstandings, which increase the possibility of the marriage breaking up.

One area of conflict I have noticed from my counseling involves the diminishing of sexual intimacy. For men, sexual intimacy is a way for the couple to connect and express their love for each other. It is a means for the couple to comfort each other, especially after the loss of a child. But for many women, the loss of a child is so devastating, they cannot even think about having sex! They are in too much pain to have any pleasure. These different reactions complicate the grief process and decrease marital satisfaction.

Joy Swift in her book *They're All Dead Aren't They?* says the deaths of their children consumed their thoughts and feelings. They also had to go through the two separate trials of the individuals who murdered their children. Despite those difficulties and the financial stress, Joy and George did not become angry at each other or blame each other.[6] Few couples react this way. Sometimes couples become angry with each other and with God—even as angry with God as Mrs. Job.

Marge and Tom were thinking about getting a divorce. The pressure on their marriage began with the death of their son. Marge was driving when the accident occurred. Although she did not cause the death, Tom was devastated and felt that Marge was responsible. He realized the police report did not refer to her culpability. But his need to blame someone, plus his own anger and grief, made him unable to forgive her. Shortly after the accident and the death of their child, they appeared in divorce court. The death of a child can overwhelm a marriage. For Mr. and Mrs. Job, however, the disaster did not end even with financial setbacks and death of their children. There was more to come.

On another day the angels came to present themselves
before the Lord, and Satan also came with them to present
himself before him. And the Lord said to Satan, "Where
have you come from?" Satan answered the Lord, "From
roaming through the earth and going back and forth in
it." Then the Lord said to Satan, "Have you considered
my servant Job? There is no one on earth like him; he is
blameless and upright, a man who fears God and shuns
evil. And he still maintains his integrity, though you
incited me against him to ruin him without any reason."
"Skin for skin!" Satan replied. "A man will give all he
has for his own life."

—Job 2:1-4

After all of his calamities, God again recommended Job.
Yet Satan had an answer:

"But stretch out your hand and strike his flesh and bones,
and he will surely curse you to your face." The Lord said
to Satan, "Very well, then, he is in your hands; but you
must spare his life." So Satan went out from the presence
of the Lord and afflicted Job with painful sores from the
soles of his feet to the top of his head.

—Job 2:5-7

Next, Satan attacked Job's physical health. Like finances
and death of children, physical illness can devastate a
marriage. According to Silver, couples who experience
chronic pain are particularly vulnerable to most common
and stressful life events. Illness or chronic pain can lead to
financial difficulty, loss of intimacy, emotional imbalance,
and changing roles."[7] When illness creates stress, the most
noticeable effect is the way the family organizes relationships. Roles that were well understood before the illness
may no longer be relevant.

Mike and Marsha have struggled for the past nine years with Mike's increasing pain from TMJ (Temporo Mandibular Joint). The chronic pain affected their marriage tremendously. Mike is less able to help around the home as the medications make him tired. He is less involved with parenting and cannot drive the boys to various school and church appointments. He is less talkative and has become distant in the marriage. Marsha says, "I want my husband back."

Couples get married and have certain expectations about roles, interactions, and patterns of communication. In an illness or with chronic pain, the healthy partner must assume more of the responsibility. Sexual intimacy diminishes because the partner with chronic pain has less interest in sex. In fact, "50%-75% report having little or no sexual relationships." Illness and chronic pain causes couples to grieve the loss of relationship.[8]

Couples who suffer this loss may experience difficulties similar to the stages of grief. (The classic stages of grief as suggested by Kubler-Ross are: denial, anger, bargaining, depression, and acceptance.[9]) A quick reflection on Mrs. Job's response when she suggested that Job "curse God and die" conveys she was in the second stage of the grief process. She was angry with God, and probably angry with Job, because the illness made him different from the man she married. All these stressors resulted in anger and alienation.

This biblical couple provides insight into how couples who are under attack can survive. It provides valuable lessons for the family, and even individual Christians. While it is certain that Satan wants to ruin the home, God wants to give couples an anchor—a safety net for marriages. God wants to ensure that couples make it. God works to prepare couples for the tough times.

How can a marriage weather the tough times? What are the steps in the process? Is it possible that trials in the marriage create resilience and prepare couples for future difficulties?

Developing Resilience in the Marriage

I (Trevor) am reading a book by physician Paul Brand and a popular Christian writer Philip Yancey entitled *The Gift of Pain*. Dr. Brand for years has been an orthopedic physician who treated Hansen patients, or lepers. For most people, the thought of dealing with pain is horrendous. But according to Brand, pain is a gift that provides the sensors that prevent self-destruction.

Brand said he became keenly aware of this one day while observing a leper who reached into a charcoal fire to retrieve a yam that another patient had dropped. Because his sensors for pain were inoperative, this patient did not feel the fire. His hand was badly burned, but he was not even aware of the damage. Brand explains that a mild level of pain or activities that cause pain protect us. A carpenter who regularly plies his trade will develop calluses on his hand that protect him from greater pain. A tennis pro develops calluses on his or her hands, a protective area that reduces the impact of pain and makes for a more effective player. This supports the truism: "No pain, no gain." From this perspective, one's marriage may need to go through some toughening in order to survive even tougher times ahead or to serve as a foundation for spiritual growth.[10]

So knowing this fact, is God teaching you a lesson for dealing with the tough times in your marriage? Was this God's strategy for Job and his wife? Did God allow Satan "to do his thing" to prepare Job and his wife for some future experience? When one experiences financial set backs, are there lessons to learn for future budgeting? When couples become parents prematurely, when their relationship is not secure, or maybe their budget is not ready for an expanded family, are these lessons for later tough times?

What are the lessons that Job and his wife can teach us about the tough times? What can this story teach about survival? What coping skills do couples need to develop? The following lessons can be essential in your marriage.

Stay connected to God.

Job did not understand where God was taking him. While Job knew God loved him, he could not fathom God's actions. Even though Job was puzzled by God's silence in the midst of his trials, Job stayed connected to God. For a couple's marriages to survive, they must stay connected to God through prayer and daily family worship. Generally, the family that prays together, stays together. This means you take God seriously, but not yourself or the situation. You take God seriously by keeping your focus on God through daily worship and prayer. You take God seriously through belief in God's Word. Words such as, "And we know that in all things God works for the good of those who love him, who have been called according to his purpose" (Romans 8:28). "God is our refuge and strength, a very present help in trouble. Therefore we will not fear" (Psalm 46:1,2 KJV). Taking God seriously means seeing God's grace and love in the midst of the tough times. We also need a good sense of humor.

Joy Swift and her husband used the deaths of their children as an opportunity to get to know the Lord more and to lean on each other. George and Joy used their grief to search for a deeper and more meaningful religious experience. They drew closer to each other. As a result, Joy and George even became pregnant and restarted their family. An indication of their adjustment was how they spent their first Christmas without the children:

> George was still working nights, and I still kept my schedule to his, though I realized that when the baby was born I'd have to adjust my schedule again. I didn't mind George's working these odd hours now. ... He offered to trade shifts with another security man for Christmas day. He had children and we both agreed that it would be nice to let him share Christmas with his family. Since we had no children, we could "celebrate" anytime.[11]

Stay connected to each other.

Job stayed connected to his wife despite her lack of faith. Job never abandoned his wife. He remained steadfast. *Don't let tragedies end your relationship.* Remember that tragedies like the loss of job or the death of child or stressful situations such as having a mother-in-law move in or even having teenage children are going to affect your marriage. Be prepared for the hard times! But do not allow these times to divide you. Continue to communicate and talk, even when it is hard. Couples need to set aside time weekly to talk to each other.

After her four children were tragically murdered, Joy Swift used the time to get close to God and closer to her spouse.[12] Tragedy need not end your marriage. Why blame each other at these times? Was it Job's fault that the children died? Was it Mr. Swift's fault that burglars killed their four children, then another child died of illness? Tragedies are not the time to blame each other.

Recently, I (Edith) was watching divorce court on TV, and there was a couple getting a divorce because the wife had an accident in which their son died. The father blamed the mother. Imagine that. Do you think she got up that morning and decided she wanted to have an accident and kill her son? It is easy to let tragedies divide a marriage.

Some people think their lifestyle regimen prevents them from debilitating diseases. This, however, is not always true. Job's illness was not due to poor diet or lack of exercise. He was stricken with illness despite his lifestyle. We can not always understand the reason for illness. There seem to be numerous spiritual reasons for physical pain, such as making one strong or even testing one's faith in God. Pain and illness may be used to cause our growth.

I (Trevor) found out one week that I had bursitis and arthritis in my right shoulder. This can be painful and debilitating. It may go away with treatment or, as with the apostle Paul, it may remain the thorn in the flesh that I will always live with. Is God using this to strengthen me? Can this condition strengthen my marriage for the tough times ahead? As part of the aging process, illness and pain will occur. As a couple, we need to become fortified to face aging together. Because marriages have many stages, our relationship will not remain the same.

In some marriages, partners become a source of disappointment and disillusionment. This was the case with Job and Mrs. Job. In fairness to Mrs. Job, she witnessed the anguish and the humiliation her husband was suffering. She could not understand why or how God could abandon him in difficult times. She was confused about Job's steadfast faith. Further, she suffered the loss of all of her children and experienced financial disaster. All these crises made her vulnerable to depression. Watching a spouse in pain can at times be more difficult than actually experiencing it. However this is not the time for division in the home. Regrettably, one's spouse can bring the most pain.

Job needed a crutch to lean on, but Mrs. Job was not available. She became part of the problem. Some partners can introduce harmful stress into the relationship. This is a time when you need good communication. Pain and suffering may prevent partners from listening or understanding each other. Pain makes self-expression hard. Suffering makes it difficult to listen.

Mrs. Job could not understand her man of faith in this time of loss. She was hurting for her husband and for her own loss, and it was hard to see beyond the pain. When one is down, it is not always possible to look up. Mrs. Job could not look up, and she discouraged Job from looking up. Husbands and wives will respond to grief differently. In times of crisis they may be on different levels of spiritual development, resulting in marital discord and difficulty. This can bring added grief because each person is caught up in his or her own grief and may resent their spouse's different grief expressions. Don't let tragedy bring separation. Support each other in the tough times. This means you need to keep praying together and for each other. Spiritual connection together is important for handling the tough times.

Here are some communications tips important for marriage in the tough times:

Keep talking to each other. This is not the time to stop talking. Find the words to express your sorrow and pain, even when those words are not the most effective. Keep talking until you find your voice. Do not use this time to accuse or play the blame game. Schedule time to talk each week. You can accomplish this in a number of ways. Go out to dinner each week just to talk. Or go for a walk and talk to each other. In the midst of crisis, you need to arrange talking time. This means you need to continue listening to each other—the type of listening that hears the pain and doesn't avoid difficult conversations.

Be respectful of each other. During the time of crisis, make sure you respect your partner' feelings. Though their reaction may be different, they are probably experiencing the crisis just as intensely. Being respectful means being polite to your partner. Courtesy is always appreciated. Treat each other lovingly and in a caring manner. This reaction through the eyes of love will demonstrate enormous compassion and empathy.

Look at the problem from your spouse's perspective. Communication is enhanced when you do this. Mrs. Job needed to understand how Job was experiencing this problem. Mrs. Job needed to avoid dysfunctional thinking patterns, which led to polarizing, and to accept Job's way of handling grief. Polarizing thinking assumes only one way of handling grief is correct. Polarizing thinking is divisive. Polarizing thinking suggests, I feel God has abandoned me; if you love me, you will feel that way too. You will then "curse God and die" because you must choose my way of handling the situation. Avoid destructive thinking.

Avoid minimizing your spouse's concern. Listen with empathy and concern. Do not downplay and react as if the problem is not that difficult. Responses such as "Don't worry about that," or "This too shall pass", or even "All things work together for good," while offered with good intentions, reflect minimization. Too often, these responses are less about reassuring our spouse and more about reassuring ourselves. These kinds of remarks attempt to squelch your spouse's reaction. Think about what happens once those remarks are offered. Your spouse is silenced.[13] Those remarks imply, "Your problems are not as big as you make them;" "You are exaggerating." Listen respectfully and do not downplay your spouse's concerns. Minimizers make a molehill out of a mountain. Unfortunately for Job, most of the people he spoke with did not minimize, but maximized the problem.

Avoid maximizing or magnifying the problem. This is the opposite of minimizing. Maximizers make every problem a disaster. They take "life events and exaggerate them until everything seems like a catastrophe."[14] This is best explained by these reflections by Teresa Ferguson:

> One evening a gentleman visited our home and David asked me to put on a cup of coffee. I did, but it got late and I wanted to go to bed. So I asked David if he would be sure to turn off the coffeepot. He said, "Sure, no problem." I went to bed.... The next morning when...I got up...and started to make the coffee. Guess what greeted me the moment I opened the door? Burnt coffee! Then I noticed the front door had been left unlocked all night...I looked around, and every light had been left on... I was so furious I wanted to run into the bathroom, rip open the shower curtain and shout, "Can't you ever do anything I ask you to do?"[15]

From this experience, Teresa recognized she was overreacting; she was being a "drama queen." Maximizers fail to differentiate between a crisis, like a hurricane or a child's death, and something less urgent, like not turning off the coffee pot or not folding towels "correctly." They perceive each event and respond to it with the same intensity. Maximizers make a mountain out of a molehill. In her interaction with her husband, Mrs. Job overreacted. While this was a crisis, it was not evidence of God's abandonment.

Avoid overgeneralizing. Overgeneralizers take one negative event and apply it to all other circumstances. They truly believe that experience is the best teacher—and that one experience provides insight into all other experiences. Overgeneralizers carry a load of anxiety, doubt, and fear. They hold on to past hurts, failures, and rejections—and recite them as evidence for their gloomy attitude toward the future."[16] Too frequently, overgeneralizers are not trust-worthy or forgiving. These attributes make overgeneralizers fear to risk new experiences in the marriage. They assume things will always be difficult and remain the same because of earlier disappointments.

Allison and Todd had been married for about five years when Allison began walking with her neighbor every day. One day it rained while she and her neighbor were walking; they got wet. Since it started raining in the middle of the walk, her shoes got wet and took several days to dry. She also caught a cold. From that time on, Todd was reluctant for her to walk on days that even looked rainy. He would fuss and discourage her going for a walk. Todd took the one incident and generalized it to all potentially rainy days. His overgeneralization and fearfulness caused friction in the marriage.

Avoid emotional reasoning. Emotional reasoning interprets feelings as if they were fact. It confuses feelings with facts and says, "I feel this way, so it must be true."[17] While your emotions are good barometers for your internal process, they are not an explanation for your spouse's behavior. Just because you feel that way does not make it true. While feelings are valid, they are not facts and cannot take the place of facts.

Avoid personalizing life events. Personalizers tend to be moody and easily hurt. They view each event as a rejection. People often call them touchy, overly sensitive, even hysterical.[18] These individuals are insecure and assume that a look makes a statement of rejection. Sometimes these destructive displays of rejection occur together. For example, Star reflects both emotional reasoning and personalizing.

Star and Sam lived in the same town with Sam's elderly grandparents. Sam was very close to his grandparents, but his grandmother had Alzheimer's. Usually his mother and other family members spent Christmas at the home of his grandparents. But due to his grandmother's illness, the family had to devise other plans. Star was still recuperating from delivering their second child right before Christmas, so imagine her surprise when Sam told the entire family to come to their home. This made Star feel unloved and unappreciated—that Sam loved his family more than her. She felt rejected and less important than the family. Sam was surprised that she felt that way. He acknowledged that this was not a wise decision, that he should have consulted her. But he did not see the decision as indicating his love for his wife. Star's feelings, while valid, were not fact. She took a hasty decision by her husband and personalized the event to mean she was not loved.

These patterns of destructive thinking are damaging to a marriage—but are heightened when the family is in crisis. We see evidence of this kind of thinking in the remarks by Mrs. Job and also Job's friends. They were overgeneralizers and also polarizing—seeing life only in good or bad. This pattern heightened Job's suffering.

Stay connected to family and friends, but filter out negative content. Well-meaning friends can cause much trouble. Although they wish to offer comfort, they can utter some judgmental statements and can say inconsiderate things that leave you even more devastated. When you are suffering, they may remind you, "You know all things work together for good to them that love God." Or, "You know God has a purpose for this." While these statements are true, timing is important. When is the best time for friends like Job's to come and share? Do you share in the midst of the trial or wait until things get better? What should one share, and how many questions should you explore?

Visits from friends should be sources of encouragement. While the visit from Job's friends was meant to encourage him, these visitors discouraged Job. They accused Job falsely and thought they could explain the trials in his life. None of us is God; none of us knows the causes of trails. We can offer only speculation. Family and friends can be supportive and helpful, but, sometimes in a crisis you need to listen to some things and filter out other things.

Stay focused on your ultimate goal. Trouble will come to everyone since these are turbulent times. The pressure of society requires more structure and direction. Everyone will need the right resources to navigate these waters.

One important tool for weathering a crisis is the family mission statement. This is a purpose statement that helps keep you on course. It keeps the family on point even though difficulty occurs. Don't allow the purpose and aim of your family to be defined by the obstacles. A mission statement, though not developed in the midst of a crisis, provides support and direction.

How do you develop a mission statement? Remember a mission statement is short, defines the purpose of your family, and incorporates the family's core values. Here are some suggestions for developing one

- Meet together as a family in a brainstorming session and share core values; these values provide the basis for your mission statement.

- Have each member write two or three lines that reflect the mission of the family.
- Incorporate these sentences into a short paragraph.
- Allow family members to reflect on the statement for a couple of weeks.
- Refine the statement to incorporate all factors essential for the family mission.[19]
- Use the mission statement as a guide for family decisions and handling crisis.
- Mission statements can be revised if the family situation changes (an extended family member joining, a loss, or a transition).

Develop a financial plan for your family

Another activity to encourage family survival for handling stress in the tough times is to develop strategies for responding to financial disaster. Financial disasters can strike the family at any time. Here are some suggestions that may help reduce financial difficulty:

Have a family budget. A budget is usually a list of planned revenues and expenses for a specific period (such as a year). It should include each month's expected expenditures and actual expenditures. One way to develop a budget is to review and analyze expenses for a specific period, such as the past three months. This provides a guide for developing a realistic budget.

List all your expenditures; develop a column for budgeted amount and actual amount for each. For example, review electricity bills for three months; the average for this period would be your expected expenditures for electricity. If your electricity expenses were $100 in May, $150 in June, and $200 in July, you would add the cost ($450) and divide by three ($150). This amount would be your expected monthly expenditure for electricity. List this amount in one column and your actual expenditures in another column. A budget should be developed collaboratively and massaged periodically. Numerous books offer help on family budgeting.

Here are a few additional money management hints to avoid financial disasters:

- Pay God first—pay an honest tithe and offering.
- Avoid debt and avoid credit cards.
- Live simply; don't live beyond your means.
- Avoid 'trust busters' in your marriage, such as:
  - Do not keep financial secrets from your spouse.
  - Do not keep hidden assets or cash.
  - Avoid secret shopping and excess expenses.
  - Avoid vices: gambling, drinking, and drugs.
- Save a percentage of each paycheck and learn to invest your money.
- Build wealth with your money.
- Plan for emergencies: Keep at least $1500 for emergencies in savings. This will reduce the need for credit card use. This money can help with cars that break down, unexpected medical expenses, a replacement refrigerator, and other family emergencies.
- Plan for the future. This includes retirement planning, investment, and increasing the family's capital.[20]

When you follow these steps, you can be in a better position to weather life's financial storms; even in the storm like Job's, there will not be despair.

Strength from Trouble

Our review of the marriage of Mr. and Mrs. Job reveals some of the factors Satan uses to destroy marriages. However, we can view these trials as the sand in the oyster of life. To produce the pearl, an oyster needs sand from the ocean. The irritating presence of the sand causes overwhelming, even destructive, forces that refine the oyster and cause it to produce a beautiful pearl. In our marital relationships, sometimes life's irritants—such as financial difficulty or the loss of a job—are the sands that force us to create a pearl. Troubles come to make marriages strong! Trouble provides marital strength and often hardens us to withstand the tough times ahead and establish a rock-solid marriage. The intent of the tough times in God's economy is to produce a pearl of marriage. The couple can rise out of their circumstances, no matter how difficult, and have the marriage that God intended.

Recent research on marital satisfaction reveals that marital happiness is not based on avoiding difficulty. Couples throughout the United States were interviewed, including a couple that had three children die, but still they remained happily married. They learned the secret of marital success for the tough times. At least three couples interviewed had been divorced and remarried to each other. Once they had an encounter with the Lord, they came back to each other. They had learned the secret of marital success for the tough times. At least three couples married for 60 years were interviewed; these couples had survived a great deal of tragedy, illness, financial difficulty, discrimination, moves, and deaths within the family—but these marriages survived. They had learned the secret of marital success for the tough times. These secrets include commitment and connection to God and to each other, consistency in their lifestyle, and patterns of love for each other and God. None of these couples fought over who does the dishes or who takes out the garbage.

Regular communication with God and each other is essential. God wants to save our marriages in the tough times and for the tough times. God knows that growth in the marriage will need the hardening of life's circumstances. Weathering life's calamities will strengthen us for the difficulties ahead. All marriages will have difficulty; use these times of stress for reflection, growth, and connection. God will not leave you in these difficulties. So learn to lean more on God.

MARRIAGE FOR THE TOUGH TIMES

Personal Reflections

Text: Book of Job

1. Reflect for a moment on the tough times in Job's family. Which setbacks have been significant for your family? Finances? Children? Illness? Family division? Condemning family or friends? (Discuss this with your family)

_____

_____

_____

_____

2. What lessons can you learn from this difficulty?

_____

_____

_____

_____

3. What are some strategies you have learned that could address this difficulty in your family? (for example, developing a budget or getting out of debt)

_____

_____

_____

_____

4. Define at least one specific action you plan to take during the next week that would begin to implement the strategies you learned?

_____

_____

_____

_____

CHAPTER 8

I Can't Get No Satisfaction: Sex in the Marriage

If there is sex after marriage, I am certainly unaware of it!

Introduction

*E*VERYBODY LOVES RAYMOND star Ray Ramano says that his comedy is inspired by real life. "After kids, everything changes," he told *Newsweek*®. "We're having sex about every three months. If I have sex, I know my quarterly estimated taxes must be due. And if it's oral sex, I know it's time to renew my driver's license."[1] Talk shows abound with features on couples who are not having sex. What happened to sex in marriage? Sexless marriages! Sexual problems in marriage! The bestseller lists include books like: *The Sex-Starved Marriage, Rekindling Desire,* and *Resurrecting Sex.* Can the Bible give us answers to this problem?

This chapter will look at the role of sexuality in marriage through the eyes of a couple whose sexual relationship is the focus of an entire book in the Bible: The Song of Solomon (also called The Song of Songs). King Solomon and Shulamite's relationship reflects the role of romance

187

and sexuality in marriage. This is the only book in the Bible that focuses on a couple's courtship, romance, and love.

This is a marriage between a country girl and a king. It is a marriage between a couple from two different social and economic statuses. It takes a young girl from the shepherd's field and places her in the palace. This is not a marriage based on solidifying alliances by bringing wealthy families together. It is a marriage based solely on love. It is the story of the marriage of the wisest man who ever lived and a country girl who stole his heart. Can we enhance modern marriages by learning about the relationship of a storybook couple?

Like all other biblical couples, this couple offers lessons for marriages today. This book is not a historical narrative. Instead it is a series of love poems written by the king to depict his love for Shulamite and her love for him. It provides the words and thoughts of the king and Shulamite for each other. The extensive conversation between these two lovers has no parallel in the Bible. The Bible provides few conversations between couples and none as extensive as this.

This book also brings some unique challenges. Scholars often view it as allegorical, with only spiritual application. It depicts love through the eyes of the king and it is not a linear tale, but more episodic.[2] In this chapter, we will not focus on these issues. We will begin with a quick review of the life of both Solomon and Shulamite to provide the context for our discussion of this couple.

King Solomon and Shulamite

King Solomon is well known. He was the son of Bathsheba and David (2 Samuel 11-12) born after their affair and subsequent marriage (See chapter 5). Solomon was crowned king prior to his father's death and was nurtured by his father until David's death. Once Solomon solidified his standing as king, God came to him and said, "Ask for whatever you want me to give you " (1 Kings 3:5). Solomon requested wisdom and the ability to listen with compassion. This endeared him to the heart of God and to the people of his kingdom.

However, Solomon was the typical polygamous Middle Eastern king. There are biblical allusions to him having 700 wives and 300 concubines (1 Kings 11:3). His various marriages to the daughters of his allies in surrounding areas are depicted in the Bible; each seemed to have been politically motivated. Thus the fact that he devoted a series of poems to this country girl who was a shepherdess reflects the depth of his love for her. This marriage was different; it was based on love with passion, a romantic love that celebrated marital sexual intimacy.

Shulamite is less well known than her husband the king. We assume she was a working woman, a shepherdess. It is clear that she was a beautiful woman who has turned dark from the sun (Song of Solomon 1:5) and was proud of her rustic appearance. She loved the country and was unpretentious. She did not know the culture of the city, nor was she a part of the royal entourage.

This country maid had beauty inside and outside that reflected the virtues and nobility of womanhood. According to Keil and Delitzsch, "That which attached her to him is not her personal beauty alone, but her beauty animated and heightened by nobility of soul." These features made the king want to remove her from the country life of a shepherdess and exalt her to royalty. The naïve country girl Shulamite transformed the king into a romantic lover, and the king transformed the country girl into a queen.[3]

This story draws us to the power of love and sexual intimacy in this relationship. Here is a couple who was comfortable with sexuality and sexual love. How did they reach this level of comfort with their own sexuality? How are sexual views developed? How do sexual views impact the marriage?

Developing Views of Sexuality

Numerous factors influence the development of our views on sex. These include messages from our family, church, community, and media. In recent discussions with college students on their views of sex and sexuality, we found that sex is a subject most families avoid. Most college students received very little information about sex and sexuality in the home. We have noticed this trend in our students for the past decade. Parents were often remiss in discussing this subject with their children. Parental silence about sex conveys a powerful message to the children that sex is not a subject their parents feel safe discussing.

Joshua was raised in a single-parent home. During marital counseling he stated, "My mother and I talked about everything." Later, when our conversation shifted to parental messages about sex, we asked, "What did you learn about sex at home?" Joshua grew silent and then admitted, "We never talked about sex, and mother was silent about this area." What did her silence mean? How did Joshua interpret it? Did he decide that sex is taboo, a dirty topic to avoid? Many Christian young people receive limited or negative messages about sex from the home.

According to our discussion with students, they are still getting mixed messages about sex. Males are allowed or expected to be sexually involved, while girls are still expected to be chaste. Parents provide neither information about the changing body and hormonal change, nor the tools to enhance the decision to be chaste. Instead, parents only say "No, don't" or "Wait." This silence or negativity affects sexual expression in marriage.

How about the church? What messages do young people get there? The church also provides very limited discussion of the subject. In our conversations, young people admitted that most churches say nothing about sex. When the church has a message, it is primarily that young people should abstain. The church does not provide any additional information about the challenges of hormonal changes and the impact of their changing body for adolescents in a highly sexualized society. In reality, the church's message about sex has evolved from a time when sex was viewed as a necessary evil, and religious leaders were encouraged to take a vow of abstinence, to its present position of sex as gift from God. Still, sex is a subject many Christians prefer to avoid. It is seldom discussed from the pulpit.

In a couple's retreat we facilitated several years ago, the subject of sex was discussed during the church service and on the day of worship. These discussions provoked conflict. Several attendees questioned discussing this subject during a church service and on the day of worship. "This is not an appropriate subject for the sabbath" or "We can discuss this another day, but not today" were common comments. There were no children present. These couples shared their displeasure in the sessions, in their written evaluations, and with us personally. These married couples saw sex as a taboo subject! We had suggested that sex was worship, and that God has ordained it for couples (Hebrews 13:4).

Still, the church and home are not the only source for information on sexuality. Society and the media are also sources today. What messages do young people get from society and media? They learn that sex is *not* taboo. Instead, it is essential for selling products and an integral component of relationships. In movies and on TV, people meet and have sex a few moments later. Sex is portrayed as essential for happiness and health. In the media, individuals seem unable to control their sexual desires. In a recent episode of a popular TV hospital show, a couple was so overcome by sexual tensions, they had a sexual tryst in one of the hospital offices. They could not wait! Sexual experience took precedent over their work, discretion, and protocol. The media's message is augmented by a rapid increase in Internet pornography. The pornography business is larger than all the top mainstream Internet companies combined.[4] Thus, today's sexual views are influenced by a confluence of factors, and these views affect sexuality in the marriage. Some of these influences, like the Internet, did not affect Solomon and Shulamite, but numerous other factors pressured their relationship.

Relationship of King Solomon and Shulamite

While we lack certain information about King Solomon and Shulamite, we can make inferences about the role of sex in the home. Solomon's parents' marriage began in an adulterous relationship. His brother Amnon raped his sister, Tamar, and Absalom slept with his father's concubines as part of the insurrection against his father (2 Samuel 11, 13-17). These incidents suggest a home where sex was a subject the family may have acknowledged and perhaps discussed. Thus this family comfort with sex and sexuality may provide the context for Solomon's expression of sexual love for Shulamite.

However, Shulamite is just as comfortable with sex and sexuality as her lover, King Solomon. Perhaps her experience as a shepherdess seeing the sheep mate led her to realize that sex was a normal component of life. Perhaps in her home and village, the older women provided insight for this young lover prior to her marriage as part of her premarital counseling. This is true today for many traditional cultures where engaged young women are taught how to provide and enjoy sexual pleasure in their marriages. In this love poem, Shulamite's comfort with romance is reflected in her search for her lover and her many invitations for him to join her in the bed. These positive attitudes about sex, supported by the home and community, provide a context for sexual pleasure in marriage. They provide great lessons for sexual preparation for marriage.

Nevertheless, couples today without this preparation can also enjoy sexual intimacy. Sexual intimacy can form the basis of a strong and committed relationship. However, sex is often the crucible in which marital difficulty emerges. Problems in communication or finances may result in sexual difficulties for some couples. Sometimes sexual difficulties may only be symptoms of marital difficulty in other areas. This is not true for all couples; in fact, for some couples, the only relationship they have is sexual.

Martin and Barbara had one son and had been separated for almost six months. The reason they separated, according to Barbara, were the intense arguments and conflict that occurred when they lived together. While they were not physically violent, their verbal arguments were hostile with lots of yelling and screaming. They were both miserable; however, she reluctantly confessed they still had great sex. While they could neither live together nor get along, Martin still came by the house each week, and they had sex. This marriage had been reduced to a sexual relationship similar to prostituting. Most couples do not allow for a relationship that is only sexual. Marital couples are instead plagued by some typical sexual problems.

Sexual Problems Often Confronted by Couples

According to researchers, *"Inhibited sexual desire is the most common sexual problem; about 50% of all long-term relationships have a partner who lacks interest."*[5] This is the classic sexless marriage. Couples in the US have sex about 68.5 times a year, or a little more than once a week.[6] Inhibited sexual desire has several causes: physical causes such as menopause and diabetes, as well as psychological causes such as anxiety, lack of affection, depression, marital conflict, work stressors, trauma, discomfort with sexual pleasure, and fatigue from working too hard.[7]

Another reason for sexless marriage is pornography. Pornography results in less interaction between spouses because the couple is not talking to each other or having sex; instead the husband (usually) is cowering "in dark rooms lit only by the glow of nude images on the screen."[8] Pornography is often a secret, and the wife is unaware of its presence in the marriage. It often makes the man feel sexually incompetent and "detours and derails a man rather than propelling him towards his wife."[9] Pornography has a negative effect on marital relationships since a man can have his sexual needs met without having to deal with the challenges of a relationship. At the same time, he does not have to leave the house to spend long hours in pursuit of other women.

Lynn and Laura have been married for 10 years, and to outside observers they have a good marriage. But Laura is upset with that Lynn, a computer buff, spends most nights on the computer. Though he is very supportive financially in their marriage, Lynn has little time for conversation and little time for sexual activity. It took years before Laura realized his late night activities were in some sense adulterous, since the time he spends at the computer are spent on pornography.

Another common sexual problem for men is *premature ejaculation*. This problem affects many men at some time during their lifetime, but "Twenty percent of males consistently have difficulty controlling their ejaculations."[10] A premature ejaculation occurs when a man comes too quickly during intercourse before his wife reaches her climax. While the primary reason for this is performance anxiety or other psychological concerns, there are also some physical causes, such as diabetes and disorders of the nervous system.[11] This is usually a problem that can be resolved with a few basic techniques that we will explore in the last section of this chapter.

Women, however, may struggle with not being in the mood or experiencing pain during sex. Many women experience these symptoms occasionally, but it become a problem if they happen persistently. Some women have physical concerns that affect their mood or cause pain during sex. Physical reasons for not being "in the mood" include "hormonal imbalances, menopause, infections or diseases like diabetes."[12] However, psychological concerns can also affect a woman's mood. These include "everyday life problems ... job worries, pressure of juggling work and family, substance abuse, depression and financial worries."[13] These psychological problems can affect women physically. Women confronted with persistent patterns of "lack of mood" or pain during sexual activity should seek professional help.

Another male sexual problem is impotency. Frequently called erectile dysfunction or ED, impotency is defined as an inability to get or keep an erection firm enough for sexual intercourse. While erectile dysfunction occurs in twenty-five percent of men 65 years are older, it is not an inevitable part of aging. It is usually has physical causes such as disease (diabetes, heart disease, or vascular problems), smoking, being overweight, injury, or a side effects of drugs.[14] Whatever problems today's couples may be experiencing, in the next section Solomon and Shulamite have suggestions to make marital love sizzling in the twenty-first century.

Lessons from Solomon and Shulamite

The first lesson

There are numerous lessons from this couple about enhancing sexuality in your marriage. The first is that *sexual love is meant to be celebrated*. Sensuality and sexuality are causes for much joy for this couple. In fact, this love poem begins with the words "Let him smother me with kisses from his mouth" (Song of Solomon 1:2 COMPLETE JEWISH BIBLE). Here is a couple that was not shy about a public display of affection. They would encourage married couples to rejoice in their love for each other. Love requires expression both publicly and privately. Solomon and Shulamite celebrated their love for each other daily— physically!

The second lesson

This couple would also share *the importance of verbal compliments* and words of affection in the sexual relationship. Compliments are important for lovers (review these passages: 1:8-12, 4:2-8; 4: 9-12, 5:2; 5:10-16; 6:4-10; 7:6-9). These lovers compliment each other incessantly. The king showers his lover with picturesque words and speaks of her beauty continually. He discusses her eyes, her teeth, her lips, and her neck. Listen to his words to Shulamite:

Your teeth are like a flock of newly shorn ewes which have come up from their washing, all of which bear twins, and not one among them has lost her young. Your lips

196

are like a scarlet thread, and your mouth is lovely. Your
temples are like a slice of a pomegranate behind your
veil. Your neck is like the tower of David, built with rows
of stones on which are hung a thousand shields, all the
round shields of the mighty men. Your two breasts are
like two fawns, twins of a gazelle which feed among the
lilies. Until the cool of the day when the shadows flee
away, I will go my way to the mountain of myrrh and to
the hill of frankincense. You are altogether beautiful, my
darling, and there is no blemish in you. Come with me
from Lebanon, my bride, May you come with me from
Lebanon. Journey down from the summit of Amana, from
the summit of Senir and Hermon, from the dens of lions,
from the mountains of leopards.

—Song of Solomon 4:2-8 NASB

It is clear from this statement that King Solomon
recognized that the mind is the most important sexual
organ. He caressed his lover not just physically, but also
with words before he even touched her. He caressed every
part of her body: her teeth, her lips, her neck, and her
breasts. He recognized the importance of words for women.
He knew that women are verbal creatures and love to hear
expressions of love. Each word became a part of foreplay.
Solomon recognized that the verbal must be coupled with
physical foreplay for good sex. The compliments are mutual
for these lovers. Shulamite says to her lover that:

My beloved is dazzling and ruddy, outstanding among
ten thousand. His head is like gold, pure gold; His locks
are like clusters of dates and black as a raven. His eyes
are like doves beside streams of water, bathed in milk,
and reposed in their setting. His cheeks are like a bed of
balsam, banks of sweet-scented herbs; His lips are lilies
dripping with liquid myrrh. His hands are rods of gold
set with beryl; His abdomen is carved ivory inlaid with

197

sapphires. His legs are pillars of alabaster set on pedestals of pure gold; His appearance is like Lebanon Choice as the cedars.

—Song of Solomon 5:10-16 NASB

Shulamite knows her lover also values words. So she bathes him in words of her love because a man's ego needs to be stroked.

The third lesson

Gifts are a necessary part of lovemaking. As you read about this couple, you see they gave many gifts of love. They didn't just talk about loving each other, but showed that love tangibly. Shulamite gave lilies to her lover (Song of Solomon 6:3). The did not give gifts just on special occasions. Solomon thought about her all the time with gifts of love. He didn't just think about her when he wanted to make love. He was always preparing for lovemaking every day. He gave her gifts "just because."

The fourth lesson

Setting the stage for lovemaking is important (Song of Solomon 1:12,13; 7:12,13). For these lovers, lovemaking didn't just happen. Lovemaking required setting the stage for love. Long before aromatherapy, these lovers knew that fragrances enhance the relationship. "Let us go early to the vineyards to see if the vines have budded, if their blossoms have opened, and if the pomegranates are in bloom—there will I give you my love" (Song of Solomon 7:12). Lovemaking is an event; it should be beautiful and fragrant, and preparation enhanced the sexual experience for the lovers.

Another feature of setting the stage included caressing and fondling. "His left arm is under my head, and his right arm embraces me" (Song of Solomon 2:6; 8:3). Caressing and fondling were essential components of foreplay as the couple moved closer to the sexual act. This couple recognized the need to touch each other as foreplay in preparation for sex. It is clear for this couple sex was not "slam, bam, thank you "ma'am," that's it." Lovemaking was expressed using all of the senses, including the sense of touch.

The fifth lesson

The couple also shows us the *necessity to get time away from everyone*. For good lovemaking to occur, the biblical couple needed time alone and away. "Arise, come, my darling; my beautiful one, come with me" (Song of Solomon 2:13). The location was not as important as the time away with each other. Spending time alone talking, touching, kissing, and making love are essential components to avoid sexless marriages. This couple would say, "Go away with your lover, just the two of you; it will enrich your marriage."

The sixth lesson

Shulamite would offer the lesson to modern wives that *a woman can and should instigate the lovemaking*. In Song of Solomon 3:1-3, Shulamite searched for her lover; she wanted him in their bed. She recognized she had a role in the lovemaking process. It was not just his job to lean over and start the process. That perspective implies that women have no interest in sex and that sex is only a male activity. Shulamite would state that sex is an activity both

199

men and women enjoy. She reached out and initiated sex. This initiation encourages excitement in the marriage. Most men want women to initiate sex sometime!

The seventh lesson

Marital love should be exclusive (Song of Solomon 4:12). One safeguard for sexuality is exclusivity. This biblical couple shared their love only with each other. Though Solomon had numerous concubines and wives, he expected exclusivity from his wives, and he had relationships only with his wives or concubines. He did not repeat his parents' mistake of adultery. He wanted Shulamite to be his own private garden, locked up just for him. He wanted her to be a garden whose gate only he could open and whose path only he could tread.

The eighth and final lesson

This couple would also say, *sex should be spontaneous.* They would advise you to, "Seek joyful and creative ways to share your love. Love each other tenderly, frequently, and unexpectedly." One challenge for married lovers is keeping sexual expression in the relationship vibrant after twenty-five years. How do you keep your sex life vibrant even after years of sexual intimacy? How do you avoid routine sex with the same position and little foreplay or forethought? This final section will explore some of these options.

Tips for Enhancing Old and New Marriages

Using the lessons provided by this ancient biblical couple, here are some ways to boost your sexual pleasure:

Put God first

Begin the sexual experience with God. Invite God into your bedroom and your bed. Pray together before sex. Thank God for sex and ask for a blessing on your future sexual experience. God invented sex and is quite comfortable with the prospect of sexual intimacy in your marriage. Research has shown that couples in a committed spiritual relationship have better sex lives. In fact, married Christian women are satisfied with their sexuality and are happier in their marriages than American women in general.[15]

Make your sexual love a celebration

When there is a celebration, it often begins with pre-planning. Think of other celebrations like Christmas or your birthday. Christmas involves months of planning and preparation. There are decorations, special meals, and gifts. It is not an afterthought. Couples should consider and plan their sexual love. Just like a holiday, there should be a build up! Plan to make the atmosphere exciting. What can you do to add spark to it? Take the time and make the room romantic, light the candles, put on incense, and prepare to share your love with each other. Fragrances will enhance the atmosphere. Change positions! Change the room! Redecorate your room just for sexual experience! Make plans to change your approach to lovemaking, since sexual love's celebration does not begin in the bed.

Kevin Lehman admonishes us to love each other all day long.[16] This means you begin the day with kisses and hugs, you call each other during the day, and you hug and kiss in the kitchen, at the washing machine, near the children's room, and throughout the day. Then once you get in bed to actually have sex, it is just the final response to a day of loving each other. View the sexual experience as body

201

communication, an opportunity to share and show your love physically. Think of ways to celebrate your sexual love all day long! Preparation also involves personal preparation. Don't get into the bed smelling like a gym; for many women this is a turn-off. Then don't rush your celebration; take sex slowly. In our modern life, everything gets rushed. There are instant grits and potatoes; however, Shulamite and Solomon would say, "Don't rush through sex." Sex is to be savored, enjoyed, and appreciated. Take your time with your lover. Enjoy each other. Make lovemaking an all-day event.

Make compliments and positive expressions an integral part of the relationship

Let your spouse know you value them and care about them. Share words of love and expression of caring with each other. Compliments are an important component of the marriage. This means complimenting your spouse on the meal, on the home décor, on the way your spouse is dressed, but it also means telling them what you like about them. It means saying, "I love your big brown eyes" or "I can't keep my hands off of your biceps or breasts." Solomon and Shulamite complimented each other from the head to the foot. In your compliments, you can include her breasts or his chest or whatever you *really* like about your spouse. Nothing is off limits! Shower your spouse with compliments when you are together, not just before you are making love but "just because" you love them.

Give gifts of love

When you love someone, you feel compelled to give to them. Gifts come in many sizes; it could be a bouquet of flowers, or it could be a massage. It could be a clean kitchen or a fishing trip. Gifts are expressions of your love.

Gifts should reflect what your partner wants. If you are an avid golfer but your spouse isn't, giving your partner a set of clubs is not a gift of love. Give your spouse a gift he or she will love. Solomon and Shulamite believed in pleasing their lovers by giving gifts. Gift-giving conveys your love when they are spur-of-the-moment, given from the heart, and desired. Gift-giving conveys the thought that when you are not here, you are still on my mind. It implies you are someone I think about when I am shopping. You are important to me. The importance of gifts in relationships is captured by O. Henry in the classic Christmas tale of the couple Della and Jim in "The Gift of Magi."[17] In this story, Della and Jim sold their most-valuable possessions to give the other a Christmas gift. For Della it was her hair, for Jim it was his watch, but love caused each to give their most valuable possession. Love must be expressed tangibly.

Giving gifts for birthdays, holidays, anniversaries and Valentines Day is expected, so consider giving them at other times. Give gifts for the end of the week! Give gifts because your spouse is sweet! Give gifts because "I love you!" Give gifts because you are the mother or father of my children! Gifts show your love and support. For some partners, an act of service is a gift of love— so washing the dishes or cutting the lawn could be a gift of love. A gift does not have to be expensive, or even cost money. Give gifts "just because"!

Recently, we conducted a family life weekend in a large southern city. We shared this information of giving gifts in the marriage and the importance of giving gifts "just because I love you." Later during the week we got a call from Paul, one of the husbands who attended the meeting. During the session his seven-year-old son, Ray, listened intently to the talk and remembered the concept of giving gifts "just because." To Paul's amazement, the next day in the grocery store, Ray said, 'Daddy, let's buy Mommy some flowers.' Paul questioned the reason. "It is not your mother's birthday or Mother's Day." Ray responded, "Daddy let's buy Mommy some flowers just because it's not Mom's birthday." Paul readily agreed, and his wife, Pauline, was ecstatic with the "just because" gift. This gift of love had repercussions. It made Paul happy to give, it made the Pauline happy to receive, and it also provided Ray an example of couple love.

Get away from everyone and spend time with each other

Plan a childless weekend or a weekend away at least once a year. Get away and spend time sharing your love with each other. This could be a romantic weekend for just the two of you or it could be a couple's retreat with your church. Arthur and Samantha had been married for more than 30 years and have an empty nest, but every three or four months they would go off on a weekend together. Once they went to Paris for a weekend.

The location is not as important as the time with each other. If you cannot afford Paris, contact your local hotel or motel for their special weekend rates and spend time alone with each other. This time alone could include sleeping late, enjoying room service with breakfast in bed, and lots of snuggling and couple time. This is not the time to worry about bills or the children. This is a time to focus on each other and your love for each other. Can't afford to go to the local motel or hotel? Then send the kids away and spend the day in bed with each other. Turn off the phone! Close the blinds! Unplug the TV! Make this time a special time for each other.

Or consider going on a couple's retreat with your church or organizations like "Marriage Encounter" or "Weekend to Remember" from Family Life Today. These weekends provide intimate time together plus enhanced learning and focusing on marital happiness. There are many different types of couples retreats. Choose one that meets the needs of your marriage.

Women, learn to initiate the lovemaking in your marriage

Husbands initiate sex more frequently than women. One counselor reports, "The number one complaint I hear from men is this issue of their wife not initiating sexual encounters."[18] Women seldom initiate sex because of cultural and biological factors. Unfortunately, women have been socialized to take a passive role in sexual activity and allow the man to be the initiators. Even with the sexual revolution, men are still the primary initiators. Most men are not willing to wait for their wife to initiate. So the husband moves in and makes the overtures, and this becomes the pattern for their marriage. The wife waits passively for her husband to initiate sex.

However, studies have found that many men like it when their wife initiates sex.[19] Matt and Laura had been married for eight years and had established the pattern that he was always the primary initiator in their relationship. "But when she initiates sex, it's definitely a turn-on," he says.[20] To increase and enhance sexual satisfaction, plan to be the initiator. Take a nap so you are not as tired. Get home early and meet him at the door ready for some intimate time together; send the children to family or friends. Call him and suggest he meet you at a hotel for a quickie at lunchtime. Shulamite was an initiator in her relationship with Solomon; she went looking for her lover. In your marriage, reach out to your husband. This will enhance the sexuality of your marriage. Plan the encounter! Do something innovative! Get a special negligee! Cover the bed with rose petals!

Leave sexy notes around for a treasure hunt that ends in the bedroom! Put candles or Christmas lights around the bed. Make your lovemaking an occasion. Be creative, and it will bring wonderful results to your marriage.

Marital love should be exclusive

While having outside lovers and affairs may seem exciting, they do not produce the kind of sexual life God intended. Affairs are usually the indication of marital distance or lack of commitment. Couples in committed relationships can really learn how to please each other. They can grow together. They can experiment with each other. A good marriage requires love that is both committed and passionate. These factors thrive best in a marriage of exclusivity. This means a marriage where the spouse does not worry about getting an STD, a marriage where there is no distraction of late-nights calls, a marriage where the spouse is not always worrying about the location of their lover, fearing they are with someone else. Marital love should be a place where the spouses feel secure and safe in the relationship. Marital sex is predicated on trust that allows the couple to do exciting things for and with each other sexually. This security allows for experimentation in positions and experimentation in location in the home.

Trust allows you to take sexual risk with each other. Make a commitment with God and your spouse to practice an exclusive marriage. God considers this commitment important enough to include in the Ten Commandments. "Thou shalt not commit adultery" is not a suggestion, but a command from God. Marital love should be exclusive. This means neither partner should be involved with pornography, nor should there be frequenting of strip clubs. (See chapter 4.)

206

Sex should be spontaneous

While planned sex can be productive, at times it should be spontaneous— unplanned, unexpected, and unpredict-able. This means sex can happen in the morning, at noon, or at night. This means sex can happen in the bedroom—or in the kitchen. It means sex can happen in the bed —or on the washing machine. Many years ago at a couple's retreat, an older couple suggested that the movement of the washing machine cycles could enhance sexual pleasure! While we have no personal experience with that, it reflects the principle of creativity in the marriage. Spontaneity means that sex can occur in a variety of positions. Sexual lovers can stand up, sit down, or lie down. One can be fully clothed or naked. One can be indoors or outdoors. One way couples can develop spontaneity in their marriage— according to Shulamite and Solomon—is to become creative in your lovemaking. For some suggestions to increase the spontaneity in your marriage, read the book *52 Ways to have Fun, Fantastic Sex—A Guidebook for Married Lovers*.[21] This book has a different activity for each week. It will bring spontaneity back to your marriage. Or you could get *Simply Romantic Nights* from Family Life (www.familylife.com) and use these ideas to add spontaneity to your marriage. Make your sexual time special!

However, for some couples struggling with sexual problems, other help may be needed.

Handling Sexual Problems in Marriage

The most common sexual problem in marriages is the *sexless marriage*. It is estimated that one in five couples have sexless marriages, that means they are having sex less than ten times a year. Research has found couples who did not have sex at all for six or more years! Couples must address these difficulties in marriage. Here are some steps that can help.[22]

1. Develop a vision of what you want in your sexual relationship.
   a. Think about what is missing.
   b. Take time to think about your sex life.
   c. What are the ingredients needed to have a better sex life?
   d. What would you have to do differently?
   e. What would your spouse have to do differently?
2. Then list the reasons you believe there is no sex in your marriage such as:
   a. Too busy or working too hard.
   b. Lack of spark in the marriage.
   c. Unresolved marital problems.
   d. Taking each other for granted or childhood trauma.
3. Choose a mutually acceptable time to discuss these observations:
   a. Begin with what you need to change.
   b. Take turns sharing and listening to each other.
4. Use tools to enhance your sexual love:
   A. Go on a weekend together to mark a renewal of marital intimacy.
   B. Look for ways to support and encourage each other.
   C. Love each other all day long.
5. Consider reading a book to discover how to enhance marital sex (for example, *The Gift of Sex*, Penner and Penner; *Resurrecting Sex*, David Schnarch; *Sex-Starved Marriage*, Michelle Weiner-Davis; *Rekindling Desire*, McCarthy and McCarthy).

A. Go on a couple's retreat that focuses on enhancing marital intimacy.

None of these suggestions work for you? You've done all this? Consider getting counseling. Find a competent sex therapist who can help you explore the reason for a sexless marriage and resolve the factors that prevent happiness in your marriage. Do not be complacent and accept this marital difficulty. Do something about it! You do not have to have a sexless marriage.

What about premature ejaculation?

According to Clifford and Joyce Penner, this is single most common problem reported at their seminars.[23] The prevalence rate in American males is estimated to range from thirty percent to seventy percent. The National Health and Social Life Survey (NHSLS) indicates a prevalence of thirty percent, which is fairly steady through all adult age categories.[24] While premature ejaculation can occur at any age, it is most common in men under 40 or in older men with other medical conditions.[25] This is a problem with a solution. Once you have excluded biological reasons, the following suggestions will help.

The Penners outline a five-step process for solving this problem. The first step is a *desire to really please each other* and to stop having selfish sex. The man and woman must decide this is a problem they can cooperate to solve. Next, *the couple must make this problem a point of verbal discussion.* After the discussion, the couple should work on pleasing each other with non-genital pleasure. This reduces the pressure to perform and teaches us to really enjoy each other. Couples who develop non-genital pleasure are ready for the next step. This step involves genital pleasure that is not sexual. Couples are encouraged to do manual stimulation, simulating sexual intercourse, then entry without ejaculation, and finally total body pleasure with ejaculation. These last few steps are considered with a change in position, with the woman on top. For specific instructions in this method, consider reading books or going to a sex therapist who can provide more specific information. It is important that couples work on sexual problems instead of ignoring them or blaming each other.[26]

What about pornography?

For couples with this problem, remember it leads to less sexual intercourse and alienates the wife. Many professionals believe that pornography is a sexual addiction and must be handled like other addictions. The husband, since it is often a male concern, must admit he is addicted and needs help. This should involve numerous types of treatment such as:

- Individual counseling.
- Couples counseling.
- Group counseling in self-help groups like sexaholics anonymous.[27]

In group counseling, a man learns to be accountable to other men and practice sexual integrity. Some men obtain sponsors they can turn to in moments of relapse.

A man must learn his triggers and develop strategies for handling these situations. For example, on a business trip how do you plan to handle the TV with X-rated stations? What can you do before you get into the room to address this concern?

- Ask the front desk to block these channels.
- Call your wife and talk with her.
- Find activities that take you out of the room.
- Learn to recognize triggers and develop methods to block thoughts that lead to pornography.[28]

Other activities to consider include marriage counseling, reading books, and keeping a journal. For more information, consider reading *Every Man's Battle* by Stephen Arterburn, Fred Stoeker, and Mike Yorkey or *Out of the Shadows: Understanding Sexual Addiction* by Patrick Carnes or *The Worth of a Soul* by Stephen Kramer.

While sexual difficulties may occur in your marriage, they should not be ignored. Communicate with each other about these problems. Sex is an essential activity for couples to talk about. Remember, God invented sex. God wants your sex life to be a time of celebration and love. Couples should include God in their sex life. Sex can be the cement in the marriage to enhance your connection. It can be the icing on your marital cake. It is a relationship-building experience—especially if it is relationship-centered and not body-centered. It assumes emotional, spiritual, and intellectual intimacy exists in your relationship.

If we follow the principles outlined in this chapter, we can join these two ancient lovers and say "Let him kiss me with the kisses of his mouth—for your love is more delightful than wine. ... Take me away with you—let us hurry" (Song of Solomon 1:2-4).

I Can't Get No Satisfaction:
Sex in the Marriage
Personal Reflections

Text: Song of Solomon 1-8

1. Reflect on the messages you received about sex while growing up. What messages did you get from your home? What messages did you get from the church? How were these messages affected by the media's sexual focus?

   _____

   _____

   _____

   _____

2. As you reflect on the common sexual problems in marriages, which has had a major impact on your marriage? Why do you think this area has been a problem?

   _____

   _____

   _____

   _____

3. Review the lessons from Shulamite and Solomon. Which one would be most helpful for your marriage? How do you plan to include this lesson in the marriage?

   _____

   _____

4. Pornography is a major problem in modern Christian marriages. How do you plan to address this problem or pornography-proof your marriage?

5. Do you think couples should plan to include sex as a regular component of their marriage? What about the Carla and Brad Muller's plan to have sex 365 days? [29]

6. What specific things can you do to spice up your sexual life?

CHAPTER 9

Take My Mother-in-Law, Please
Making Out-laws into In-laws

Introduction

A POPULAR JOKE: What is the difference between outlaws and in-laws? Outlaws are wanted. One of the many problems that confront couples today is that of in-laws. This one marriage problem serves as the source of many jokes. There is even a website with numerous mother-in law jokes.[1]

While mother-in-law jokes may make us all laugh, in-law problems are no joke. Research has shown that marital success decreases with in-law problems. This chapter will focus on two couples whose marriages were affected differently by in-laws. For the marriage of Moses and Zipporah, the response of his siblings, Miriam and Aaron, challenged the marriage—while Naomi, Ruth's mother-in law, blessed Ruth and Boaz's marriage.

How do couples deal with problem in-laws? Is it true that when you marry a person, you also marry his or her family? What can you do to reduce tensions with in-laws? Let's look to these biblical marriages for assistance.

Reflection on Two Biblical Couples

Moses and Zipporah

This is a marriage that began with a man on the run. Moses, who was adopted by Pharaoh's daughter although he was an Israelite, was forced to flee his country and his position of power because of one rash act. One day while surveying the land, he noticed an Egyptian beating a fellow Hebrew. Moses impetuously killed the Egyptian. When Pharaoh heard of his action, he tried to kill Moses. But Moses fled to the land in Midian (Exodus 2:15). This is the first strand in this story.

The other strand involves the seven daughters of the priest of Midian. As shepherdesses, these girls were responsible for keeping their father's sheep. One of the tasks that caused them difficulty was watering the sheep. Each day when they went to water, other shepherds would come along and drive them away. The women would have to wait until the men finished watering their flock, and then come back. The result: It took them longer to water their sheep.

At this well, the lives of our two characters intersect: Boy meets girl. Moses, the fugitive, arrived and went to the well to wait for assistance. The seven daughters of the priest of Midian came to the well to water their sheep. At the well, the girls were accosted as usual, but this time something different happened. A bold, muscular Egyptian, Moses came to their rescue. He confronted the other shepherds, who fled. Then he even watered the sheep.

Moses' chivalrous action reflected his sense of justice and concern for human rights—seen earlier when he killed an Egyptian overseer who unmercifully beat a Hebrew.

However, Moses probably expected some compensation for his kindness at the well—a meal or a place to stay. None of this happened. The sisters, while grateful for his assistance, followed their custom of not speaking to strange men. So they left Moses at the well.

Once their father learned of Moses' act of kindness, he urged all his daughters to invite Moses to dinner. Moses' dinner invitation was the first step in his relationship with this family and Zipporah. Their home became a place for Moses to stay; his place to stay became a job offer. Ultimately, his boss the priest, offered Moses his daughter Zipporah in marriage.

The Bible provides no information about the courtship of this couple. We do not know whether theirs was a love like Jacob and Rebekah. The Bible does not address whether Moses had to work for years to pay for his bride. The Bible provides no information about a dowry. What is known is that the interaction at the well ended in a marriage between the rescuer, Moses, and the shepherdess, Zipporah.

This couple settled down into the routine of a shepherd, which Moses became along with his wife and their sons. This couple lived happily in Midian. It is estimated that Moses lived there forty years. While this couple remained in Midian, there seemed to be no in-law problems—even though Zipporah had six sisters and her parents. In fact, Moses and his father-in-law seemed to have developed a good relationship. Then God called Moses and commanded a career change, and the rest is the history of freeing the Hebrews from the Egyptians.

When Moses had successfully freed the Israelites from Egyptian bondage and they were wandering in the desert, we get further insight into the relationship between Moses and Jethro, his father-in-law. This incident occurs on a visit from Jethro, who came to return his daughter to her husband, Moses.

Jethro sent word that he was coming for a visit, and Moses met him with a kiss (Exodus 18). While visiting, Jethro observed Moses at work judging the people—which involved an entire day giving them guidance and direction. So he gave Moses some advice. "What you are doing is not good," Jethro said. "You and the people who come to you will only wear yourselves out" (Exodus 18:17,18). Jethro proposed that Moses delegate some of this responsibility. Choose men, train them, and allow them to assume some of your responsibility. Moses appreciated the advice and implemented it. This advice was not an issue of conflict or difficulty for Moses and Jethro. The suggestions strengthened the relationship between son-in-law and father-in-law. We see no difficulty between Moses and his wife's family.

However, this couple did have some in-law problems. They came from Moses' siblings: Aaron and Miriam. While traveling in the wilderness, Moses was confronted with his siblings making openly critical remarks about Zipporah. Numbers 12:1 says, "Miriam and Aaron began to talk against Moses because of his Cushite wife, for he had married a Cushite." This duo did not think Zipporah was good enough for their brother. They thought he listened to his wife and her father too much—and excluded seeking them for advice. Their grumbling and complaining resulted in dissension in the family and ultimately caused God to respond, striking Miriam temporarily with leprosy (Numbers 12:3-10). This divine intervention reveals something about God's response to this type of family division. God would prefer that families not be divided by the struggles of in-laws.

However, this is not the only biblical example of in-law relationships; another example worth exploring involves Ruth and Boaz.

Ruth and Boaz

Ruth and Boaz's marriage developed because of a daughter-in-law's love for her mother-in-law. Ruth was married to Naomi's son. When he died, she remained with her mother-in-law. Eventually, Naomi decided to return to her home in Bethlehem of Judah. But Ruth declined to stay with her own family—and religion—in the land of Moab. Instead, Ruth uttered these immortal words: "Don't urge me to leave you or to turn back from you. Where you go I will go, and where you stay I will stay. Your people will be my people and your God my God" (Ruth 1: 16,17). What a testimony to a loving relationship with a mother-in-law! While these two widows were sad and destitute, they were not alone. They had each other. They were able to negotiate a move, find a job, and eventually develop a plan to get Ruth another husband.

This mother-in-law and the daughter-in-law had a relationship that was mutually beneficial. Ruth decided she would go to work to support the two of them, and she did this with Naomi's blessing and encouragement. As a worker in the field, Ruth's industriousness and reputation for caring for her mother-in-law made her stand out from other workers. Ruth's conscientiousness, and her concern for Naomi, were soon noticed by Boaz, the landowner. Boaz began to make sure that she got plenty of gleaning from the field.

His generosity gave Naomi an idea. She developed a plan to get Ruth a home and a husband. She suggested a way to notify Boaz, an older man, of Ruth's interest in him as a near kinsman. Throughout this course of action, Naomi directed each step of the process, and Ruth dutifully followed her mother-in-law's instructions. Naomi's suggestion allowed Ruth to claim her inheritance and eventually marry Boaz.

Ruth was ignorant of the cultural nuances associated with the near kinsman. But her relationship with Naomi yielded positive results: a marriage to Boaz and the birth of a son who was grandfather of King David—which put her in the lineage of the Messiah. This relationship had long-term, lasting benefits. The women of the village told Naomi that Ruth's love was "better to you than seven sons" (Ruth 4:15). What a testimony to the power of good relationships with one's in-laws! In an age when women were not as valuable as men, Ruth was considered better than seven sons! What a difference in these two stories. One ended with division and leprosy, while the other ended with the birth of a child of promise. As we juxtapose these two stories, we can clearly see that in-law relationships can have a powerful effect on a marriage.

Similarities and Differences

It is interesting to reflect on the similarity between these two couples. Both began the marriage with *baggage*. Moses was fleeing his country because of his conviction for murder. Ruth had been married before and was a barren woman in a time when this was viewed with suspicion. Often it is the baggage that complicates the marriage and relationships with in-laws.

Both couples had *mixed marriages* with different ethnicity. Moses was an Egyptian Jew, and Zipporah was from the land of Midian. Ruth came from the country of Moab, and Boaz was a Jew living in Judah. Both couples experienced a mix of religious beliefs and cultures. Cultural differences often cause discord in marriages and increase the likelihood of in-law discontent.

Both marriages also reflected *class differences*. Ruth was destitute and a gleaner in the fields of Boaz, a wealthy landowner. While Moses' family members were slaves, he was raised in the home of Pharaoh, which meant he was treated as royalty. Zipporah, however, was a shepherdess. Finally, the couples had *religious differences*. Ruth was a recent convert to Judaism, and Zipporah, whose father was a priest, seemed to have a worship style different from Moses.

Despite the similarities, the relationships with in-laws were totally different. After the death of both her husband and her sons, Naomi decided to return home. Here we see the results of a different relationship. Both of Naomi's daughters-in-laws at first wanted to go with her. Why? The quality of the relationship with her daughters-in-laws is a key point. Naomi's warmth and character must have been attractive. She must have shown a love that her daughters-in-law found appealing. The Seventh-day Adventist Commentary states: "Naomi was an ideal mother-in-law; she did not press even her legitimate claims upon her daughters-in-law, but left them entirely free to make their own choices."[2] Although both Orpah and Ruth were fond of their mother-in-law, Orpah eventually returned to her home. But Ruth passionately requested that Naomi not ask her to return to her own country.

What made this relationship work? A review of their relationship suggests some beneficial lessons (Ruth 2). Naomi knew when and how to give advice. She was not constantly trying to tell Ruth what to do. Sometimes she just supported Ruth's interest. When Ruth wanted to go to work, Naomi stated, "Go ahead, my daughter" (Ruth 2:2). Later, Naomi orchestrated the steps in the courtship of Ruth and Boaz. In this relationship, Ruth trusted Naomi's advice. Why? Naomi had consistently been a model of love and support. She was more than a mother-in-law; she was like a mother.

In the marriage of Ruth and Boaz, we see the power of good in-law relations. Naomi, the ex-mother-in-law, acted as a nurse for the baby of Ruth and Boaz. Amazing! This was not her grandchild! It is her ex-daughter-in law's child! The women in the village said, "Naomi has a son" (Ruth 4:17). In this relationship, we see the power of love; and it transcends kinship roles and responsibilities.

This bond, a model of good in-law relationships, reminds me of a wedding I attended. The bride was a widow, and her deceased husband's father gave her away at the ceremony. In her new marriage, her relationship with her in-law who lived near her home remained the same. The new husband became like a son to the family. Good in-law relationships are developed individually and do not depend on the relationship with the relative.

How different the relationship of Miriam and Aaron, Moses' siblings, with Zipporah. They talked against Zipporah and made her life difficult by making fun of her (Numbers 12:1). This negative relationship with their Ethiopian sister-in-law reveals Miriam and Aaron's ethnocentrism. The criticism affected their bond with Moses, and God intervened. The Lord punished Miriam and Aaron for their treatment of Zipporah and Moses.

This relationship between Miriam and Aaron and Zipporah stands in stark contrast to that developed by Moses with his father-in-law, Jethro. Moses lived peacefully with Jethro for forty years. We also see the nature of their relationship in Exodus 18:7 when his father-in-law brought his wife back to him, and they greeted each other with a kiss. When Jethro came up with a novel plan to aid Moses' work and suggested he develop a chain of command, "Moses listened to his father-in-law and did everything he said" (Exodus 18:24). The nature of the relationship, based on trust and support, enabled Moses to adhere to Jethro's advice.

Blessings result from a positive relationship with in-laws. What lessons can these two couples teach us—and how can our in-law relationships improve?

Lessons for In-law Relationships

Both Jethro and Naomi are valuable wellsprings of information and development. What an advantage to have four parents encouraging and supporting the growth and development of the marriage. This is God's plan.

Advice for Mothers-in Law and Fathers-in-Law

1. Recognize good relationships as a biblical injunction. God is pleased with intergenerational acceptance. God blessed Naomi and Ruth, but God punished Miriam and Aaron. God supports positive intergenerational relationships. Make every effort to reach out and have good relationships with your child's spouse. God wants families to love and support each other.

> My dear children, let's not just talk about love; let's practice real love. This is the only way we'll know we're living truly, living in God's reality. It's also the way to shut down debilitating self-criticism, even when there is something to it. For God is greater than our worried hearts and knows more about us than we do ourselves.
> —1 John 3:18-20 THE MESSAGE

God's plan is for families to love each other, avoid criticism, and respect each other. So God is pleased when families get along.

2. Establish relationships of support and encouragement. Mothers-in-law (MIL) and fathers-in-law (FIL) should reach out and support their child's spouse. Once your child is married, support the couple and the decisions they make. If at all possible, actively support and encourage them. It is not your role to try to sabotage this relationship. This was the behavior of Miriam and Aaron, and God punished them for it.

When our daughter got married, we decided we would do whatever it takes to support their relationship. Originally, we sent them books they could read to enhance their marriage. We sent so many books, they asked us to stop; they could not read them all! Then we shared DVDs and tapes, so they could obtain the information effortlessly, by just watching. Finally, we decided to send them to a couple's retreat each year. We believe in marriage enrichment, so we paid for the retreat. This is our gift each year, and we believe it will have more benefits than a china pattern dish set or the latest gadgets. We have provided similar gifts of books, tapes, or DVDs to the young couples in our extended family.

Support and encourage the marriage of your child. Once they are married, the decision has been made; it is too late to change it. What benefit comes from your criticizing and complaining about your child's spouse? It does not enhance the marriage—but strains your child's relationship with you. It may cause your child to defend his or her partner and stay in a truly negative relationship longer. Who wants to be proven wrong? Who wants to hear "I told you so"? The biblical lesson is to support and encourage your child's marriage.

Some may be saying, "But you do not know my son-in-law or my daughter-in-law." Unfortunately, some sons-in-law and daughters-in-law are hard to support. If you cannot encourage or support them, then ask God to help you say *nothing*. Instead, make the marriage a subject of prayer. Place this couple daily before Christ. Call the name of your child in prayer daily. Call the name of your in-law in prayer daily. If we believe all things are possible with Christ, then turn this marriage over to Jesus. This will be hard, but it is better to be silent and prayerful than to be extremely critical.

Tom and Mary got married secretly despite their parents' opposition. Soon the problems that both sets of parents feared did occur. But the couple did not seek parental advice or assistance— because they knew what response they would get. When they finally did share, it was just as they expected. Both sets of parents remained unsympathetic, said that the marriage was against their wishes, and proceeded to criticize the couple's decision. The response of their parents actually drew this couple closer—but isolated them from the family.

Negative remarks will not enhance the marriage. Criticism will not encourage growth. Growth and development in relationships only occur under the gentle nurturance of love.

3. Give advice upon request and infrequently. Once children become adults, parents often struggle with developing the correct balance with them. Children go from a complete state of dependence on the parents at birth to a complete state of independence in adulthood. Parents go from feeding and changing diapers to parenting their adult offspring, in their own homes, as though they were children.

Learning to relate to an adult child is a challenge. What is the appropriate relationship with these adults, whom we once fed, bathed, and potty-trained? How do you relate to someone who was once so dependent on you? We see the best rule of thumb in the example of Naomi and Jethro;

both gave advice—but only when it was appropriate. Both waited until there was clearly an opening or request for directions. Only then did they give specific advice. They gave advice cautiously, and Jethro suggested that Moses consult with God.

4. Next make your advice optional, not a requirement. Listen to Jethro's advice to Moses. It was optional, "*if you do this…*" (Exodus 18: 23). Jethro recognized that you give adult children the option; you cannot issue them commands. Naomi also followed this policy. She asked Ruth, "My daughter, should I try to find a home for you?" (Ruth 3:1,2). In-laws should give advice infrequently, with options, and—if possible—upon request.

This means parents must sit silently and watch, instead of speaking. It means parents must get permission to share their suggestions. Being an in-law and parent of adult children requires restraint. If you struggle with being quiet, ask God to help you. Ask for God's direction for times to speak and times to be silent. Only in times of clear danger—such as child abuse or domestic violence—should you provide unsolicited suggestions and advice.

During the years we lived in Florida, Trevor's parents came to live with us. I looked with dread to their coming. Why? My mother-in-law was extremely neat, but I was much more relaxed. How could we live together with such different lifestyles? We did—and quite successfully. One example of how this worked occurred on a Friday afternoon. I was rushing around trying to cook for the next day. I am one of those chefs who cooks one dish; makes a mess, and goes to another spot to cook another dish and make another mess. By the time I completed the dinner, the entire kitchen would be a mess. Then I would clean the entire kitchen. My mother-in-law's style was diametrically different. She cleaned as she worked; when she finished meal preparation, the kitchen would be spotless.

On this particular day, she wanted to help me. But each time she came into the kitchen, it was a bigger mess. She could not work in such disorder, but she never said a word. Instead, she mentioned she was going out for an errand. Not until she mentioned the third errand did I recognize the problem. While I could work in disorder, she could not! I thought about this dilemma. I wanted her to help me, but I would have to adapt if I wanted the help. I recognized I could work in either setting: neat or disorder. So, even though she had not said a word, she taught me two valuable lessons. She taught me the lesson of not giving advice unless it is requested, and she also taught the lesson of how to get help in the kitchen. Her gracious approach with me made a difference.

5. Have clear boundaries. Do not go into your adult child's home as an owner, but as a visitor. This means you do not open pots, question the cleaning practices, or straighten the towel cabinet without permission. When you are a visitor, you observe the home without feeling a responsibility to transform or fix it. As a visitor, you may not like how the home is decorated, but you usually keep this information to yourself. You may not be fond of how the towels are arranged in the cabinet, but you do not rearrange them. Treat your adult child's home just as you would the home of any other adult you are visiting. Your child's home is not a reflection of the quality of your parenting! You tried to teach some concepts when they were in your home—now let them implement or not implement these concepts.

Enter their home with some emotional detachment. It is not your home. You do not have to agree with the décor,

227

the aesthetics, the standard of care, or the house rules. It is not your home. This is hard! When I go to my children's homes, I sometimes try to get them to adapt the values and standard of care that I would prefer. But this only creates tension and distrust. So keep silent. Do not say a word unless there is a request. Then share your opinion—but in a limited fashion. Do not give a full-course meal when your child wants only a snack. *Make this a matter of prayer.* Ask God to help you keep quiet. Remember: "Don't shoot off your mouth, or speak before you think…" (Ecclesiastes 5:2 The Message).

One area that requires good boundaries is child care. The same principle applies to your role with the grandchildren. While it is understandable that grandparents want what is best for the grandchild, assume parents want the same thing. Even if you disagree on what is best, suspend your judgment unless it is a matter of life or death. Assume the best and allow these new parents to raise their children in a manner they deem best. Do not go into the home of your adult child and criticize their parenting style, especially in front of the child. Do not suggest they are incompetent. If they are doing something you believe is harmful, do not correct them in front of the child. Here are some steps you should take as it relates to child care:

1. Ask God for direction on how best to handle this situation.
2. Choose an appropriate time and approach.
3. Ask if they would like to hear a suggestion. Carefully and prayerfully offer your alternative suggestions.
4. Leave the situation for them to resolve themselves. They now know your suggestion, but as adults they are not compelled to follow your suggestion.

There are, of course, exceptions when in-laws should intervene in marriages—such as child abuse or neglect. Recently in the town where we live, a mother allowed her three children to starve to death. In a case like this, the grandparents have the right and obligation to step in. When a child has physical marks of abuse or has not eaten in several days, grandparents should take more responsibility. This would, of course, be true even if these were not your grandchildren. Remember, ask God to instruct you before you intervene. "The effectual fervent prayer of a righteous man availeth much. " (James 5:16 KJV).

6. Accept your son-in-law or daughter-in-law just as they are. Once your child has married someone, accept the new person as a member of the family. The choice has been made. Your role is not to try to break up this marriage. Your role is not to prove your child made a mistake. Your role is not to rescue your child. What God has joined together, let no in-law break asunder. Your new son-in-law or daughter in-law needs your love, support, and encouragement. Pray for your new son-in-law or daughter in-law daily. If there is an area that needs changing, submit this area to God in prayer. Pray for your new "child."

Commit to do everything you can to support the marriage. Here are some things that will support the couple: pray for their marriage daily, send them books to enhance their marriage, pay for them to attend marriage enrichment seminars, and provide emotional and financial support upon request. Ruth loved Naomi because Naomi accepted her as she was. Moses listened to Jethro because he treated this foreigner and fugitive murderer as his son. These examples provide a model for us as parents-in-law.

Four or five years ago at a women's retreat, my roommate shared that although she had been married for more than twenty years, her mother-in-law still did not think she was good enough for her son. This couple had children and had no intentions of breaking up. Still, the mother-in-law persisted in making her life miserable. This is not following the biblical plan. The marriage exists, so *get over it!* Your child has made a decision, so accept your son- or daughter-in-law. It is not nagging that changes lives. It is the Holy Spirit that changes lives. Pray for them and let God do his work!

If FIL or MIL want to follow God's direction for their relationship with adult children, these suggestions will provide the framework for a better interaction. Just as FIL and MIL have a role to play, so adult children can enhance this relationship by following these guidelines:

Advice to Adult children

1. Respect and listen to in-laws. Seek out advice from your parents and in-laws. They have lived a full life and may have suggestions that will help you. Both Ruth and Moses listened to their in-laws and were blessed. Taking advice does not make you a child or dependent on them. If the advice is good, listening makes you wise. As an adult you can pick and choose what you adhere to, but recognize there are some topics that are your in-laws' area of expertise. If your father-in-law was an accountant, finances would be an area of his expertise. He would be a person to seek financial advice from. Many in-laws would welcome the opportunity to help. If your mother-in-law is a great cook, ask for her recipes and use them for great meals. When I got married, I knew my Jamaican husband wanted to eat rice and peas. I knew nothing about this Jamaican dish, so I asked my mother-in-law. She graciously gave the recipe, and I still have it— although I do not need to refer to it anymore. Seek advice and follow it.

When you get unsolicited advice, listen respectfully and reflect on the advice. If the advice seems wise and godly, then follow it. If the advice seems unsuitable, feel free to discard it. The key is being respectful and reflecting on the usefulness of the advice. You do not have to follow the advice, but you should listen to it respectfully.

2. **Do not put in-laws down.** Avoid thinking negatively of your in-laws and making derogatory remarks. While jokes about mothers-in-law are numerous, don't feel compelled to use them on your in-laws—especially if the stories do not fit your situation or they put your mother- or father-in-law down. God's response to Miriam's criticism of her sister-in-law was leprosy. God encourages harmonious relationships in the family, so avoid negativity. Recognize the strengths of your in-laws— not just their limitations. All individuals have strengths and weaknesses. Usually we see only our friend's strengths and see only our enemy's weaknesses. Individuals are more complex than this; most have positive and negative traits. Avoid focusing on the negative. Look for ways to focus on the positive traits.

Unfortunately, some in-laws can be difficult. In these cases, you may struggle to see positives. Ask your spouse to help you see them. Ask God to help you recognize and appreciate their strengths. Make a list of your in-laws' strengths and use them as the basis for compliment. While this is hard, try to view the situation from their perspective. Ask God to help you understand that in-law better. If a better relationship does not result from your efforts and prayers, then accept the limitations of the relationship. Be pleasant and respectful, but maintain clear boundaries.

3. **Accept them just as they are.** You cannot change your in-laws. They have been this way for years—long before you

came into the family. It is not your role to change others. Give up the trying to change your mother-in-law or father-in-law and just accept them as they are—warts and all. You can only change yourself. You have limited choices in the relationship. One is to accept him or her, unconditionally. Another is to change yourself and your feelings about the in-law. Finally, you could marry another spouse, but we do not recommend that. Besides, your new spouse would also have family, which again requires acceptance.

4. If possible let your spouse handle issues with the family member. If there is a misunderstanding, if possible let your spouse talk with his or her parent. Do not confront your in-laws alone. Allow them the opportunity to talk with their own child. When Miriam and Aaron talked about Zipporah, it was Moses who went to his siblings. He did not expect Zipporah to address the problems with his siblings. This decision was pivotal because it did not increase tensions in the family between in-laws. Instead, siblings talked with each other, and this provided a better basis for discussion. Miriam, the sister who watched over Moses in the basket in the Nile River, had a history with her brother. Your spouse and his family have a history. Your spouse knows how best to approach them. Your spouse knows the words to say, the way to frame the discussion, and the best means to help the family see a different perspective. This burden should be the responsibility of the family member, not the in-law.

5. Be loving to your in laws. Children often sing, "'Tis love that makes us happy, 'tis love that speeds the way, it makes us kind ...." Another song states, "Love makes the world go 'round." These two sentiments express the importance of love in the family. As Christians, it is essential we convey love. So in your relationships with in-laws, spread love, share love, express love. As you love, the quality of your relationship will transform and grow. "Finally, all of you, live in harmony with one another; be sympathetic, love as brothers, be compassionate and humble. Do not repay evil with evil or insult with insult, but with blessing because to this you were called so that you may inherit a blessing" (1 Peter 3:8,9).

In-law jokes aside, these lessons are pivotal to establish a good home life. It is clear from the story of Miriam and her leprosy that denigration of your in-law is not acceptable. God desires our family life be harmonious.

We still have one other aspect of this story to explore. Miriam received God's punishment because of her position. At the Red Sea, she led the women in the victory song (Exodus 15). She was instrumental in creating harmony and peace, thus God had greater expectations for this sister-in-law. The same principle applies today. When the tensions arise between you and your in-laws, remember, "With leadership comes responsibility." Thus, if you are a mother-in-law or a father- in-law, the burden of responsibility is yours for confessing your faults, for making amends, and for taking the first step toward reconciliation. Do not wait for your daughter- or son-in-law to make amends; begin the process. Say, "I am sorry." You make the overtures because you have seniority; you have the responsibility to aid healing by beginning the process in your family. This is a story of hope and restoration!

While jokes about in-laws are guaranteed to get a laugh, family tensions are not funny. The wear and tear on the traditional family is complicated by in-law difficulties. God's plan can make a difference in your marriage. Take the effort to make your outlaws into in-laws. It will transform your family and your life.

Take My Mother-In-Law, Please
Making Out-laws into In-laws
Personal Reflections

Text: Ruth 1:3-5, 3:7-11, 4:13,14 selected texts
Numbers 12; Exodus 18

1. What are some of the most difficult in-law problems
    you have experienced? Would your spouse agree these
    are problems?

    _____

    _____

    _____

    _____

2. How have you tried to resolve difficulties with in-laws?
    What have been the results?

    _____

    _____

    _____

    _____

3. What makes in-law problems so challenging for you?
    What are the emotional issues that make it hard to let
    go in relationships with adult children?

    _____

    _____

    _____

    _____

4. Reflect on tools listed in this chapter. Which ones do you think would help in your relationship with your in-laws? When might you plan to incorporate this tool into the relationship?

_____

_____

_____

_____

5. Extended families living under one roof are the norm in many cultures. Why do you think this is a source of jokes in the US? How might this attitude affect our relationships?

_____

_____

_____

_____

CHAPTER 10

What's Love Got To Do With It!

Domestic Violence: The Levite and the Concubine

Judges 19:1-27

When the men would not listen to his host, the husband seized his concubine and thrust her outside to them. They had relations with her and abused her all night until the following dawn, when they let her go. Then at daybreak the woman came and collapsed at the entrance of the house in which her husband was a guest, where she lay until the morning. When her husband rose that day and opened the door of the house to start out again on his journey, there lay the woman, his concubine, at the entrance of the house with her hands on the threshold. He said to her, "Come, let us go"; but there was no answer.

—Judges 19:25-28, NAB

Introduction

IT WAS A $1.4 million wedding. It featured a wedding party of eighty, all friends and family, 1,000 guests, a twelve-piece orchestra, and a 7.76-carat diamond ring. Flowers were flown in from around the world. The bride's dress "took nine months to make. All of the crystals on the gown were hand-sewn. The headpiece was sterling silver, hand designed."[1]

> Although it was a chilly, overcast spring day, guests shuffled through the revolving doors of the hotel's grand ballroom. What awaited them on the other side resembled Paris in April: gurgling fountains, an orchestra, lots of soft candlelight, and the aroma of roses, calla lilies and cymbidium.
>
> In the midst of this fantasyland, the bride appeared—wearing a platinum-colored satin designer gown... The bodice, which was covered in Swarovski crystals, blossomed into a full skirt with floral embroidery trimmed in even more crystals. The 50-foot train nearly covered the 200-foot aisle that the bride walked down with her father. Evangelist Dr. Juanita Bynum, author of the best-selling *Matters of the Heart,* was marrying another preacher, Bishop Thomas W. Weeks III.[2]

Advertised on TBN, it was a Christian fairy tale wedding of the century. The bride obtained the wedding she always dreamed of, and *if* this was a real fairy tale, the story would end with the report that "they lived happily ever after." But five years later, Dr. Bynum and Bishop Weeks were back in the news—this time for an appalling offense. Bishop Weeks was accused of beating his wife in the parking lot of a hotel. The couple had met for reconciliation, but the reconciliation did not occur. Instead it led to an argument and a physical assault that a hotel bellman broke up by pulling Weeks off Bynum. In a public parking lot, Bynum was allegedly beaten, choked, and stomped to the ground by her husband. He was arrested and charged with felony aggravated assault, threats, and two counts of simple battery.[3] A case of domestic violence occurring after a fairy-tale beginning—and between two pastors!

Domestic violence occurs in all races, ethnic groups, religions, and classes. It even affects celebrities such as Ike and Tina Turner. The 1984 song and 1993 movie, *What's Love Got to Do with It?*" are based on a relationship marred by domestic violence. We have dealt personally with domestic violence among couples who are church members. This chapter hopes to provide help for desperate couples who are in a cycle of abuse and don't know how to extricate themselves. What should couples do?

Let's call them Tim and Tanya. They were a young couple in our church who had been married only a few years. He was tall and handsome; she was pretty, lively, and willowy. They had a whirlwind romance and a very brief courtship—yet decided to get married against everyone's advice. Advice like, "It's too soon, you hardly know each other," was brushed aside because, "We love each other." They got married and had a little girl. About a year later, Tim and Tanya were in our office for counseling.

In the midst of the session, he said sarcastically, "It doesn't take a rocket scientist to figure that out," and she lunged for his throat. The anger and pain in the room were stifling. We had to stand between the couple and remove her from the room. There it was, domestic violence occurring before our eyes in a counseling session. If they were willing to fight in our office, what happened at home behind closed doors? That day we saw this attractive couple from our church fighting—domestic violence in the church.

Too often, the Christian community avoids discussing domestic violence. According to the Federal Bureau of Investigation, in 2001 a spouse or intimate partner committed over 1,300 murders—four homicides a day among couples.[5] Unfortunately, as the two stories we cited at the beginning of this chapter show, domestic violence is prevalent in the Christian community.

It is a subject churches avoid, and some may questions our including it in a book for couples on saving their marriages. Here are some reasons we include it: Many authorities believe that domestic violence in the church equals domestic violence in society. Family violence is not new; it is as old as Cain and Abel—the first recorded example of family bloodshed, when Cain killed his brother Abel (Genesis 4). Domestic violence is a subject for Christians because every fifteen seconds in the United States, a woman is beaten[6]

Judges 19:1-27 provides a context for us to understand domestic violence, its causes, and some characteristics that are typical of many batterers. This story will give us some insight into batterers and domestic violence as revealed in the Levite, the main character of the narrative.

Levite and Concubine

The narrative begins with a Levite who takes a concubine, or secondary wife, from Bethlehem of Judah. The Bible states that after the marriage, she was unfaithful and returned to her father's home. After four months, the Levite went to get her. But on the return trip they were accosted by the men of Gibeah to have sex. The Levite pushed his wife out the door as a substitute—in an attempt to save himself—and she was either beaten unconscious or killed by the mob.[7] The story raises several questions: What was the role of the concubine? What does the Levite's actions convey about batterers? Why did the concubine and other women stay in these types of relationships?

The first issue for us to explore is the role of a concubine. According to the *Seventh-day Adventist Bible Commentary,* this

240

role is that of a lesser or secondary wife as part of a polygamous relationships. She was not just a mistress to the Levite,
but a lesser wife. Still, her name is never mentioned.[8]

We know little about this relationship prior to this incident.
The Bible states she was unfaithful (Judges 19:2), but it is
unclear in this case what being unfaithful means. It is doubtful
it meant an extramarital affair, since in this society an affair
resulted in death. There were strict rules about infidelity for
women (Deuteronomy 22:22-24). In this society, a woman
was expected to leave her parents' home and remain with her
husband regardless of difficulty. The act of leaving her husband
and returning home could be seen as an act of unfaithfulness.

Why did she leave? There are several possible explanations. Perhaps she disliked her role as a lesser wife like Leah
and Penninah, other lesser wives. Since she was not number
one, she grew tired of having to try harder. Possibly her
extra efforts did not yield the results she desired. Perhaps
she was dissatisfied with the Levite's treatment of her. Or
perhaps she expected to be loved and valued, but the Levite
did not provide this support. As the story progresses, this
man provides clues to why she might have left.

In the culture of that day, leaving her husband was an
affront to their marital relationship and probably a shameful
event to her parents. While staying in Egypt, I learned that
Arab women often left their parents' home and went to stay
with the family of their spouse. Halim Barakat defines this as
patrilineal descent, which supports a patriarchal tradition.
Under this system, women cannot leave the house without
permission, which limits interaction with their family of
origin. So when the concubine left, seemingly without permission, this would have been shameful for her and her parents.[10]

Nevertheless the Levite, after four months, went to get
his wife to bring her home. When he arrived, we read in
Judges 19:3, she welcomed him in. The time apart seems

241

to have dimmed the pain that caused her to leave. His willingness to come and get the concubine pleased her. Not only did she welcome the Levite into the family home, but also her family was thrilled he had come, taking away the family's shame. The concubine's father was so pleased that the Levite had come to get his wife, he wined and dined him for several days.

Late in the afternoon of the fifth day, after several days of lavish hospitality, the Levite decided it was time to leave and return home. He began his journey against the advice of his father-in-law. It was too late to reach home, and they would have to stop for the night. In those days without modern hotels, the Levite carefully chose a location to spend the night. He was unwilling to spend the night with the heathens, so he went to Gibeah, a city with fellow Israelites of the tribe of Benjamin. Unfortunately, his arrival did not encourage the usual gracious, hospitable response. The Levite and his wife found themselves in the main square of the city until dark. This city did not seem a safe place. Its failure to meet his expectations of hospitality gave them a foreboding of difficulty.

Finally an old gentleman, who was not even a native of the city, took them in. Then this fascinating story took a horrible twist. The men of the city came and asked for the Levite, to have sex with him. (Judges 19: 22). The story sounds strangely similar to the account of Sodom and Gomorrah. Their elderly host instead offers not only his virgin daughter, but also the Levite's concubine (Judges 19:24). The man refused to send the Levite. The women could be sacrificed, but not the male guest.

We find the response to this offer in Judges 19:25: "But the men would not listen to him. So the man took his concubine and sent her outside to them, and they raped her and abused her throughout the night, and at dawn they let her go."

This disturbing story is compounded by the Levite's response in the morning. After a night of sexual abuse, this woman crawled back to the house and fell at the door. The Levite came out the door and simply said: "Get up, let's go" (Judges 19:28). What a response to a woman ravished by a crowd all night!

What does this story reveal about domestic violence and men who abuse women? What are some of the contemporary lessons we can learn from this story?

Characteristics of Batterers

This Levite provides some insight into male batterers. While a few batterers—five to seven percent—are women, the vast majority of batterers are men. Here are the primary traits of male batterers:

1. *Men who beat woman have a callous view of women and a strong sense of male superiority.*[11]

The Levite's and the old man's attitudes reflect a low view of women. They did not respect these two women, the daughter and the concubine. It is astonishing that these men offered the crowd two women, a virgin daughter and a concubine, instead of the Levite's servant (Judges 19:3,11). Reflecting the time and society, they made the offer with no consideration for consequences to these women.

Instead, the Levite sent his concubine outside to these men. We see the prevalence of this thinking in their treatment of the concubine that night. These men had a callous, demeaning view of women—one personality trait of abusers. Such views may have been characteristic of that culture and era. But men who beat women still have a strong sense of male superiority, resulting in them thinking that men deserve more respect and obedience than women. This is amplified by abusers in Christian homes who demand adherence to "Wives submit" (Ephesians 5:22). They may then use lack of submission as a excuse for abuse. We will explore this later.

2. *Men who beat women use controlling behavior to get their way.*[12]

The old man offered both women. But the Levite took his wife by force and thrust her outside. He shoved her outside to protect himself. She was forced to endure abuse all night while the Levite slept (Judges 19:25).

Consider the wife of a church deacon who came for counseling. Her husband was a respected businessman. They came to church each week: he a church leader and she, his pretty wife, with their handsome children in tow. What a lovely sight—a happy Christian family! He made a lot of money, but he felt he must be in charge. She feared disagreeing with him; there were negative consequences. "I am really scared of him," she confessed. "Last night he threw me down the stairs. It is getting worse. At first it was just a push or shove, maybe a slap, but now I am really afraid of getting hurt. I don't know what he will do next; he is unpredictable. In his business, he is compassionate and kind to the customers—but not at home." This church deacon's picture-perfect wife and their handsome children saw another man—a man who wants complete control at home.

3. *Men who beat women expect their partners will meet all their needs.*[13]

Remember the response of the Levite the next morning, after he had a good sleep. He told her to get up and go. The concubine had been abused all night and had finally crawled to the door. The next morning, he was concerned only about leaving. He needed to go. His needs were paramount. His callous remarks tell volumes about his character. His behavior seems to explain why she left him in the first place. Abusive men believe their partners are responsible for their happiness. They say things like, "If you love me, I'm all you need and you're all I need."[14] This emotional and psychological dependence on the female partner is unrealistic and demanding.

4. Their relationship seems to reflect the cycle of abuse.[15]

Equipped with two donkeys and a servant, the Levite had left the hills of Ephraim to go to Judah to get this woman. Once there, he persuaded his wife to return to him; she must have viewed his willingness to come get her as a positive sign. Yet in one night, he was willing to sacrifice her life to save his own. Like many women who are victims of domestic violence, because the concubine decided to return to him, she lost her life. Men who abuse women will do whatever it takes to drive them away—and whatever it takes to get them back. This phenomenon does not happen just in marriages.

She was a coed at a Christian college. She came from an intact family and was dating a popular young man on campus. She was thrilled that he liked her and proud to be seen with him. The first time he slapped her, she was shocked. But she made excuses. "It is no big deal. I probably shouldn't have gotten smart with him. He is under a lot of stress. I am lucky to be dating someone who is cute and popular." She minimized the importance of the slap and told herself, *After all, it is finals week, and he is under a lot of stress to get good grades for graduate school. It is probably just an exception.* But when he choked her, she got scared. After that, it became a regular thing: a slap, a kick, or a shove. She said, "I felt confused, especially since right after he hits or slaps me he would be so sorry. He would be tearful and always promised never to do it again. He brought me flowers and candy. So, I know he loves me, and he is going to be a doctor maybe after he gets out of school when there is less stress, he will get better. I will wait until then."

She was a college student, an unmarried female, and a victim of violence. Her relationship reflects this cycle of abuse. The cycle begins with a period of positive relationships and/or apologies, followed by a period of building tension. During this stage, the woman attempts to calm the man to avoid the inevitable explosion. Eventually, the explosion occurs and the couple returns to the honeymoon period. This pattern is typical in relationships where domestic violence occurs. (See diagram below.)

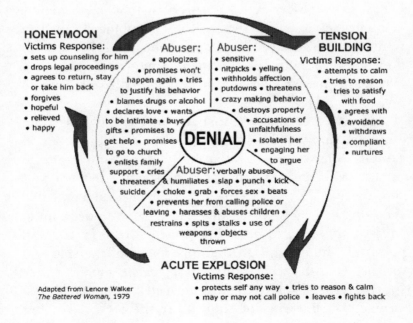

HONEYMOON
Victims Response:
• sets up counseling for him
• drops legal proceedings
• agrees to return, stay or take him back
• forgives
• hopeful
• relieved
• happy

Abuser:
• apologizes
• promises won't happen again • tries to justify his behavior
• blames drugs or alcohol
• declares love • wants to be intimate • buys gifts • promises to get help • promises to go to church
• enlists family support • cries
• threatens suicide

DENIAL

Abuser:
• sensitive
• nitpicks • yelling
• withholds affection
• putdowns • threatens
• crazy making behavior
• destroys property
• accusations of unfaithfulness
• isolates her
• engaging her to argue

Abuser: verbally abuses & humiliates • slap • punch • kick • choke • grab • forces sex • beats • prevents her from calling police or leaving • harasses & abuses children • restrains • spits • stalks • use of weapons • objects thrown

TENSION BUILDING
Victims Response:
• attempts to calm
• tries to reason
• tries to satisfy with food
• agrees with
• avoidance
• withdraws
• compliant
• nurtures

Adapted from Lenore Walker
The Battered Woman, 1979

ACUTE EXPLOSION
Victims Response:
• protects self any way • tries to reason & calm
• may or may not call police • leaves • fights back

246

6. *Men who abuse women do not take responsibility for their actions*[17]

We see this in the Levite. He never recognized his role in his concubine's death and abuse. Scripture is not clear that she was dead after a night of abuse. But he apparently made no effort to determine her well-being. Some commentators suggest she was unconscious. If so, his callous disregard may have contributed to her death.[18] After her death, he used it to begin a war, and he seemed really upset. Yet like many male batterers, he placed the blame outside himself. He could not see his role in the abuse—and did not blame himself for her death.

In a group I co-lead for male batterers, this failure to take responsibility is obvious. I often hear, "She knew if she did that, I would get upset." Or "she really tried to upset me." The men in the group feel their violence was an impulsive response. "When she said that, I lost control." The men do not recognize their own anger escalating. Instead, they attempt to project responsibility for their anger and abuse on the victim. Interesting, these men are able to control their anger at work and in other settings. The men do not hit, punch, or kick the boss, co-workers, customers, or anyone outside the home! Only at home do these men become abusive.

These are just a few of the common characteristics of abusers that are evident in this story. Recognizing these characteristics leads to the next question: Why do women remain in a relationship like this? Or why do women enable this abuse to continue?

Reasons Women Stay

Just as batterers have numerous common characteristics, there are many explanations why women remain in these relationships. Some, like the concubine in our story, stay because of *traditional beliefs about a woman's role*.[19] They may believe God wants them to remain in this relationship.

In her mid-thirties and a devout Christian, she came to me at a woman's conference. She said, "My husband beats me, but I am not leaving."

I asked, "Why would you stay?"

"I believe the Bible," she said, "and I know I am to submit to my husband in all things. Besides, my boys really need their dad. I can't raise the boys by myself." She continued, "I do not want you to tell me how to get out of the relationship. I just want some suggestions to avoid severe abuse. What should I do? I also need help with the boys. What can I do to make sure my boys do not grow up to become abusive?"

Her beliefs about a woman's role required that she remain in the relationship. She wanted the boys to grow up with a father. Divorce was not an option because it went against God's word, so she remained in the relationship—despite the pain of abuse.

Women who are immigrants may remain in abusive relations because of societal pressures. For these women, leaving is not an option. Women are expected to remain in a relationship even if it is abusive.

Some women remain so their children can have a father.[20] Many women are unwilling to assume the difficult role of single parent, especially if the man is supportive financially. Or the woman may believe it is essential for her children, especially boys, to have a father. The woman in the scenario above believed boys could not reach their potential without male influence. So she remained in a dangerous situation "because of the children."[21]

Some women remain in abuse relationships because of economic dependency, since women earn less than men.

In 1990, women's average weekly pay was approximately seventy-seven percent of men's average weekly pay.[22] Economics is an important reason women stay.

>...a study of 426 battered women found that income and employment were more important considerations than such psychological characteristics as self-esteem (General Facts About Domestic Violence). Women who lack job skills and are financially dependent on their spouses face the choice of living in poverty. The poverty rate for 1995 showed that female-headed families made up 32.4% of the poor in the U.S. Their earnings were less than $15,000 per annum.[23]

Consider the attractive wife of a millionaire, let's call her Sarah, who came to counseling like Nicodemus in the night—afraid and teary. Her husband had lots of money; they had a beautiful home and lovely children. But when she disagreed, she became a victim. "I have no money of my own," she said. "I was a artist. I am from another country. While my husband has millions of dollars, and I have several cars and maids; it still hurts when he hits me. What should I do? I cannot afford to raise the children by myself? I could never live like this if I left."

One reason this woman remained was her economic dependency. Where could she work with her limited skills? Why would she leave her lovely home and children for a shelter? Her husband was a respected member of the community, but she was a foreigner. If she left him, where could she go? So she remained with an abusive man for economic stability.

The issue of *poor self-esteem* provides another explanation for a woman's choice to remain in an abusive relationship. Self-esteem usually refers to self-evaluation. The worth you place on yourself has to do with how lovable and capable you believe you are. Although self-esteem has many facets—including physical, social, and spiritual self-esteem—women with low self-esteem may believe they deserve to be mistreated. They blame themselves for the abuse. They even feel the abuse is warranted, especially if the woman comes from a home where as a child, she either experienced or witnessed abuse.

Unfortunately, domestic violence increases poor self-esteem, creating a vicious cycle. Domestic violence lowers the self-esteem of all women, even those who originally had a healthy sense of self. Living in an abusive relationship fosters poor self-evaluation; the woman begins to question how lovable and capable she is. A woman with poor self-esteem begins to denigrate herself more because she is living in an abusive relationship. These questions increase her dependency on this man, who seems to control her destiny. They also increase her fear—one more reason women remain in abusive relationships.[24]

The batterer has threatened her many times about the consequences of leaving. He has said, "I will hurt you or kill you if you leave." So leaving becomes less of an option. One of the most dangerous times for an abused woman is when she tries to leave. This danger is why the location of most domestic abuse shelters is kept secret. These women are *more* vulnerable when they separate than when they remain. "Battered women seek medical attention for injuries sustained as a consequence of domestic violence significantly more often after separation than during cohabitation; about 75% of the visits to emergency rooms by battered women occur after separation."[25] Similarly, more calls are made for intervention and assistance from law enforcement *after* separation. One study revealed that abusive men committed half of the homicides of their spouses and partners after separation.[26]

She came from a middle-class religious family and had met her husband at church. Not long after their marriage, the family began to suspect abuse. She feared to talk with them about the abuse, and soon her husband limited her contact with her family. Finally she shared her plight with her family, got the courage to leave, and got her own apartment with an undisclosed address. Things were looking up for her. She was moving up in her job. She had filed for divorce and had even begun to date again. Unfortunately, her husband was watching her. He did not know where she lived, but he knew where she worked. So he came to her job and stabbed her to death. The penalty for leaving her husband was death—just what he had threatened.

Isolation makes it hard for women to leave.[27] Abusive men are controlling and make every effort to separate a woman from her family and friends. This leaves her few people to talk with, masking the pattern of abuse. Talking to family or friends becomes a source of disagreement between the woman and her partner. Upset about the abuse, the family offers only one solution, leave him.

A woman in an abusive relationships cannot always share with friends, who question her logic for staying. They may become angry with her for remaining. The abused woman may choose to avoid outside contact because of this condemnation. This decision, in turn, causes her to become more isolated and increases her chances of being abused. Embarrassment over the abuse also increases isolation. Meanwhile, her family and friends grow more frustrated that she remains in the relationship.

Sometimes isolation is caused by disbelief from family or friends, since the spouse seems like such a nice guy. The church, which is often a source of solace for women, may not be available. The pastor may believe a good wife should stay and try to be a better wife. In some cases the pastor may not believe there has been abuse. Dr. Renee Drum shares a story of a pastor who said, "I don't know why Sue went to your shelter. John said he never hit her."[28] He refused to acknowledge that a deacon could be guilty of such an act. Naturally, this pastor failed to support the victim.

Without a social network and isolated from family and church, many women *do not believe anyone will help them.*[29] There may not be a shelter in the community. In 2005 according to the National Center for Domestic Violence, *out of 35,000 towns and cities in the United States,* there were only 1,637 emergency shelters for abused women.[30] *This is* less than half the number of animal shelters! *Feeling isolated, these women stay because they do not know where to get help—or if their town even has a shelter. Women may not know what services are available and may not believe they can receive help.*

Finally, some women *confuse the fact that these men need them desperately with love.*[31] Because these men need them, the women remain. I have frequently heard victims of domestic violence say, "He cannot make it without me." This behavior reflects elements of co-dependency not love. *Co-dependency* is a term originally used in families of alcoholics. The enabling partner, whose behavior supported and helped the alcoholic partner, was called *co-dependent.* This pattern results in a dysfunctional relationship with others. Co-dependent people are addicted to helping someone. They need to be needed.[32]

The reasons women remain in abusive relationships are complex. Some leave one abuser—and select another abuser. Women in serial relationships with abusive partners reflect the characteristic of co-dependency. Like the biblical concubine, many women leave and return. In fact, most women leave a number of times before they finally leave. Unfortunately for the concubine, death took away this option.

Equally confusing is why men remain in the relationship. What is their rationale for domestic violence? In the
case of the Levite who had another wife, why did he travel
for several days to get the concubine? We have to raise the
question: What's love got to do with it?

Why Resort to Domestic Violence?

Returning to our story of the Levite, his actions raise
questions that beg for an answer. Domestic violence has
nothing to do with love! The Levite's deeds were not
motivated by love as defined in 1 Corinthians 13:

> Love is patient, love is kind. It does not envy, it does not
> boast, it is not proud. It is not rude, it is not self-seeking,
> it is not easily angered, it keeps no record of wrongs.
> Love does not delight in evil but rejoices with the truth.
> It always protects, always trusts, always hopes, always
> perseveres.
>
> —1 Corinthians 13: 4-8

If domestic violence is not about love, what is battering
about? It's about being *in control, establishing your power,*
and *proving that you are the man.* This need drives the
batterer toward abuse. Interestingly enough, these men
are not abusive outside the home. They are not abusive at
work or when hanging out with the boys. They express their
need to be in control only at home. The power wheel below
explains various ways that abusers manifest their control
and power in domestic violence. The man may use finances;
emotional, sexual, and physical abuse; and isolation as
tools of control—ways to establish power and demonstrate
authority in the home. Why would these men need to
manifest power over women in this demeaning way?

In our professional experience with male batterers, abusive men often have low self-esteem and are extremely dependent emotionally on women. They desperately need these women to take care of them. This dependency increases their sense of vulnerability and makes them uncomfortable and fearful. He tries to cover this discomfort with bravado, intimidation, and violence. This gives him a sense of power.

In cultures where men are taught that women should be treated like children—not allowed to drive or go out without a male escort—domestic violence is a natural component of a male- dominated culture. But it is still motivated by the need for power and control.

Is domestic violence ever a response to a woman's desire? Do some women want a man to hit her? Do some women do things just to get hit? While folklore may support this kind of thinking, research and the Bible do not! There is never a reason to hit a spouse.

Reflect on some of the biblical couples we have studied: Eve shared the forbidden fruit with Adam, Rebekah deceived Isaac, David killed Bathsheba's husband, and Gomer was unfaithful. In none of these cases was domestic violence ever seen as the solution. God did not tell Adam to hit Eve, nor did Isaac beat Rebekah.

Indeed, God told Hosea to "Go, show your love to your wife again" (Hosea 3:1). God told him to love Gomer as the Lord loves Israel. He told Hosea to buy her back because she was in some kind of debt or slavery. God did not suggest he buy her back and make her a slave. God did not say to buy her back and beat her. God did not say buy her back and remind her every day what a mess her life was in. God told Hosea to return to Gomer and *love* her. He did not speak of punishment for her misdeeds.

Domestic violence has no place in the Christian home. The biblical proclamation of male headship and female submission does not support or encourage domestic violence! What are the lessons the Levite and his concubine can teach us?

Lessons to Learn about Domestic Violence

1. Question traditional male concepts.

This story of the Levite and concubine questions some long-established beliefs and recognizes their negative impact on marriage. Headship does not mean domestic violence.

It is not a reason for male dominance. It does not mean the husband, like the Levite, has the right to thrust his wife out to be abused all night. Ephesians 5: 21-30 provides the basis for a much different understanding of male headship:

> Submit to one another out of reverence for Christ. Wives, submit to your husbands as to the Lord. For the husband is the head of the wife as Christ is the head of the church, his body, of which he is the Savior. Now as the church submits to Christ, so also wives should submit to their husbands in everything. Husbands, love your wives, just as Christ loved the church and gave himself up for her to make her holy, cleansing her by the washing with water through the word, and to present her to himself as a radiant church, without stain or wrinkle or any other blemish, but holy and blameless. In this same way, husbands ought to love their wives as their own bodies. He who loves his wife loves himself. After all, no one ever hated his own body, but he feeds and cares for it, just as Christ does the church—for we are members of his body.

We must resolve several issues to understand male headship: What is male headship in the Christian home? What is submission? What does it mean to love your wife like Christ? We will explore each of these concepts.

According to Klyne Snodgrass, "Head in this context suggests 'responsible for.' The husband has a leadership role, though not in order to boss..."[4] These roles do not imply inferiority of the woman to the man. We also see this in the apostle Peter's explanation of the equality of genders in 1 Peter 3:7. Male headship means the man is the spiritual head of the household. Headship means responsibility for the spiritual leadership of the family. The husband calls the family to worship and leads the family in worship. The husband prays for the family constantly. As the spiritual head, he has additional responsibility for the family's spiritual and emotional health.

Headship is not about privilege, but responsibility. The husband provides the spiritual model for the family. Headship is an organizational principle and refers to different roles in the marriage. The man is the authority, the titular head of the family. He works with his wife for organizational proficiency. In times of family disagreement and tension, as the Christlike figure, the husband as leader must seek forgiveness first, just as Hosea went to his wife.

Submission means support, according to Dr. Constable. It means respecting the husband. Respect plus love plus support equals an attitude of submission.[35] God commands it as a part of the mutual submission he requires of all Christians. The wife voluntarily submits to her husband's authority for the successful running of the family organization. She recognizes his role and allows him to lead. This submission operates among equals. This submission recognizes some of their basic needs—of the male ego to be respected and appreciated—and of the women for love and protection. God the Creator developed a model that would address these needs and provide an organizational structure for the family.

How does this function? Decision making can help explain this process. Decision making involves mutual submission to listen to your partner's opinion. In their discussion, love is required from the husband and respectful support is required from the wife. They make mutual decisions that respect the partners' differences and strengths. But if the couple has a deadlock, the husband, in the role of the head, makes the final decision. But his love causes him to consider strongly his wife's view.

Finally, husbands must love like Christ. Reflecting on Christ's role with the church gives us further insight. Christ, as head of the church, never emotionally or physically abuses us, the church. In fact, Christ loved the church so much, he died for us. Our submission to God—while required—is not demanded. God loves the church whether it is submissive or not. The church's reaction does not determine God's love for us. Unlike the Levite, God would not thrust the believer out the door to be abused all night. Instead, Christ's headship meant he assumed the responsibility to go out suffer for us. Headship never excuses abuse. This leads to our next lesson from this couple.

2. *Recognize the meaning of true love.*

The Levite and the concubine's relationship did not reflect the true meaning of love. Love, as depicted in 1 Corinthians 13:4-8, requires Christlike behavior on the part of both husband and wife. According to Ellen White, the husband is to be the "house-band...binding by his strong earnest devoted affection the members of the household."[36] Love in a relationship cannot be commanded; it does not involve fear. 1 John 4:18 states, "There is no fear in Love. But perfect Love drives out fear, because fear has to do with punishment." What does love have to do with fear? A relationship based on fear does not reflect the true meaning of love.

Love does not involve any of the behaviors manifested in the power wheel, such as verbal abuse, breaking objects, or making threats (See page 254). Any time force is used in a relationship—even for a good cause—it reflects the evil one's techniques, not God's. Force and fear do not foster love; only love activates love. True love requires making your spouse's needs paramount. When you serve as a channel of God's love, the childhood pain brought into the marriage can be healed. Reflect again on Hosea's gift of love to Gomer. It was transforming.

Growing up, Misty felt animosity from her brothers and favoritism from her mother. This was painful and resulted in poor self-esteem and intermittent depression. Then she met Michael. Although his childhood had also been painful with the death of his mother, he was kind and compassionate. He valued her presence in his life. He felt she was beautiful inside and out. He worked hard to become the husband Misty needed—even joining a men's group. Experiencing this true love transformed Misty. She developed into a competent and caring wife, mother, and worker. Her love was also comforting to Michael as he, like Isaac, received comfort after his mother's death. Both Michael and Misty were transformed by true love.

3. *Recognize the difference between interdependence and co-dependence in the marriage.*

Interdependence involves depending on each other in a relationship of mutual support, love, and respect.[37] This is far different from co-dependency, which involves two people in an unhealthy relationship showing tolerance for inappropriate behavior and a desperate need for the other. When a spouse really can't make it without you, there is a problem in the relationship. No one needs to be that dependent. Don't confuse this desperate need with love. It is not the role of a spouse to save or rescue someone. Only God can do that. Remember, a co-dependent partner is addicted to helping someone. This spouse has an inordinate need to be needed. One role of social work is to help those who are in need and vulnerable. Professionally speaking, I (Edith) know that these services are offered to those in need. But this profession has limits. Likewise, it is not the spouse's role to be a social worker to their partner in marriage. The desperate need to be needed leads to the next lesson from the Levite and the concubine—the importance of self-esteem.

4. A healthy self-esteem is an essential ingredient of effective relationships.

Recognize your inherent value as God's child. Self-esteem is the ability to form an identity and then attach a value to it. It is based on being lovable and capable. This is complicated for women, according to Jean Baker Miller, since a female's sense of self-worth involves feeling that "she is part of relationships and is taking care of the relationships."[38]

While relationships are important for assessing our sense of self, relationships should not determine our self-esteem. This naturally leads to Godly self-esteem: the ability to form an identity by recognizing and appreciating the value God places on you. John 3:16 states that, "For God so loved the world that he gave his only son ..." (ESV). You were that valuable to heaven. Nothing can separate you from the love of God in Christ Jesus (Romans 8:35-39). Our relationship with God should increase our sense of self-worth and decrease involvement in an abusive relationship.

5. Get out of any abusive relationship.

Finally, if you are involved in an emotionally, financially, or physically abusive relationship, get out. Do not remain in an abusive relationship; there is no biblical basis for staying. God wants to free you from negative, destructive relationships. The Bible provides ample reasons for leaving. Marriage is meant to reflect the relationship of God and the church. Abuse does not reflect that relationship. God provides you with choices—not force and fear. The basis for the relationship between Christ and the church is true love. A quick review of the marriages we discuss in this book should discourages abusive relationship.

Finally, 1 Corinthians 6:19 states that our bodies are God's temples requiring special attention and care. How could physical or emotional abuse be acceptable to God's temple? Who would disregard God's presence in the body and justify abuse? Abusive relationships do not reflect God's character or Christian principles; there are no acceptable reasons for domestic violence. Abuse is unacceptable. It should be opposed in the church as well as in the community. This stance will reduce the isolation and limited resources that allow for abuse.

6. *The church should provide a safe haven for vulnerable and abused women.*

Church members should refuse to ignore abuse when it occurs in the family, among friends, among church members, and among neighbors. Turning a deaf ear and blind eye does not reflect Christian attitude. Men who are abusive function best in situations where women are isolated. Therefore, churches should serve as an integral component of society's network to support women. Churches should maintain contact with the women in their congregations to reduce isolation. Church leaders should address abuse from the pulpit. Have an anti-domestic violence day!

Your involvement could provide a lifeline to an abused person. Do not become discouraged if they do not leave at first. Most women in abusive relationships attempt to leave five to seven times before they actually succeed. Your concern will help that process. Finally, parents should teach their children—both sons and daughters—that abuse is always unacceptable.

The story of the Levite and concubine is one of the saddest relationships in this book. But it provides valuable lessons for Christians today. It reminds us that domestic violence has nothing to do with love. It provides a context for exploring the role of headship and submission—and reveals the true nature of headship in the marriage. While this marriage ended in tragedy, it encourages individuals in abusive relationships to take action to save lives: their own.

WHAT'S LOVE GOT TO DO WITH IT!
Domestic Violence: the Levite and the Concubine

Personal Reflections

Text: Judges 19:1-27

1. Do you know of someone in a violent domestic relationship? What should be your response to this person's situation?

    _____

    _____

    _____

    _____

2. What can you do to encourage your church to become more actively involved in issues related to domestic violence? What can your church do to make these women feel less alone?

    _____

    _____

    _____

    _____

3. Which form of abuse is most prevalent in your relationships: verbal, emotional, physical, or sexual?

    _____

    _____

    _____

    _____

4. What are some steps you plan for personal protection, such as developing a safe place, packing a bag, and others?

_____

_____

_____

_____

5. How do you differentiate between love and inappropriate neediness in a relationship? When does need become co-dependency or abuse?

_____

_____

_____

_____

6. Why would women, especially African American women, avoid using the legal system (police and courts) to address domestic violence in a relationship? Why does this complicate the nature of the relationship?

_____

_____

_____

_____

Concluding Thoughts

A S WE HAVE looked at several marriages in the Bible, we have seen that each has its own unique experiences. So we must raise the issue that every marriage will have a different starting point, and each is unique. There is no "perfect match," and all marriages require that the couples work hard. Each of us will need to expend an enormous amount of effort to save our marriage—which is valuable for our present home, our immediate community, our church, and our society.

If we go back to the statistics we quoted at the beginning of the book, we must conclude that saving this institution is important not only for the larger society, but also for the individual. For both macro and micro reasons, we need to provide the best solutions to save marriages. Those statistics are daunting:

- About half of all marriages end in divorce.
- One in three females has been sexually molested.

- Forty percent of couples admit they lie to each other about financial items.
- Sixty percent of men and forty percent of women are involved in extramarital affairs.

Edith and I feel that human beings have tried so many other approaches to saving marriages. Biblical models may be just what we need to create a space where this process can be negotiated. After considering these biblical marriages, it is clear that all have apparent fault lines, None would seem like a perfect match—or even an ideal match—yet through time they were tested and survived. Human relationships are fraught with inconsistencies, so we need models and mentors to facilitate survival.

As we have looked at these ten models, it is our hope that you see through the lens of these couples' experiences a potential success strategy you can forge for your own marriage. The lessons we have extracted from the couples we encountered are valuable to implement in marriages today. Each martial experience may not have a similar pattern to yours; our task has been to provide you with the resources to find paradigms you can use in your unique marriage. It is our hope that you will use this book as a tool to create skills to save and build your marriage.

Bibliography

Allen, C. *10 Mistakes that Women Make During Sex.* 2007-2009. Http://www.simplemarriage.net/10-mistakes-women-make-during-sex (accessed March 2009, 2009).

Arterburn, Stephen, Fred Stoeker, and Mike and Yorkey. *Every Man's Battle: Winning the War on Sexual Temptation one Victory at a Time.* Colorado Springs, Colorado: WaterBrook Press, 2004.

Bader, E. and P. T. Pearson, *In Quest of the Mythical Mate: A developmental approach to diagnosis and treatment in couples therapy.* New York: Routledge.

Ballas, C. *Inhibited Sexual Desires.* 2005. http://healthguide. howstuffworks.com/inhibited-sexual-desire-dictionary. htm (accessed March 8, 2008).

Barakat, Halim. *The Arab World: Society, Culture and State.* Berkeley, California: University of California Press, 1993.

Barker, Robert L. *The Social Work Dictionary.* Washington, D.C: NASW Press, 1995.

Bird, Jim. Nine Steps towards a healthy step-family. http://departments.weber.edu/chfam/TOPICS/NINE. STEPSHTML. (accessed April 26, 2008).

Brown, J. and D. Christensen. *Family Therapy Theory and Practice* (2nd ed) Belmont, California: Thompson-Wadsworth, 1999.

Chapman, Gary. *The Five Love Languages: How to Express Heartfelt Commitment to Your Mate.* Grand Rapids, Michigan: Zondervan Publishing,1995.

Chapman, Gary. *Five Love Languages.* Chicago: Northfield Publishing, 2004.

Cook, David C. *God's Little Instruction Book for Men.* Colorado Springs: Honor Books, 1996.

Cline, V. *Treatment and Healing of Sexual and Pornographic Addictions from Morality in Media .* April 15, 2008. http:// www. obscenitycrimes.org/vbctreat.cfm.

Constable, Thomas L. Notes on Ephesians, http://www. soniclight.com/constable/notes/pdf/Ephesians.pdf (accessed January 4, 2009).

Crary, David "Interracial Marriages Surge across US" *USA Today* (April 12, 2007) http://www.usatoday.com/ news/health/2007-04-12-interracial-marriage_n.htm, (accessed May 26, 2009).

Davidson, Marilyn J., Cooper, Cary L. *Shattering the Glass Ceiling: The Woman Manager.* London: Paul Chapman Publishing, 1992.

Deal, Deal. Successful Step Families, http://www.successful-stepfamilies.com/home.php (accessed February, 2008).

DeCoteau, D "Signs of an Affair—How To Spot Them and Prevent Them Before They Occur." *Signs of an Affair—How To Spot Them and Prevent Them Before They Occur EzineArticles.com.* http://ezinearticles.com/?Signs-of-an-Affair-How-To-Spot-Them-and-Prevent-Them-Before-They-Occur&id=531309.

Deveny, Kathleen. "We Are Hot in the Mood." *Newsweek®*, June 2003.

Dictionary.com http://dictionary.reference.com/browse/interdependence (retrieved January 4, 2009).

Domestic Abuse Intervention Project. http://www.theduluth-model.org/wheelgallery.php (accessed May 26, 2010).

Domestic Violence Shelters in the US-2005 www.ncdsv.org/images/DVSheltersUS.pdf (*accessed December 3, 2008*).

Domestic Violence: Why do women stay? Why don't they leave? (2004-2008) Women's Web (accessed December 24, 2008 from http://www.womensweb.ca/violence/dv/leave.php/.

Drumm, René, Marciana Popescu, Gary Hopkins, and Linda Spady. Abuse in the Adventist Church vol 184, *Adventist Review* (October 11, 2007), 8-11.

Edelman, Marian Wright. *Measure of Our Success* New York: Harper Collins Publishers, 1993.

Edelman, Marian Wright. Biography, Children's Defense Fund, (retrieved August 5, 2008). http://www.childrens-defense.org/site/PageNavigator/People

Ferguson, David, & Ferguson, Teresa. *Intimate Encounters*, Austin, Texas: Relationship Press, 1997.

Fontenot, A. (2008) Profile: Tina Turner at About. Com (accessed December 20, 2009 from http://oldies.about.com/od/soulmotown/p/tinaturner.htm)

General facts about domestic violence http://home.cybergrrl.com/dv/stat/statgen.html (accessed December 29, 2008).

Goldenberg, H. and I. Goldenberg. *Counseling Today's Families.* 4th edition. Pacific Grove, California: Brooks/Cole Thomson, 2002.

Goldenberg and Goldenberg. *Family Therapy: An overview* (5th ed.) Pacific Grove, California: Brooks/Cole, 2000.

Golson, Barry and Robert Scheer. "Jimmy (Carter), We Hardly Know Y'All." *Playboy*, November 1976.

Gottman, John. *Why Marriages Succeed or Fail: And How You Can Make Yours Last*. New York: Simon & Shuster, 1994.

Gray, John. *Men are from Mars, Women are from Venus*. New York: Harper Collins Publishing New York, 1992.

Harley, William "His Needs, Her Needs," Marriage Builders: Building Marriages That Last, http://www.marriage-builders.com/graphic/mbi5060_qa.html (accessed March 20, 2008).

Harley, William "Coping with Infidelity: How Should Affairs End?" Marriage Builders: Building Marriages That Last, http://www.marriagebuilders.com/graphic/mbi5060_qa.html (accessed March 20, 2008).

Hart, Barbara J. (1992) Children of Domestic Violence: Risk and Remedies. CASAnet Resources (accessed December 29, 2008 from http://www.casanet.org/Library/domestic-abuse/risks-remedies.htm#).

Henry, O. *The Gift of the Magi:The Four Million. http://www.sa.org.* http://www.sa.org.

Hopeful Solutions for Sexless Marriages. http://www.hopefulsolutions.net/sexless/marriage.htm.

Interracial marriage flourishes in U.S.—Race & ethnicity, http://www.msnbc.msn.com/id/18090277/from/toolbar (accessed April 27, 2010).

Kahlenberg, Rebecca. (2001) "The I Do's and Don'ts of Intercultural Marriage." *Washington Post*, (11-22-2001).

Kahn, J. and London, K. "Premarital Sex and the Risk of Divorce." *Journal of Marriage and the Family*, Vol. 53, No. 4. Nov. (1991), 845-855.

Keil, C. and Delitzsch, F. *Commentary on the Old Testament.* Grand Rapids, Michigan: Eerdmans Publishing, 1973.

Kinnon, Joy B. "Wedding of The Year." *Ebony* (Johnson Publishing), February 2004.

Kulman, G. (2004) Stages of Marriage (retrieved January 12, 2006, from www.stayhitched.com/media.htm)

Lehman, Kevin. *Sex Begins in the Kitchen.* Ventura, California: Regal Books, 1995.

Lerner, Harriet. *The Dance of Intimacy.* New York: Harper & Row, 1989.

Luskin, Frederic, *Forgive for Good.* New York: Harper-Collins, 2002.

Marharaj, Subadra (2000) Violence in marriage—why do women stay? http://www.uic.edu/classes/socw/socw517/whywomenstaymaharaj.htm (accessed December 24, 2008).

Marquardt, E. *Between Two Worlds: The Inner Lives of Children of Divorce.* New York: Random House, 2005.

Miller, Jean Baker *Toward a New Psychology of Women.* Boston: Beacon Press,1986, 5.

Mother-in-laws-http://www.motherinlawstories.com/mother-in-law_jokes_page.htm n.d.)

Muller, Charla with Betsy Thorpe. *365 Nights: A Memoir of Intimacy.* New York: Berkley Books, 2008.

Nichols, M. and Schwartz, Richard C. *Family Therapy: Concepts and Methods.* 5th edition. Boston: Allyn and Bacon, 2001.

Penner, Clifford and Penner, Joyce. *52 Ways to have Fun, Fantastic Sex: A Guidebook for Married Lovers.* Nashville, Tennessee: Thomas Nelson Publishers, 1994.

Penner, Clifford and Penner, Joyce *The Gift of Sex.* Nashville, Tennessee: Thomas Nelson Publishers 2003.

Pittman, Frank, *Private Lies: Infidelity and the Betrayal of Intimacy*, New York: Norton and Company, 1989.

Powell, Blaine http://www.2-in-2-1.co.uk/marriageclinic/infidelity/affairs/index2.html (accessed May 20, 2008).

Power and Control Wheel (2008) Why Women Stay in Abusive Relationships? (accessed December 24, 2008 from http://www.mchenrycountyturningpoint.org/ cycleofviolence.html)

Premature Ejaculation. http://www.medic8.com/healthguide/ dictionary.htm (accessed March 29, 2008).

Premature Ejaculations. http://www.emedicine.com/med/ topic643.htm.

Randall, K. (2003) What's Love Got to Do with It. (accessed February 22, 2007 from (http: www.utexas.edu/features/ archive/2003/love.html).

Robinson, B. A. (2003) Sample Problems that May Arise in an Interfaith Relationship. (retrieved August 5, 2008 from Religious Tolerance.Org. http://www.religioustoler-ance.org/ifm_prob.htm).

Ropelato, J. "Internet Pornography Statistics Retrieved on March 10, 2008." March 10, 2008. http://internet-filter-review.toptenreviews.com/internet-pornography-statistic.html#anchor1 (accessed 2008).

Ross, D. S. and Ross, R. Interfaith Weddings. (retrieved August 8, 2008 from Love Track http://www.love-track. com/cc/cc_f_one_rabbirev.html, http://www.interfaith-family.com/article/issue75/cavaan.phtml).

Rubin, A. (1970) "Measurement of Romantic Love." *Journal of Personality and Social Psychology*, Vol. 16, 265-273.

Safe@work (2000) Facts and Statistics about Domestic Violence. http://www.safeatworkcoalition.org/dv/ factsandstats.htm (accessed December 12, 2008).

Scarf, Margie. *Intimate Partners: Patterns in Love and Marriage.* New York: Ballantine, 1987.

Scott, Elizabeth. (2007) Conflict Resolution Mistakes to Avoid, *About.com Health Disease and Condition.* http:// stress.about.com/od/relationships/tp/conflictres.htm (retrieved September 6, 2007).

Sexaholics Anonymous. http://www.sa.org.

Sexual Problems in Men. 1995-2008. http://www.mdecinenet. com/script/main/art.asp?articlekey (accessed March 25, 2008).

Skeptical Brother (2007) Juanita Bynum files for Divorce. (retrieved December 20, 2008 from http://skeptical-brotha.wordpress.com/2007/09/06/juanita-bynum-files-for-divorce/.

Smedes, Lewis B., *The Art of Forgiving.* Nashville, Tennessee: Moorings, 1996.

Smedes, Lewis B., personal communication, February 1991.

Smith, Reger. Two Cultures: One Marriage. *College and University Dialogue: An International Journal of Faith, Thought and Action,* 1996.

Snodgrass, Klyne. *The NIV Application Commentary.* Grand Rapids, Michigan: Zondervan Publishing House, 1996, 295.

Sprecher, Susan. (2002) "Sexual satisfaction in premarital relationships: associations with satisfaction, love, commitment, and stability." *Journal of Sexual Research,* August 2002, 1-5.

Stritof, Bob. and Sherri. (2008) How to fight Fair in Your Marriage, About.com: Marriage. http://marriage.about. com/cs/conflictandanger/ht/fightfair.htm (retrieved January 5, 2008).

The Seventh-day Adventist Bible Commentary, Vol. 2, *2 Samuel 11*, Washington, D.C.: Review and Herald Publishing Association: volume 2, 1972, 645-649.

The Seventh-day Adventist Bible Commentary, Vol. 3, Song of Solomon. Washington, D.C.: Review and Herald Publishing Association, 1954, 477.

The Seventh-day Adventist Bible Commentary, Vol. 2, *Ruth.* Washington, D.C.: Review and Herald Publishing Association, 1954, 430.

The Seventh-day Adventist Bible Commentary, Vol. 2, *Judges*. Washington, D.C.: Review and Herald Publishing Association, 1954, 407-409.

Tucker-Ladd, Clayton. http://www.psychologicalselfhelp. org. *We're not in the Mood:Sex After Marriage*. 2000. http://www.nomarriage.com/articlesexless.html (accessed March 25, 2008).

Turning Point (2008) Cycle of Violence accessed December 30, 2009 from http://www.mchenrycountyturningpoint. org/cycleofviolence.html

US Census Bureau, Interracial Tables, Table 1: Race of Wife by Race of Husband: 1960, 1970, 1980, 1991, and 1992, http://www.census.gov/population/socdemo/race/ interractabl.txt (accessed August 5, 2008).

Vaughn, Peggy. *The Monogamy Myth: Personal Handbook for Recovering Affairs*. New York: Newmarket Press, 1989.

Van Pelt, N. (1980). *To Have and To Hold*. Nashville, Tennessee: Southern Publishing Association.

Vine, W.E. (1966) *An Expository Dictionary of New Testament Words*. New Jersey: Revell Company.

White, Ellen. *The Story of Redemption*. Mountain View, California: Pacific Press Publishing Association, 1947.

White, Ellen, *The Story of Patriarchs and Prophets*. Mountain View, California: Pacific Press Publishing Association, 1958.

White, Ellen G. *Ministry of Healing*. Mountain View, California, Pacific Press, 1942.

White, Ellen G. *Adventist Home*, Nashville, Tennessee: Southern Publishing Association, 1952, 211.

White, Ellen (Manuscript 39), Vol. 3 The Seventh-day Adventist Commentary, Washington, D.C.: Review and Herald Publishing Association, 1910, 1139.

Wilcox, B. and Nock, S. "Her" Marriage after the Revolutions. *Sociological Forum* 22 (1), (2007), 103-110.

Wilson, A. (1985) Bookrage Staff. "Fences." (retrieved January 23, 2008 from http://www.bookrags.com/studyguide-fences/>. Fences.

Wingfield, M. "Secret of Eve: Survey Shows Christian Wives Sexually Active, Satisfied." *Kentucky Western Recorder*, 1998. www.medicinenet.com/script/main/art.asp?articlekey. www.medecinenet.com.

Wolthius, Randall. (2008) Essential Ingredients of a Healthy Marriage, Pine Rest Christian Mental Health Services, http://www.pinerest.org/resources/today/marriage/ingredients.asp (retrieved May 7, 2008).

Williams, G. Co-Dependency Test and Definition. http://www.way2hope.org/codependency-test-definition.htm (accessed December 31, 2008).

Endnotes

Introduction

1. Les Parrott and Leslie Parrott, *Saving Marriage Before It Starts* (Zondervan, Grand Rapids, Michigan 1995), 13.
2. Dan Hurley, "Divorce Rate: It is not as high as you think" *The New York Times (April 19, 2005)* http://www.divorcereform.org/nyt05.html (accessed August 31, 2009).
3. J. F. Walsh and V. Forshee, "Self-efficacy, self-determination and victim blaming as predictors of adolescent sexual victimization" *Health Education Research: Theory and Practice (1998). her.oxfordjournals.org/cgi/reprint/13/1/139.pdf (accessed August 31, 2009).*
4. *Jena McGregor, "Love and Money" Smart Money (February 9, 2004),* http://www.smartmoney.com/personal-finance/marriage-divorce/love-money-15383/?print=1 *(accessed January 26, 2008).*
5. *Peggy Vaughn, The Monogamy Myth: Personal Handbook for Recovering Affair (Newmarket Press, 1989).*

6. *Jennifer Crockett and Marisa Beebe, "Making the Case for Marriage" Forever Family, entry posted 2001,* http://www. foreverfamilies.net/xml/articles/benefitsofmarriage.aspx *(accessed January 26, 2008).*

7. *Crockett and Beebe, Making the Case for Marriage.*

8. *African American Healthy Family Initiative, Administration for Children and Family (July 8, 2005).* http://www.acf. hhs.gov/healthymarriage/pdf/aahmi.pdf *(accessed January 27, 2008).*

9. *William D. Antonio, "Walking the Walk on Family Values" Boston Globe (October 31, 2004)* http://www.boston.com/ news/globe/editorial_opinion/oped/articles/2004/10/31/ walking_the_walk_on_family_values/ *(accessed January 27, 2008).*

Chapter 1

1. W. Bradford Wilcox and Steven Nock, "'Her' Marriage after the Revolutions" *Sociological Forum* 22, no. 1 (February 14, 2007) 103-110.

2. August Wilson, Fences *BOOKRAGS STAFF*. Retrieved January 23, 2008 from http://www.bookrags.com/ studyguide-fences/>. Fences 2001.

3. Ellen White, *The story of Patriarchs and Prophets.* (Mt. View, California: Pacific Press Publishing Association), 54.

4. Ellen Bader and Peter Pearson, In Quest of the Mythical Mate a developmental approach to diagnosis and treatment in couples therapy. (New York: Routledge, 1988), 8-11.

5. Ibid. 8-11.

6. Patricia and Gregory Kuhlman, Stages of Marriage 2003 www.stayhitched.com/media.htm (accessed January 12, 2006).

7. bid.

8. Bader & Pearson 1988, 11.

9. Patricia and Gregory Kuhlman, 2003.

10. Ibid.

11. Ibid.

12. Zick Rubin, Measurement of Romantic Love, *Journal of Personality and Social Psychology 16,* no 2 (1970) 265-273.

13. David Ferguson and Teresa Ferguson, *Intimate Encounters.* (Austin, Texas: Relationship Press, 1997) 1-13.

14. Harriet Lerner, *The Dance of Intimacy.* (New York: Harper & Row, Publishers, Inc. 1989), 39.

15. John Gray, *Men are from Mars, Women are from Venus.* (New York: Harper Collins Publishing, 1992).

16. Lerner, 1992.

17. Elizabeth Marquardt, *Between Two Worlds: The Inner Lives of Children of Divorce.* (New York: Random House, 2005).

18. Clifford Penner and Joyce Penner, *The Gift of Sex.* (Nashville: W Publishing Group, 2003), 329.

19. Ellen White, *The story of Patriarchs and Prophets.* (Mt. View, California: Pacific Press Publishing Association, 1958), 57.

Chapter 2

1. Clara Moskowitz, Love at First Sight Might be Genetic, *LiveScience,* (April, 2009). http://www.livescience.com/culture/090408-genetic-love.html (accessed May 6, 2009).

2. Elizabeth Scott, Conflict Resolution Mistakes to Avoid. *About.com Stress Management (June, 2007): from* http://stress.about.com/od/relationships/tp/conflictres.htm *(accessed September 6, 2007).*

3. W. E. Vine, *An Expository Dictionary of New Testament Words,* (New Jersey: Revell Company. 1966,) 128.

4. Randall Wolthuis, Essential Ingredients of a Healthy Marriage. (2008) Pine Rest Christian Mental Health Services, http://www.pinerest.org/resources/today/marriage/ingredients.asp (accessed May 7, 2008).
5. John Gottman, *Why Marriages Succeed or Fail: How You Can Make Yours Last*. (New York: Simon & Shuster, 1994) 45.
6. Ibid, 57.
7. Nancy Van Pelt, *To Have and To Hold*. (Nashville, Tennessee: Southern Publishing Association, 1980) 90-93.
8. Bob Stritof and Sheri Stritof, How To Fight Fair in Your Marriage—Conflict Management in Marriage, About.com;Marriage. (http://marriage.about.com/cs/conflictandanger/ht/fightfair.htm (accessed January 5, 2008) 2008
9. Nancy Van Pelt, 93.

Chapter 3

1. Emily Bouchard, Famous Step-Parents Answer Challenging Blended Family Questions (May 07, 2008) https://www.amazines.com/article_detail.cfm/483525?articleid=483525 (accessed 05/11/09).
2. Hank Arends, Mother's Day is Time to Reflect on Timeless Role, *StatesmanJournal.com* (May 9, 2009) http://www.statesmanjournal.com/article/20090509/COLUMN1001/905090321/1100/COLUMN (accessed 05/11/09).
3. Ron Deal, Successful StepFamilies (2008) http://www.successfulstepfamilies.com/home.php (accessed February, 2008).
4. Irene Goldenberg and Herbert Goldenberg, *Counseling Today's Families*. (Pacific Grove: Brooks/Cole Thomson 2002) 165-167.

5. Robert Barker, *The Social Work Dictionary* .(Washington, DC: NASW Press, 1995) 365.

6. Irene Goldenberg and Herbert Goldenberg, *Family Therapy: An Overview.* (Belmont: Wadsworth Publishing, 2000) 74.

7. Michael Nichols and Richard C. Schwartz, *Family Therapy: Concepts and Methods.* (Boston: Allyn and Bacon, 2007) 137.

8. Goldenberg and Goldenberg, *Family Therapy: An Overview,* 31.

9. Joseph Brown and Dana Christensen, *Family Therapy Theory and Practice* (Pacific Grove: Brooks/Cole, 1999) 57-59.

10. Ibid. 113-135.

11. Jim Bird, "Nine Steps Towards a Healthy Step-Family, A Weddingday.com (2000-2001) http://www.a-weddingday.com/articles/HealthyStepFamily.html (accessed April 26, 2008).

12. Ibid.

13. Ibid.

14. Goldenberg and Goldenberg, 2000, 253.

15. Jim Bird, Aweddingday.com.

Chapter 4

1. Margie Scarf, *Intimate Partners: Patterns in Love and Marriage* (New York: Ballantine, 1987) 136.

2. Peggy Vaughan, *The Monogamy Myth: Personal Handbook for Recovering Affair* (Newmarket Press, 1989) 6.

3. Barry Golson and Robert Scheer, Jimmy (Carter), We Hardly Know Y'All. *Playboy,* November 1976.

4. Relationships, "Couples-Heavy Heartaches" Affairs, BBC.co.uk, http://www.bbc.co.uk/relationships/couples/heartaches_affairs.shtml (accessed May 19, 2009).

5. *Seventh-day Adventist Bible Commentary Volume 2,* 2 Samuel 11, (Washington, D.C.: Review and Herald Publishing Association, 1972) 647.
6. Peggy Vaughn, *The Monogamy Myth,* 30-31.
7. William Harley, "Coping with Infidelity: How Should Affairs End?" Marriage Builders: Building Marriages That Last, http://www.marriagebuilders.com/graphic/mbi5060_qa.html (accessed March 20, 2008).

Chapter 5

1. BBC On This Day—1950-2005, "1981: Charles and Diana Marry" http://news.bbc.co.uk/onthisday/hi/dates/stories/july/29/newsid_2494000/2494949.stm (accessed May 20, 2008).
2. Karl F. Keil and Franz Delitzsch, *Biblical Commentary on the Old Testament,* Vol. 10, Hosea. (Grand Rapids, Michigan: Eerdmans Publishing, 1973), 36-37.
3. *The Seventh-day Adventist Bible Commentary,* vol. 5, Hosea (Washington, D.C: Review and Herald Publishing, 1955) 888.
4. Ibid. 888.
5. Keil and Delitzch, 36-37.
6. *SDA Commentary,* 888.
7. Blaine Powell, "Affairs: How Affairs Develop" *2-in-2-1-Marriage Clinic,* 2001 under Infidelity, http://www.2-in-2-1.co.uk/marriageclinic/infidelity/affairs/index2.html (accessed May 20, 2008).
8. D. DeCoteau "Signs of an Affair—How To Spot Them and Prevent Them Before They Occur." *Signs of an Affair-How To Spot Them and Prevent Them Before They Occur EzineArticles.com.* http://ezinearticles.com/?Signs-of-an-Affair-How-To-Spot-Them-and-Prevent-Them-Before-They-Occur&id=531309 (accessed May 21, 2008).

9. Susan Sprecher, "Sexual satisfaction in premarital relationships: associations with satisfaction, love, commitment, and stability." *Journal of Sexual Research,* Vol 39. No. 3 (August 2002) 190-196.

10. Joan Kahn and Kathryn London, "Premarital Sex and the Risk of Divorce." *Journal of Marriage and the Family,* Vol.53. No.4 (Nov 1991) 845.

11. Lewis Smedes, "Forgiveness and Marriage" (lecture Marriage Festival, Huntsville, Alabama, 1994).*

12. Frederick Luskin, *Forgive for Good* (New York: Harper-Collins, 2002).

13. Lewis Smedes, *The Art of Forgiving* (Nashville: Moorings, 1996) 6.

14. Luskin, 2002.

15. Smedes, 1996, 7.

16. Ibid.

17. Lewis Smedes, lecture, 1994.

18. Ibid.

19. BBC on this Day/20/ November " 1995 Diana admits adultery in interview," http://news.bbc.co.uk/onthisday/hi/dates/stories/november/20/newsid_4341000/4341436.stm (accessed May 22, 2008).

20. Lewis Smedes, 1996.

21. Darold Bigger, "Journeying Through Personal Grief" *Ministry Magazine,* vol. 70. no 11 (November, 1997), 6-9.

22. Sara Schilling,"Walla Walla Couple Celebrate Time for Forgiveness" Tri-City Herald.com (April 12, 2009) www.tri-cityherald.com/901/story/541277.html (accessed May 21, 2009).

23. Lewis Smedes, lecture, 1994.

24. Smedes, 1996, 7.

25. Smedes, lecture, 1994.

26. Ibid.

Chapter 6

1. Children's Defense Fund "Marion Wright Edelman Biography" found under Children's Defense Fund Leadership and Staff, http://www.childrensdefense.org (Retrieved August 5, 2008).
2. US Census Bureau, Interracial Tables, Table 1: Race of Wife by Race of Husband: 1960, 1970, 1980, 1991, and 1992, http://www.census.gov/population/socdemo/race/interractab1.txt (accessed August 5, 2008).
3. David Crary, "Interracial Marriages Surge across US" *USA Today* (April 12, 2007) http://www.usatoday.com/news/health/2007-04-12-interracial-marriage_n.htm, (accessed May 26, 2009).
4. Deborah Ross and Roger Ross, Creative Ceremonies: Interfaith Marriages, Love Track http://www.love-track.com/cc/cc_f_one_rabbirev.html (accessed August 8, 2008).
5. Ellen White, (Manuscript 39), Vol. 3 *The Seventh-day Adventist Commentary,* Washington, D.C.: Review and Herald Publishing Association, (1910) 1139.
6. B.A. Robinson, "Facts About Inter-Faith Marriages" Religious Tolerance.org (December 15, 1999) http://www.religioustolerance.org/ifm_fact.htm (accessed August 5, 2008).
7. B.A. Robinson " Specific Problems that May Arise from a Inter-Faith Marriage" Religious Tolerance.org (July 4, 2003) http://www.religioustolerance.org/ifm_fact.htm (accessed August 5, 2008).
8. Marion Wright Edelman *Measure of Our Success*, (New York: HarpersCollins) 1993.
9. Interracial marriage flourishes in U.S.-Race & ethnicity-msnbc.com http://www.msnbc.msn.com/id/18090277/ (accessed April 27, 2010).

10. Rebecca Kahlenberg, The I Do's and Don'ts of Intercultural Marriage. *Washington Post*, (11-22-2001) 12.

11. Ibid, 12.

12. *The Seventh-day Adventist Bible Commentary*, Vol. 3 (Washington, D.C.: Review and Herald Publishing, (1954), 477.

13. David C. Cook, *God's Instruction Book for Men* (Colorado Springs: Honor Books, 1996).

14. Gary Chapman, *The Five Love languages*, (Chicago: Northfield Publishing, 2004) 17,18.

15. Rebecca Kahlenberger, The I Do's and Don'ts of Intercultural Marriage, *Washington Post*, (11-22-2001) 12. Reger Smith, Two Cultures: One Marriage. *College and University Dialogue: An International Journal of Faith, Thought and Action.* (1996) 1-3.

Chapter 7

1. Joy Swift, *They're All Dead Aren't They* (Boise, Idaho: Pacific Press Publishing Association, 1986) 49-51.

2. Sari Harrar and Rita Demaria, *The 7 Stages of Marriage: Intimacy, Laughter and Passion Today, Tomorrow, Forever,* (New York: The Reader Digest Association, 2007) 30.

3. Gary Chapman, *The Four Seasons of Marriage* (Wheaton, Illinois: Tyndale House, 2005) 17.

4. Electronic Library, http://www.articler.com/881429/How-Financial Stress-Threatens-A-Marriage.html.

5. Electronic Library, http://www.associatedcontent.com/article/311431/the-rise-fall-of-casy-serin-a-wouldbe.html n.d.

6. Joy Swift, *They're All Dead Aren't They,* 189.

7. Julie K. Silver, *Chronic Pain and the Family: A New Guide* (Cambridge, Massachusetts: Harvard University Press Family Health, 2004) 20-21.

8. Ibid. 26.
9. E. Kubler-Ross, *On Death and Dying* (New York, New York: Scribner, 1997) 147.
10. Paul and Yancey, Philip Brand, *The Gift of Pain* (Grand Rapids, Michigan: Zondervan Publishing House, 1993) 6.
11. Joy Swift, *They're All Dead Aren't They,*130.
12. Ibid.131.
13. David and Theresa Ferguson, *Intimate Encounter*s (Austin, Texas: Relationship Press, 1997) 180
14. Ibid. 168.
15. Ibid.167.
16. Ibid. 170.
17. Ibid. 173.
18. Ibid. 163.
19. Stephen Covey, and Sandra Covey. *The Seven Habits of Highly Effective Families.* (New York, New York: Golden Books Publishing, 1997).
20. Cheryl Broussard, and Michael Burns, *What's Money Got to Do With It* (Oakland, California: MetaMedia Publishing Inc., 2002).

Chapter 8

1. Kathleen Deveny "We are not in the Mood," *Newsweek*® (June 30, 2003).
2. H. D. M. Spence, The Pulpit Commentary, *Song of Solomon.* (London: Funk & Wagnall Company) 7, 8.
3. F. Delitzsch and C. Keil, Commentary of the Old Testament (since 1869) Vol. 6, *Song of Solomon.* (Grand Rapids: William B Eerdmans Publishing Company, 1973), 4, 5.
4. J. Ropelato. "Internet Pornography Statistics Retrieved on March 10, 2008." March 10, 2008. http://internet-filter-review.toptenreviews.com/internet-pornography-statistic.html#anchor1 (accessed 2008).

5. Clayton Tucker-Ladd. http://www.psychologicalselfhelp. org. *We're Not in the Mood: Sex After Marriage* . 2000. http://www.nomarriage.com/articlesexless.html (accessed March 25, 2008).

6. Tucker-Ladd, *We're Not in the Mood: Sex After Marriage.*

7. C. Ballas, *Inhibited Sexual Desires.* 2005. http:// healthguide.howstuffworks.com/inhibited-sexual-desire-dictionary.htm (accessed March 8, 2008).

8. Stephen Arterburn, Fred Stoeker, and Mike Yorkey. *Every Man's Battle: Winning the War on Sexual Temptation One Victory at a Time.* (Colorado Spring, Colorado: WaterBrook Press, 2004).

9. Arterburn, Stoeker, and Yorkey. *Every Man's Battle.*

10. Clayton Tucker-Ladd, *We're Not in the Mood* .

11. *Premature Ejaculation.* http://www.medic8.com/health-guide/dictionary.htm (accessed March 29, 2008).

12. Clayton Tucker-Ladd. http://www.psychologicalselfhelp. org. *We're not in the Mood:Sex After Marriage* . 2000. http://www.nomarriage.com/articlesexless.html (accessed March 25, 2008).

13. Ibid.

14. Ibid.

15. M. Wingfield, "Secret of Eve: Survey Shows Christian Wives Sexually Active, Satisfied." *Kentucky Western Recorder*, 1998.

16. Kevin Lehman, *Sex Begins in the Kitchen.* (Ventura, California: Regal Books) 1995.

17. O. Henry, *The Gift of the Magi:The Four Million. http:// www.sa.org.* http://www.sa.org.

18. Allen, C. *10 Mistakes that Women Make During Sex.* 2007-2009. Http://www.simplemarriage.net/10-mistakes-women-make-during-sex (accessed March 2009).

19. Ibid.

20. *Sexual Problems in Men.* 1995-2008. http://www. mdecinenet.com/script/main/art.asp?articlekey (accessed March 25, 2008).
21. Clifford Penner and Joyce Penner. *The Gift of Sex.* (Nashville: Thomas Nelson Publishers, 2003).
22. *Hopeful Solutions for Sexless Marriages.* http://www. hopefulsolutions.net/sexless/marriage.htm.
23. Clifford and Joyce Penner. *The Gift of Sex*, 268.
24. *Premature Ejaculation.* http://www.medic8.com/health-guide/dictionary.htm (accessed March 29, 2008).
25. Ibid.
26. Clifford and Joyce Penner. *The Gift of Sex*, 268.
27. *Sexaholics Anonymous.* http://www.sa.org.
28. V. Cline, *Treatment and Healing of Sexual and Pornographic Addictions from Morality in Media*. April 15, 2008. http:// www. obscenitycrimes.org/vbctreat.cfm.
29. Charla Muller with Betsy Thorpe. *365 Nights: A Memoir of Intimacy*. (New York: Berkley Books, 2008).

Chapter 9

1. http://www.motherinlawstories.com/mother-in-law_jokes_page.htm n.d.
2. *Seventh-day Adventist Bible Commentary*, Volume 2 Ruth. (Washington, D.C.: Review and Herald Publishing Association 1954) 430.

Chapter 10

1. Joy B. Kinnon, "Wedding of The Year," *Ebony* (Johnson Publishing), February 2004, from http://findarticles.com/p/articles/mi_m1077/is_4_59/ai_112861729 (accessed December 12, 2008).
2. Ibid.

3. Skeptical Brother, "Jaunita Bynum Files for Divorce," Http://skepticalbrotha.wordpress.com (September 6, 2007).

4. Robert Fontenot, (2008) Profile: Tina Turner at About. Com retrieved on 12/20/08 from http://oldies.about.com/od/soulmotown/p/tinaturner.htm (accessed May 23, 2010).

5. Safe@work (2000) Facts and Statistics about Domestic Violence. http://www.safeatworkcoalition.org/dv/factsandstats.htm (accessed December 12, 2008).

6. Amnesty International (2008) Violence Against Women—a fact sheet http://www.amnestyusa.org/violence-against-women/violence-against-women—a-fact-sheet/page.do?id=1108440 (accessed December 20, 2008).

7. D. A. Carson, *The New Bible Commentary the 21st Century Edition*. Judges (Downers Grove, Illinois: Inter-Varsity Press, 1994).

8. *Seventh-day Adventist Bible Commentary, Judges. Vol 2,* (Washington, D.C.: Review and Herald Publishing Association, 1954) 407-409.

9. D. A. Carson, The New Bible Commentary, *Judges.*

10. Halim Barakat, The Arab World: Society, Culture and State. (University of California Press, 1993).

11. AARDVARC.org, Inc (2008) Domestic Violence Statistics http://www.aardvarc.org/dv/statistics.shtml. (accessed December 12, 2008).

12. Ibid.

13. Ibid.

14. Ibid.

15. Turning Point (2008) Cycle of Violence retrieved 2/30/08 from http://www.mchenrycountyturningpoint.org/cycleofviolence.html

16. Ibid.

17. AARDVARC.org, 2008.

18. D. A. Carson, *The New Bible Commentary, Judges.*

19. Domestic Violence: Why do women stay? Why don't they leave? (2004-2008) Women's Web http://www. womensweb.ca/violence/dv/leave.php/ (accessed December 24, 2008).

20. Subadra Marharaj, (2000) Violence in Marriage —why do women stay? http://www.uic.edu/classes/socw/socw517/whywomen-staymaharaj.htm (accessed December 24, 2008).

21. Domestic Violence: Why do women stay? Why don't they leave? (2004-2008) Women's Web. (retrieved December 24, 2008).

22. Marilyn J. Davidson, Cary L. Cooper, *Shattering the Glass Ceiling: The Woman Manager,* (London: Paul Chapman Publishing, 1992) 82,138.

23. Subadra Marharaj, 2000.

24. Ibid.

25. Barbara J. Hart, (1992) Children of Domestic Violence: Risk and Remedies. CASAnet http://www.casanet.org/ Library/domestic-abuse/risks-remedies.htm#. (accessed December 29, 2008).

26. Ibid.

27. Domestic Violence: Why do women stay? Why don't they leave? (2004-2008).

28. Rene' Drumm, Marciana Popescu, Gary Hopkins, and Linda Spady. Abuse in the Adventist Church vol 184, *Adventist Review* (October 11, 2007) 8-11.

29. Domestic Violence: Why do women stay? Why don't they leave? (2004-2008).

30. *Domestic Violence Shelters in the US-2005* www.ncdsv.org/ images/DVSheltersUS.pdf (*retrieved December 30, 2008*).

31. G. Williams, Co-Dependency Test and Definition. http:// www.way2hope.org/codependency-test-definition.htm (accessed December 31, 2008.

32. Ibid.
33. Domestic Abuse intervention Project. ttp://www.theduluthmodel.org/wheelgallery.php (accessed May 26, 2010).
34. Klyne Snodgrass, *The Application Commentary* (Grand Rapids, Michigan: Zondervan Publishing House, 1996) 295.
35. Thomas L. Constable, Notes on Ephesians http://www.soniclight.com/constable/notes/pdf/Ephesians.pdf (accessed January 4, 2009).
36. Ellen G. White, *Adventist Home*, (Nashville: Southern Publishing Association, 1952) 211.
37. Dictionary.com http://dictionary.reference.com/browse/interdependence (retrieved January 4, 2009).
38. Jean Baker Miller, *Toward a New Psychology of Women* (Boston: Beacon Press 1986) 5.

CPSIA information can be obtained at www.ICGtesting.com
Printed in the USA
LVOW081236170212

269052LV00001B/7/P